ETHICAL CRITICISM: READING AFTER LEVINAS

ETHICAL CRITICISM: READING AFTER LEVINAS

Robert Eaglestone

Edinburgh University Press

© Robert Eaglestone, 1997

Edinburgh University Press
22 George Square, Edinburgh

Typeset in 11/13 pt Adobe Caslon
by Hewer Text Composition Services, Edinburgh
and printed and bound in Great Britain at the University Press, Cambridge

A CIP record for this book is
available from the British Library

ISBN 0 7486 0967 9 (hbk)
ISBN 0 7486 0955 5 (pbk)

The right of Robert Eaglestone
to be identified as the author of this work
has been asserted in accordance with
the Copyright, Designs and Patent Act (1988).

To Geraldine

'The caress of love, always the same, in the last accounting . . . is always different and overflows with exorbitance the songs, poems and admissions in which it is said in so many different ways'

Emmanuel Levinas

CONTENTS

ACKNOWLEDGEMENTS

I am grateful to the library staff at the University of Wales, Lampeter, and the Upper Reading Room at the Bodleian, Oxford, for being so helpful. I would like to thank Simon Critchley and Tim Woods for their encouragement and comments. I also want to thank Peter Middleton, who read some of the manuscript in a different form. Most of all in this respect, I want to thank Lawrence Normand, who supervised with quite astounding care and dedication the doctoral dissertation from which this developed. At the University of Wales, Lampeter, I owe thanks to David Walford for introducing me so meticulously to Heidegger, and to the whole philosophy department, especially R. R. Rockingham-Gill, Bernard Weiss, David Cockburn and Janey Hartwell. I also owe a great debt of thanks to all in the English department at Lampeter, and especially to Barbara Dennis, Rebecca Ferguson and Allen Samuels, and to Connie Gudla in the Computing Centre. I would like to thank the staff of the English departments at Manchester, Southampton, Middlesex and Westminster Universities, and at Royal Holloway, University of London. Thanks too, to Jackie Jones at Edinburgh University Press for her help and enthusiasm. In addition, I am indebted the following friends and colleagues for their encouragement and support: Janice Allen, Mary Baker, Kim Brown, Susan Brown, Amanda Crawley, Sarah Dimmerlow, Patrick Finney, Malcolm Geere, Andrew Gibson, Nick Hoare, Alex Hollingsworth, Robert Mighall, Peter Mitchell, Hugh Osborne, Sue Pitt, Jonathon Reé, Mike Shanks, Gavin Stewart, Richard Tennant, Michael Tierney, Julian Thomas and Tom Webster. I could not have managed at all without the love and unstinting support of my parents and family. Thank you. Finally, I would like to thank Geraldine Glennon for all sorts of things.

ABBREVIATIONS

WORKS BY LEVINAS

EE   Emmanuel Levinas, *Existence and Existents*, trans. Alphonso Lingis (London: Kluwer Academic Publishers, 1988)

EI   Emmanuel Levinas, *Ethics and Infinity: Conversations with Phillipe Nemo*, trans. R. A. Cohen (Pittsburg: Duquesne University Press, 1985)

OBBE   Emmanuel Levinas, *Otherwise than Being: or, Beyond Essence*, trans. Alphonso Lingis (The Hague: Martinus Nijhoff, 1981)

RIS   Emmanuel Levinas, 'Reality and its Shadow', in *The Levinas Reader*, trans. Alphonso Lingis, ed. Seán Hand (Oxford: Blackwell, 1989), pp. 129–43

TI   Emmanuel Levinas, *Totality and Infinity: An Essay on Exteriority*, 3rd printing, trans. Alphonso Lingis (London: Kluwer Academic Publishers, 1991)

OTHER WORKS

AR   Paul de Man, *Allegories of Reading* (London: Yale University Press, 1979)

BT   Martin Heidegger, *Being and Time*, trans. John Macquarrie and Edward Robinson (Oxford: Blackwell, 1962)

ED   Simon Critchley, *The Ethics of Deconstruction* (London: Blackwell, 1992)

ER   J. Hillis Miller, *The Ethics of Reading* (New York: Columbia University Press, 1987)

FG   Martha Nussbaum, *The Fragility of Goodness: Luck and Ethics in Greek Tragedy and Philosophy* (Cambridge: Cambridge University Press, 1986)

HH   J. Hillis Miller, *Hawthorne and History: Defacing it* (Oxford: Blackwell, 1990)

LK   Martha Nussbaum, *Love's Knowledge: Essays on Philosophy and Literature* (Oxford: Oxford University Press, 1990)

OG   Jacques Derrida, *Of Grammatology*, trans. Gayatri Chakravorty Spivak (London: Johns Hopkins University Press, 1976)

OW   Martin Heidegger, 'On the Origin of the Work of Art', in *Poetry, Language, Thought*, trans. Albert Hofstadter (London: Harper Row, 1971), pp. 17–87

VM   Jacques Derrida, 'Violence and Metaphysics', in *Writing and Difference*, trans. Alan Bass (London: Routledge and Kegan Paul, 1978), pp. 79–153

VP   J. Hillis Miller, *Versions of Pygmalion* (London: Harvard University Press, 1990)

Introduction

—— • ——

THE UNCERTAIN TOPOGRAPHY OF CRITICISM

Inquiring, learning, knowing and reasoning are forms of responsible relationship with other people and with our world. They attest to the priority of ethics even in our knowing. Facing another person my free spontaneity is called into question. I am answerable and am summoned, obliged, called into responsibility. Intelligibility itself is born through language in community, and rational discourse is about bearing responsible witness and justifying that witness before others.

David Ford[1]

It is easy to see that we are living in a time of rapid and radical change . . . that . . . will inevitably affect the nature of those disciplines that both reflect our society and help to change it . . . this is nowhere more apparent than in the central field of . . . literary studies. Here . . . the erosion of the assumptions and presuppositions that support the literary disciplines in their conventional form has proved fundamental.

Terence Hawkes[2]

Does criticism, a strange form of 'inquiring, learning, knowing and reasoning', have ethical obligations? If it does, what are they and how do they appear?

An explicit concern for ethics has been at the heart of literary criticism since its inception in a modern and modernist form at around the time of the First World War. However, with the passing of time and as the discourse of criticism changes, this ethical grounding has become insecure. The ethical 'assumptions and presuppositions that support the literary disciplines' have been eroded or displaced. This insecurity is problematically understood as the result of what is named, reductively, 'literary theory'. 'Theory', especially deconstructive theory, has often been accused of lacking an ethics, of being amoral. 'Theory-mongers' are 'devilish tempters who claim to offer higher forms of thought and deeper truths and insights – the intellectual equivalent of crack . . . cancerous radiation comes from the head of Derrida and Foucault'.[3] The old maps of criticism and its ethical commitments have utterly changed, but the newer maps of criticism are unclear. What is ethical criticism after 'literary theory'?

In order to answer this question, to draw this map, it might seem important to provide a strict definition of criticism. However, because the central ethical and connected epistemological presuppositions of criticism have changed and are in dispute, it is precisely the definition of criticism that is in contention. In 1978, Hayden White wrote that 'contemporary literary criticism does not constitute a coherent field of theory and practice. The contours of criticism are unclear, its geography unspecified, and its topography therefore uncertain.'[4] The topography of criticism and theory is even more uncertain now. This lack of clarity and uncertainty is reflected in the name of the academic discipline which teaches criticism: Literary Studies, English, English Studies, Literary Criticism.

It is exactly the question of definition (of de-finition, the question of limits) that is taken up in debates over criticism and 'theory'; indeed, Paul de Man argued that 'the main theoretical interest of literary theory consists in the impossibility of its definition'.[5] To offer a definition is already to engage with the debate; even to hesitate to offer definitions is to make a stance, about the uncertainty of making a definition. Four attempts at a 'definition' will illustrate this problem clearly and show the depth of the uncertainty in critical discourse.

Leavis, perhaps the most significant figure in the development of criticism in the UK, notoriously refused to define 'criticism'. Leavis wrote that it 'is not possible to draw a firm line around the field of study of English literature, though where its centre is should be plain'.[6] In his famous debate with Wellek, Leavis argued that the 'critic's aim is, first, to realize as sensitively and completely as possible this or that which claims his attention; and a certain value is implicit in the realizing'.[7] His definitions, apart from their assumptions of gender, remained vague, specifying that a critic is to have 'sensibility', a quality which, Chapter 1 argues, is inextricably interwoven with 'value' and with ethical concerns.

In the USA, René Wellek's and Austin Warren's extremely influential *Theory of Literature* took a similar, if more fully argued, position. Drawing on both Russian formalism and Ingarden's phenomenological work, they argued against approaches based on biography, psychology, sociology, philosophy or history and suggested that the 'natural and sensible starting point for a work of literary scholarship is the interpretation and analysis of the works of literature themselves'.[8] Like Leavis, they understood criticism to consist of reasoned judgements 'formulated . . . on the basis of some sensibility, immediate or derivative'.[9]

In contrast, the critical left, following the lead of thinkers like Raymond

Williams, argued for a more politically engaged definition of criticism. Terry Eagleton argued that criticism was 'born of a struggle against the absolutist state'.[10] It should 'show the text as it cannot know itself, to manifest those conditions of its making (inscribed in its very letter) about which it is necessarily silent'.[11] The aim of criticism is to study 'the laws of the production of ideological discourses as literature'.[12]

Poststructuralist thought offers yet another definition of criticism. Geoffrey Hartman suggests that criticism should aim 'at a hermeneutics of indeterminacy . . . a type of analysis that has renounced the ambition to master or demystify its subject (text, psyche) by technocratic, predictive or authoritarian formulas'.[13] Hartman, in contrast to the others, understands criticism as a genre in its own right: 'literary commentary may cross the line and become as demanding as literature: it is an unpredictable or unstable genre that cannot be subordinated, a priori, to its referential or commentating function.'[14] This definition obviously differs from the previous three. It seeks to displace the distinction between literature and criticism; it questions the ability of criticism to provide an 'answer' or a stable interpretation; it suggests that the relationship between society and writing may be more complex than the other definitions assume.

These four different versions of criticism not only illustrate how definitions are created by and for argument, for ideological and rhetorical reasons. They also show the uncertain topography of criticism, and how the ethical belief which founded and gave direction to criticism has disappeared.

CRITICAL ORIENTATIONS: GRAPHI-READING AND EPI-READING

Although a definition of criticism appears to be impossible, Denis Donoghue offers an approach to criticism by an understanding of how it functions. In Donoghue's schematic, any act of criticism, any reading, is one of two sorts, either an 'epi-reading' or a 'graphi-reading'. This distinction draws on and considerably refines Wellek's and Warren's distinction between the 'intrinsic' and 'extrinsic' study of literature. Epi-reading 'is predicated on the desire to hear . . . the absent person'.[15] The epi-reader 'moves swiftly from print and language to speech and voice and the present person' and understands 'reading as translation' from words to acts (p. 146). Epi-reading transposes 'the written words on the page into a somehow corresponding situation of persons, voices, characters, conflicts, conciliations' (p. 101). For an epi-reader, language is transparent, a window through which the world of people, actions and events can be seen. Epi-readers include Gerard Manley Hopkins ('who loved words because he loved, or prayed to love, the God he construed as Word': p. 147); Georges Poulet (the book 'the reader holds in his hands is no longer a mute object but the consciousness of another': p. 106); Kenneth Burke; Paul Ricoeur (the 'act of interpretation . . . restores written words to speech and thence to the shared realm of intention and reference': p. 123).

Donoghue contrasts this with graphi-reading, which prioritises language, text and reading over a nostalgia for the human and seeks to engage with texts 'in their virtuality' (p. 200): it represents, in Geoffrey Hartman's words, 'the eclipse of voice by text' (p. 200). It makes 'each word a unit of whatever attention the sceptical reader chooses to bring to it' (p. 206), and prefers allegory over symbol, metonymy over metaphor and grammar over rhetoric. Graphi-reading reads the words and refuses to pass beyond, or create a world behind, them. Jacques Derrida is obviously a graphi-reader, as is Paul de Man, who 'ascribes to language the life an epi-reader would ascribe to an artist' (p. 186). All deconstructive criticism is graphi-reading, suspicious of a nostalgia for a person within a text. Roland Barthes and Stéphane Mallarmé, for whom 'the pure work of poetry invokes the disappearance of the poet's voice' (p. 153), are also graphi-readers.

It is significant that Donoghue does not offer strict definitions. Instead, he provides heuristic analyses, explaining why each critic or writer is an epi- or graphi- reader. Donoghue makes clear that neither graphi-reading nor epi-reading are a critical practice as such: they represent 'a stance, an attitude, a prejudice' (p. 146, p. 199). They represent a mode or orientation of criticism, not an actual methodology. They are contrasting ways of understanding the textual, of understanding what the text is and how it works. Each mode has a huge sweep, taking in a vast number of critical and interpretative projects and stances. Most significantly, each mode of reading offers a different approach to the question of the ethics of criticism.

Chapter 1 will suggest that the modernist, humanistic model of criticism, inaugurated early in the century, is fragmented, self-contradictory, confused and flawed. It will show how and why its 'presuppositions and assumptions' have been eroded. Chapter 2 illustrates a vigorous restatement of this critical model by examining the work of Martha Nussbaum. Nussbaum's work represents a clear example of epi-reading as a mode of criticism. More importantly, it offers an ethical justification for this sort of reading or critical orientation. However, the chapter suggests that her work is problematic, especially in relation to language. Following this, Chapter 3 considers the deconstructive criticism of J. Hillis Miller as a significant example of graphi-reading. Miller, in response to attacks on deconstruction and deconstructive criticism, argues the case for an ethics of criticism in *The Ethics of Reading* and its sequel, *Versions of Pygmalion*. Chapter 3 analyses these two works and suggests that Miller's conclusion, although it high-lights the problems of language Nussbaum ignores, does not establish a satisfactory relation between literature and the ethical.

Neither epi-reading nor graphi-reading offers a way of clarifying or justifying the ethics of criticism. Epi-reading passes through literary language to picture a world it creates: it ignores the specific qualities of language on which it claims to be concentrating. Graphi-reading concen-trates on the language, but seems unable to offer anything apart from the actual language of a text which might be considered ethical, or lead to an ethics of criticism. It is at this stage that the thought of Emmanuel Levinas becomes relevant to the debate.

Levinas has been described as 'the greatest moral philosopher of the twentieth century' and his philosophy hailed as a way to uncover 'an ethical demand in the postmodern'.[16] His work has been a significant and profound influence on many contemporary thinkers, such as Irigaray and Lyotard. More specifically, Levinas is a central figure in the work of Jacques Derrida. The relationship between Levinas's thought, literature and criticism – what Levinas's work means for ethical criticism – has not been analysed in detail.

Where Levinas's philosophical work has been linked to critical issues, it has been principally in relation to reading his philosophy as Judaic. Much commentary on Levinas could take as its motto Jabès's comment that 'unreason is the Jew's vocation. It means believing in his mission'.[17] Although the intersection of Judaism, critical interpretation and philoso-phy, especially continental philosophy, is particularly fruitful, it is not the subject of this book.[18] Rather, it takes Levinas at his word when he claims that his religious writing and his philosophical writing are separate: 'I always make a clear distinction, in what I write, between philosophical and confessional texts. I do not deny that they ultimately have a common source of inspiration.'[19]

This 'common source' does not mean, as some commentators have suggested, that he is 'translating' Judaic thought into philosophy.[20] He has said that

> I have never aimed explicitly to 'harmonise' or 'conciliate' both traditions. If they happen to be in harmony it is probably because every philosophical thought rests on pre-philosophical experiences, and because for me reading the Bible has belonged to these founding experiences.[21]

Whether his inspiration is biblical or a less specific but equally powerful
'ethical-political impulse to resist the "fundamental conceptual system
produced by the Greco-European adventure"', it is clear that Levinas
does not wish his philosophy to be confused with his work on religion or
theology.[22] As Catherine Chalier writes, his 'philosophical writings are
indeed philosophical because he does not yield to the temptation of
substituting the authority of a certain verse or of a certain name to the
philosophical requirement of argumentation'.[23] It is by working through
the philosophical, rather than by opposing it to, or integrating it with,
religious thought, that Levinas uncovers the ethical.

Emil Fackenheim wrote that

> philosophers keep on acting as if, philosophically, there is no
> difference between the six million and one child dying of cancer,
> just as theologians keep on acting as if, theologically, the 'case' of
> Auschwitz were 'covered' by Good Friday or the ninth of Av. So far as
> most philosophers and theologians are concerned, there simply is no
> Holocaust.[24]

If Levinas can be understood as a philosopher without reference to
Jewish thought, this is not to argue that he is a philosopher of the sort
Fackenheim discusses. Indeed, Maurice Blanchot suggests, in fact, that
it is the thought of the Holocaust that 'traverses, that bears, the whole
of Levinas' philosophy'.[25] Levinas's work is an attempt to reshape
philosophy after the Holocaust. One of the two dedications of
Levinas's second major work, *Otherwise than Being*, is to 'the memory
of those who were closest among the six million assassinated by the
National Socialists, and of the millions on millions of all confessions
and all nations, victims of the same hatred of the other man, the same
anti-semitism'. Adriaan Peperzak writes that 'anti-semitism became for
Levinas the equivalent of antihumanism and that to be a Jew is identical
with being human'.[26] If there is a Judaism at the heart of Levinas's
thought, it is a 'Judaism' which is not limited to the Jewish people, but
to all peoples. Zygmut Bauman argues that

> the Holocaust was not simply a Jewish problem, and not an event in
> Jewish history alone. The Holocaust was born and executed in our
> modern rational society, at the high stage of our civilization, and at the
> peak of human cultural achievement, and for this reason, it is a
> problem of that society, civilization and culture.[27]

It as at this level that Levinas's thought relates to the Holocaust, and, in its
challenge to our 'society, civilization and culture' 'can make us tremble'.[28]

CRITICAL DIRECTIONS:
CRITICISM, LITERATURE AND EMMANUEL LEVINAS

Neither graphi-reading nor epi-reading, as understandings of critical orientations, offer a satisfactory solution to the problem of the ethics of criticism. In the light of this, and bearing in mind Levinas's challenge to philosophy, the argument turns to Levinas's philosophical thought on ethics. However, in relation specifically to the issue of literary criticism, Levinas's thought raises a problem. From his earliest work, Levinas's philosophy shows a deep-seated antipathy – and sometimes outright hostility – to art. If Levinas is as opposed to the aesthetic in general as these writings suggest, a Levinasian ethical criticism would be impossible. At best, it would resemble the Holy Roman Empire ('not Holy, not Roman, not an Empire') by being unfaithful to Levinas's work and lacking critical rigour ('not Levinasian, not ethical, not criticism'). Chapter 4 explores the reasons for Levinas's distrust of representation in general and the aesthetic in particular.

It is through Derrida's deconstruction of *Totality and Infinity* that the issues of criticism and ethics re-emerge: this is the subject of Chapter 5. Derrida's exacting essay, 'Violence and Metaphysics', suggests, amongst other things, that Levinas's thought in *Totality and Infinity* does not engage with the problems that language itself raises. In response, Levinas rearticulated his philosophy with a new awareness of language. *Otherwise than Being* aims to show how the 'ethical signifies within ontological language' by introducing the concepts of the saying and the said.[29] Levinas' ethics is not one set of guiding principles, laws or rules but rather the 'ethics of ethics', the ethical understanding which underlies any principles, rules or laws. It is because of this, and the way that this is made manifest in language, that Levinas's work comes to be relevant to the issue of the ethics of criticism.

Levinas's approach to language allows both the ethical commitment to the world that the critical orientation of epi-reading demands and the acute concentration on the actual language of literary texts asked for by graphi-reading. His work could be seen as moving from epi-reading through to graphi-reading and then beyond the opposition of the two. A Levinasian understanding of the ethics of criticism does not provide a methodology or type of literary theory, but rather a justification of a variety of approaches to literature. Levinas's work offers an ethical justification for the influx into criticism of the new and challenging questions, called 'theory'. It offers a new and different way of attending to the ethical in the textual, and of the responsibility inherent in reading. Criticism must be sensitive to the way in which language reveals the other and our responsibilities to the other. Levinas's philosophy offers a future for an ethical criticism.

NOTES

1. David Ford, 'Obedience and the Academic Vocation Today: Lessons for Universities', *Cambridge; The Magazine of the Cambridge Society*', Vol. 35 (1994–5), pp. 90–5 (pp. 93–4).
2. Terence Hawkes, 'General editor's preface' to the New Accents Series. See Peter Brooker and Peter Humm, *Dialogue and Difference: English into the Nineties* (London: Routledge, 1989), p. x.
3. G. R. Elton, *Return to Essentials* (Cambridge: Cambridge University Press, 1991), p. 41.
4. Hayden White, *Tropics of Discourse: Essays in Cultural Criticism*, paperback edn (London: Johns Hopkins University Press, 1985), p. 261.
5. Paul de Man, *The Resistance to Theory* (Minneapolis: University of Minnesota Press, 1986), p. 3.
6. F. R. Leavis, *The Critic as Anti-Philosopher: Essays and Papers*, ed. G. Singh, (London: Chatto and Windus, 1982), p. 187.
7. F. R. Leavis, *The Common Pursuit* (London: Chatto and Windus, 1952), p. 213.
8. René Wellek and Austin Warren, *Theory of Literature* 3rd edn (Harmondsworth: Peregrine, 1985), p. 139.
9. Wellek and Warren, *Theory of Literature*, p. 251.
10. Terry Eagleton, *The Function of Criticism* (London: Verso, 1984), p. 9.
11. Terry Eagleton, *Criticism and Ideology* (London: New Left Books, 1976), p. 43.
12. Eagleton, *Criticism and Ideology*, p. 97.
13. Geoffrey Hartman, *Criticism in the Wilderness* (London: Yale University Press, 1980), p. 41.
14. Hartman, *Criticism in the Wilderness*, p. 201.
15. Denis Donoghue, *Ferocious Alphabets* (London: Faber & Faber, 1981), p. 146.
16. Zygmunt Bauman, *Modernity and the Holocaust*, 2nd edn (Oxford: Polity Press/Blackwell, 1993), p. 214. *Postmodernism: A Reader*, ed. Thomas Docherty (London; Harvester, 1993), p. 26.
17. Edmond Jabès, *The Book of Questions*, trans. Rosmarie Waldrop (Connecticut: Wesleyan University Press, 1976), p. 125.
18. For an overview of Judaism and literary theory, see G. Douglas Atkins, 'Dehellenising Literary Criticism', *College English*, Vol. 41 (1980), pp. 769–79; José Faur, *Golden Doves with Silver Dots: Semiotics and Textuality in Rabbinic Tradition* (Bloomington: Indiana University Press, 1986); Harold Fisch, *Poetry with Purpose* (Bloomington: Indiana University Press, 1988). For the interrelation of Judaism, philosophy and literary theory, see Susan Handelman, *The Slayers of Moses: The Emergence of Rabbinic Interpretation in Modern Literary Theory* (Albany: State University of New York Press, 1982); Susan Handelman, *Fragments of Redemption: Jewish Thought and Literary Theory in Benjamin, Scholem and Levinas* (Bloomington: Indiana University Press, 1991); Jill Robbins, *Prodigal Son/Elder Brother: Interpretation and Alterity in Augustine, Petrarch, Kafka and Levinas* (London: University of Chicago Press, 1992); Jacob Meskin, 'The Other in Levinas and Derrida: Society, Philosophy, Judaism', in *The Other in Jewish Thought and History*, eds Laurence J. Silberstein and Robert L. Cohn (London: New York University Press, 1994), pp. 402–23.
19. Richard Kearney, *Dialogues with Contemporary Continental Thinkers* (Manchester: Manchester University Press, 1984), p. 54.
20. See, for example, P. N. Lawton, 'A Difficult Freedom: Levinas' Judaism', *Tijdschrift voor Filosofie*, Vol. 4 (1975), pp. 681–91; Rudolph J. Gerber, 'Totality and Infinity: Hebraism and Hellenism – The Experiential Ontology of Emmanuel Levinas', *Review of Existential Psychology and Psychiatry*, Vol. 7 (1967), pp. 177–88; Adriaan Peperzak, 'Emmanuel Levinas: Jewish Experience and Philosophy', *Philosophy Today*, Vol. 27 (1983), pp. 297–30; Christopher Norris, *Derrida* (London: Fontana, 1987), pp. 194–237; Herman Rapaport, *Heidegger and Derrida: Reflections on Time and Language* (London: University of Nebraska Press, 1989), pp. 218–19.
21. Emmanuel Levinas, *Ethics and Infinity: Conversations with Philippe Nemo*, trans. Richard A. Cohen (Pittsburg: Duquesne University Press, 1985), p. 24.
22. Michael J. MacDonald, 'Jewgreek and Greekjew: the Concept of Trace in Derrida and Levinas', *Philosophy Today*, Vol. 35 (1991), pp. 215–27 (p. 218). He is citing Derrida's 'Violence and Metaphysics', in *Writing and Difference*, trans. Alan Bass (London: Routledge and Kegan Paul, 1978), pp. 79–153 (p. 82).

23. Catherine Chalier, 'Emmanuel Levinas: Responsibility and Election', *Ethics: Royal Institute of Philosophy Supplement: 35*, ed. A. Phillip Griffiths (Cambridge: Cambridge University Press, 1993) pp. 63–74 (p. 63).
24. Emil Fackenheim, *To Mend the World: Foundations of Jewish Thought* (New York: Schocken Books, 1982), p. 11.
25. Maurice Blanchot, 'Our Clandestine Companion', in *Face to Face with Levinas*, ed. Richard A.Cohen (Albany: State University of New York Press, 1986) pp. 41–50 (p. 50).
26. Adriaan Peperzak, 'Emmanuel Levinas: Jewish Experience and Philosophy', p. 297.
27. Bauman, *Modernity and the Holocaust*, pp. x and xiv.
28. Derrida, 'Violence and Metaphysics', p. 82.
29. Simon Critchley, *The Ethics of Deconstruction* (Oxford: Blackwell, 1992), p. 7.

1

·

ETHICS AND THE END OF CRITICISM?

The development of literary criticism as an autonomous discourse, separate and distinct from philology, history or philosophy, with its own practices, ideals and structure, is the key to understanding why ethical concerns are central to criticism in the Anglo-American world. Criticism is a recent invention. Only in the last century, after the onset of modernity and 'the death of God', have literary works, as opposed to biblical or philosophical works, been actively interpreted. A specific discourse – literary criticism – has grown up around this need for interpretation. Anglo-American criticism combines an unprecedented concern for ethics and interpretation with the deployment of nationalist, imperialist, institutional and pedagogical power. In its early years, this discourse quickly established a model of how interpretation of literary texts should work. This model was a modernist model, reflecting contemporary ideas and attitudes, even though these ideas were sometimes contradictory. Although it represented only one way of interpreting, one *way of doing* criticism, it quickly became the dominant model, or paradigm, of criticism, not just in nascent 'English' departments in North America and the UK, but over a number of disciplines that sought to use literary works. Now the term criticism, or literary criticism, is generally invoked to mean this one particular modernist method. 'Criticism', for example, is opposed to a particular 'theory': this only means that one set of presuppositions and one way of interpreting – criticising – texts is opposed to another.

The defining feature of this established modernist paradigm of criticism is a commitment to a modernist humanist ethical position. A number of assumptions, about method for example, are derived from this ethical position and make up the infrastructure of this paradigm. The issue of the ethics of criticism has arisen because this modernist critical paradigm is slowly fracturing. Its assumptions about method have been questioned and shown to be inconsistent and self-contradictory. More significantly, both the humanist ethics and the way in which those ethics can underlie a critical practice, have come into question. New ways of criticism, with different and as yet implicit understandings of ethics, have rapidly evolved, both causing and resulting from the slow collapse of the paradigm of modernist criticism. This chapter sets the scene for the rest of the book by outlining the development of literary criticism into an autonomous discipline in relation to its concern for ethics. It goes on to explore the way in which contemporary writers have sought to defend the modernist critical paradigm against what they name 'theory'. It is the collapse of this paradigm that calls for the re-evaluation of the ethics of criticism.

THE HISTORY OF CRITICISM?

[I]t is a fact too often forgotten that the real content of the school and college subject which goes under the name 'English Literature' is not literature in the primary sense, but criticism. Every school student in British education is required to compose, not tragic dramas, but essays in criticism.

Chris Baldick[1]

Although the history of the development of criticism has been told several times, these histories, with the occasional exception, have failed to highlight the central importance of ethics for criticism. The years following the First World War saw the invention of a new form of criticism which became a discipline with its own specific concerns and assumptions, and relying on a fundamental understanding of ethics.

However, offering an outline of the development of criticism is not straightforward. A full, detailed history of criticism, separate from biographies and memoirs, which concentrates on the actual construction of the institutional discipline – on those things beyond its 'pure intellectual', social or personal histories – has yet to be written. Moreover, as Hayden White argues, any historical account is a construct, based on deep-seated ideological, 'epistemological, aesthetic and moral' positions.[2] Any history of criticism will be the result of the position of the historian. In addition, and more problematically still, any history of literary criticism will also be the result of the writer's critical and theoretical approaches to literature: certain approaches will emphasise certain readings and ways of reading. Three examples will also make these difficulties clear and illustrate the way in which ethical considerations, so important to criticism, are written out of histories of criticism.

Wimsatt's and Brooks's *Literary Criticism: A Short Introduction* outlines the arguments of philosophers and writers on literature from Plato on. Isolating these thinkers from their historical context suggests that each of them engaged in the same ahistorical enterprise, criticism, and so generates the illusion that all through history the 'great minds' have wrestled in the same way with the same problems. Moreover, their approach is 'that of proponents of a theoretical perspective that has already won its way and become 'normalised', as a prevalent . . . dominant, discourse'.[3] Indeed, all the significant thinkers they cover seem to tend towards Wimsatt's and Brooks's own New Critical position. The work's final paragraph proclaims that the great theories of poetry have asserted its 'special character' as 'a tensional union of making with seeing and saying'.[4] This text shows how all the major approaches have taken as central poetry's importance and value as poetry in itself. This is a New Critical understanding of poetry: ethics and politics are reconfigured in New Critical readings to exist as important only through the 'well wrought urn' or the 'verbal icon' of the poem.

Harry Blamires's *A History of Literary Criticism* is another typical account and has a similar structure.[5] The chronological list of critics implicitly suggests that criticism has always been essentially the same activity, and that Horace (pp. 12–14), Bede (pp. 35–8), Campion (pp. 59–61), Hazlitt (pp. 237–44), Ruskin (pp. 260–7), Winters (pp. 353–6) and Cixous (pp. 373–80), for example, all undertook basically the same task. It fuses a large number of writers from different discourses, with different aims and from very different times, contexts and cultural milieux together. It implies a lack of historical change and ignores the particularities of historical context. It also reduces any difference in thought or argument to a mere 'family difference', a squabble between members of the same institution.[6] Just as Leavis formed a critical great tradition of fiction, so histories which offer chronological lists form a fictional great tradition of criticism.

Terry Eagleton's history of criticism falls prey to a similar problem. Subtitled 'From the *Spectator* to Post-structuralism', it sweeps all the criticism from the mid-eighteenth century to the present day into a schema which understands criticism as either revolutionary or reactionary. Modern criticism first appears 'in intimate empirical engagement with the social text of early bourgeois England' in opposition to 'the absolutist state'.[7] In Eagleton's history, in support of his own critical practice,

> criticism was only ever significant when it engaged with more than literary issues . . . The period of the Enlightenment, the drama of Romanticism and the moment of *Scrutiny* are exemplary cases in point. It has only been when criticism, in the act of speaking of literature, emits a lateral message about the shape and destiny of a whole culture that its voice has compelled widespread attention.[8]

Eagleton's amalgamation of these different historical moments – the Enlightenment, Romanticism and the mid-twentieth century – reduces the very different intellectual, political and institutional concerns which motivated the 'critics' and writers in these different periods. Eagleton abolishes these historical contextual differences in order to make his larger point about the social role of criticism, a point which echoes and supports his own critical practice.

These contrasting examples illustrate both the impossibility of an 'objective' history of criticism and the way in which ethics has been overlooked in criticism's history. The development of criticism's modernist paradigm will show, in comparison, how profound a concern criticism has had for ethics. To supplement these histories of criticism by outlining the significance of ethics is not to offer a 'truer' history, but rather to draw out the often ignored significance of ethics for contemporary critical practice.

THE BIRTH OF MODERNIST CRITICISM

It would seem . . . that while the study of great literature is good and ennobling, as drawing the mind upward and bracing it to the consideration of sublimity and beauty, it cannot be said to have an actively moral effect.

H. Nettleship[9]

As the finer parts of our emotional tradition relax in the expansion and dissolution of our communities, and as we discover how far out of our depth the flood-tide of science is carrying us . . . we shall increasingly need every strengthening discipline that can be devised . . . The critical reading of poetry is an arduous discipline: few exercises reveal to us more clearly the limitations under which, from moment to moment, we suffer. But, equally, the immense extension of our resources is made plain.

I. A. Richards[10]

The first quotation, part of a debate in Oxford over 'English' as a subject, dates from 1890. It is clear, here and in other contemporary documents, that the idea that criticism might be ethically valuable is simply not present.[11] The second comes from the end of I. A. Richards's seminal *Practical Criticism* from 1929. For Richards, the criticism of literature can play a key part in making existence in the world better and more moral: because it is 'arduous' it reveals our 'resources' to ourselves, and so the extent and power of our own humanity. The change of viewpoint between these two writers – and the positions they exemplify –is the result of the evolution of the humanist, autonomous modernist paradigm of literary criticism, which introduced a new understanding of the interrelationship between ethics, literature and criticism.

In the last quarter of the nineteenth century, a professor of English, in both the UK and the USA, was either teaching a watered-down course on classical rhetoric or was a philologist. Criticism – in the sense of analysing literary texts as literary texts – simply did not exist as a discipline, and any suggestion that it should was regarded with suspicion. There was, for example, a long and acrimonious debate at Oxford University in the 1880s and 1890s. Nettleship summed up the issues: for him, the issue is 'whether the modern European languages and literatures [including English] are worthy of being treated as a serious subject of University study'.[12] He concludes that they are, but only if they include history as a large component and are deeply philological. For Nettleship, philology is

> the handmaid, but the indispensable handmaid, of literature and history . . . I believe also that philology is a necessary adjunct to the academical study of literature; that the academical study of literature, without philology, is a phantom that will vanish at the dawn of day.[13]

When the English School at Oxford University was set up in 1893, it taught only literary history, Anglo-Saxon, German, philology and biography; the English syllabus was similar in other universities, including Cambridge.[14] Teaching and writing about works of literature at this time was 'gossipy, and often highly metaphorical, description and unspecific praise' or involved 'introducing boys to the golden passages of Shakespeare and the poets'.[15]

This was changed radically, as a new context and cultural mission was about to locate itself in the nascent discipline. Recent work by Gauri Viswanathan has provided a new and unsettling history for the development of 'English'. She suggests that

> what has conventionally been thought of as a discipline created entirely by and for British youth was first created by early nineteenth century colonial administrators for the ideological pacification and reformation of a potentially rebellious Indian population and then re-imported back to England for a very different but related use there.[16]

For Viswanathan, the 'eurocentric literary curriculum of the nineteenth century was . . . a vital, active instrument of western hegemony in concert with commercial expansionism and military action'.[17] In 1813, the new charter for the East India company increased their responsibility for 'native' education and, at the same time, demanded that the company no longer interfered in 'native' religion. As a result, 'English' was invented as a way of educating the 'natives' in the 'English way of life' without religious conversion. As a result, not only

> did British educational ideology get maximum advantages from the employment of morally trained men for those who ran the country, but such employment was impressed upon the general public as beneficial to its own moral character. The importance of English Literature could not be exaggerated; as the source of moral values for correct behaviour and action, it represented a convenient replacement for direct religious instruction that was forbidden by law.[18]

Indeed, the 1835 English Education Act officially required the natives of India to submit to the study of English literature.

The idea that the study of literature has 'civilising values' was brought to Britain by thinkers and educators like Matthew Arnold, aiming to 'recivilise' a fissiparous England. In the United States, this need to bind an imaginary national community together was even stronger. As Arnold writes in *Culture and Anarchy*, culture

> seeks to do away with classes; to make the best that has been thought and known in the world current everywhere; to make all men live in an atmosphere of sweetness and light, where they may use ideas, as it uses them itself, freely – nourished and not bound by them.[19]

What is crucial here is the way in which Arnold binds cultural value with ethics. The emancipatory ethical mission – who could resist a world which offered sweetness and light to everybody? – and the oppressive, homo-genising features of the imposition of a single (male, 'English', European) culture come across at the same moment here. It was where and when this concern for the ethical through culture fed into the institutional growth of English that 'modern criticism' was born. This event can be dated – in as much as any event of this sort can be dated – to the origin of the English Tripos at Cambridge in 1917.

As the title of Tillyard's memoir on the events suggest, there was a 'revolution' in English at Cambridge in 1917. Previously, 'the moral and cultural potentialities of the subject were being strangled'.[20] Now a new form of 'English' emerged, 'freer than the scope of any School of English in any British University'.[21] Although Tillyard has his own agenda (and one beyond offering a practical example of how to be successful by following Cornford's academic-political tract nearly to the letter), the radical originality of the new 'subject' is clear.[22] The origins and key assumptions of this new discipline, in the UK and the USA, have been explored by a number of critics and historians. The importance of F. R. Leavis, of *The Calendar of Modern Letters* which evolved into *Scrutiny*, of the evolution of New Criticism in the USA, of the inheritance from Arnold and the belief that literature and criticism had a humanist ethical mission to repair a fractured modern world are all familiar themes.[23]

To name this new paradigm of criticism modernist is not only to stress its difference from what went before it, but also to suggest that it shares with Anglo-American high literary modernism – especially the modernism of T. S. Eliot – an attempt to maintain an ethical viewpoint.[24] What is principally at issue here is not the content of the ethical positions taken by these writers and critics, which might often be considered repugnant, but the fact that their ethical concerns are behind their critical practice: ethics and culture are intertwined. This explicit concern for the ethical, which becomes a humanist position, and a number of methodological presuppositions, which are a consequence of this humanism, serve as the defining features which make this new paradigm of modernist criticism different from earlier writing on literature.

THE ETHICS OF MODERNIST CRITICISM

Selya Benhabib describes the condition of modernity as one in which 'disenchantment has taken place [and] . . . truth, goodness, beauty no longer have a unifying source'.[25] The response to this, for the modernist writer or critic, is to 're-enchant' the world by 'an act of will and decision; the difference between an enchanted and a re-enchanted universe is that the validity and meaningfulness of the latter do not derive from objectivity – from the facts themselves – but from the subjective act that lends objectivity meaning'.[26] For meaning to exist in the modern world, it must be actively created. This general, Nietzschean formation appears, perhaps most clearly, in the aesthetic. In pre-modernist poetry, meaning was established in narrative (for example, the story of the Fall) or in presence assumed in writing (for example, the poet speaks to us of the development of his/her mind and poetic sensibility): the poem is meaningful in itself. In modernist poetry, fragments of language and shifting voices are put together to make up a poem in an act of will: the poem is not a unified meaningful object in itself, but actively created. There was an analogous change in thought about writing on literature. Prior to modernist criticism, the meaning of a literary text – although not other sorts of texts – was assured, self-evident and did not (or seemed not to) require interpretation. Writing about vernacular literature – if it did anything apart from offer generalities – elucidated terms or words philologically, or related the work to the author's life. However, as a result of modernity, criticism developed into a way of self-consciously wresting meaning from literature, or interpreting.

It is impossible to offer interpretation without presuppositions: each exegete, or critic, 'approaches the text with certain specific questions or with a specific way of raising questions'.[27] Since the new paradigm of criticism offered not gossip, description or praise of a literary work, but interpretation, the ideas and ideals of the interpreters became central to their critical practice. The modernist critics, having discovered their power as interpreters, and in the light of the Arnoldian/colonial understanding of literature as offering civilising virtues, read the texts they interpreted as presenting a basically humanistic ethical position. Solipsistically, the humanist ethical position of the critics 'discovered' humanism in the works that they read which, in turn, justified the ethical underpinnings of their criticism. Implicitly or explicitly, these critics were humanists, reacting against what they saw as the threat to humanism from technology, political creeds and the world. At its heart, modernist criticism understands itself as an ethical act, 'uncovering' the way in which literature seeks to 'mend the world' and revealing universal human values, the 'eternal verities of literature'.

This ethical heart leads on to six key presuppositions which make up the critical methodology of this modernist humanism. These assumptions are not cut and dried rules, but rather reflect general paradigmatic presuppositions made by almost all modernist critics. They are:

1. Disinterestedness. The critic or critical method claims to be able to make an objective reading and judgement of a text.
2. Practical criticism. Modernist criticism, especially in its US New Critical version, takes as its basic methodology the activity of 'practical criticism'. This is not just a pedagogic tool but is claimed to be a near-scientific reading of an 'empirical' text. It is because this practical criticism appears to be disinterested that modernist criticism in general can lay claim to being objective.
3. Sensibility to the literary text as aesthetic object. Modernist criticism, paradoxically perhaps in the light of its relationship to modernity in general, understands the literary text as an aesthetic object, isolated from the all the world save other literary texts. In dealing with a literary text, the individual's sensibility is the key feature, determining the value of both the individual and the text itself.
4. A 'commonsense' approach to language. For modernist criticism,

language is not, in itself a problem: the meanings of words, if ambiguous, are transparent and can be determined.

5. A canon. This critical approach sets up and argues for a canon of great works. Leavis' 'great tradition' and Eliot's essay 'Tradition and the Individual Talent' are examples of this.

6. The civilising mission of the university. The university, and especially for Leavis, the English school, represents the most significant proponent of this modernist humanism. Pedagogy was vital for modernist criticism.[28]

These radical new concerns found their most famous and influential expositors in the Leavises, but they are not just their views. Eliot's criticism, too, was highly influential and of the same mould.[29] Tillyard describes its arrival in Cambridge in 1920 as an 'eruption'.[30] The ethical turn of criticism can also be seen in I. A. Richards, who was considered the most influential contemporary critic, especially in the USA. Richards begins his immensely important *Practical Criticism* with three claims:

> to introduce a new form of documentation to those who are interested in the contemporary state of culture . . . to provide a new technique for those who wish to discover what they feel about poetry . . . to prepare the way for educational methods more efficient than those we use now in developing discrimination.[31]

Here, the modernist critical claims and their novelty are apparent: the ethical and cultural concern; the appeal to discrimination and sensibility; the pedagogic imperative.

This new consensus about the moral and ethical value of literature and criticism not only formed English as a university subject and criticism as a discipline; it also went hand in hand with the growth and simultaneous institutionalisation of literary criticism from 1917, boosted and given state sanction by the Newbolt report of 1921. The report argues that 'literature is not just a subject for academic study, but one of the chief temples of the Human spirit, in which all should worship'. More than this, the 'professor of Literature in a University should be . . . a missionary'. Literature and its criticism are, in the Newbolt report, centrally ethical and the literary critic – a missionary, no less – must spread its word.[32] This consensus has shaped its form, approaches and history ever since.[33]

The current and widespread debate over the ethics of criticism exists because this paradigm, its ethical concerns and its critical assumptions are collapsing or have collapsed. This model of ethical criticism no longer works and what is described as 'literary theory' reveals this.

THE END OF THE MODERNIST PARADIGM

Fundamental and far-reaching changes in literary studies, often compared to paradigmatic shifts in the sciences, have been taking place during the last thirty years.

Michael Payne and Harold Schweizer[34]

Modernist humanism is being challenged by the spectrum of ideas often incongruously lumped together as 'postmodernism'. Postmodernists 'describe *modern* ideals of science, justice, and art, as merely modern ideals . . . unable to legitimize themselves as universals' (italics added).[35] In the discourse of criticism, this challenge appears in a distinction drawn between 'criticism', meaning the modernist criticism, and 'theory'. This potential paradigm shift, between a discipline dominated by one specific method and its implicit presuppositions opposed to a wide range of approaches which make explicit their presuppositions, has inaugurated a continuing 'crisis'. For some, this 'crisis' is positive. Chris Baldick, for example, argues that 'crisis' is 'an appropriate, even favourable, condition' for a discipline 'professing criticism'.[36]

However, many critics and writers are opposed to the dissolution of the modernist, humanist critical paradigm. They argue that there is a state of 'anxiety' or of more general 'mistrust'.[37] 'Modern criticism has lost its sense of purpose' as 'sceptical assumptions about meaning' and 'subversive and unruly concerns . . . [have] erupted' into the discipline.[38] More dramatically, the situation has been described as 'intellectual gang warfare, with factions slugging it out over textual and institutional turf' or as 'a state of cold war'.[39] There has been a 'theoretical revolution', the 'paradigm [is] in crisis' or in 'intellectual disarray', racked with 'metacritical quarrels'.[40] More polemically still, a 'fraud' has been perpetrated by 'hackademe' on literature, the public, students and everybody concerned.[41] These writers, and others who oppose 'theory' equally vehemently, offer a way of analysing the current state of the modernist critical paradigm because, almost without exception, they adhere to some or all of the methodological assumptions of the modernist critical project, and certainly to its humanist ethics. They represent the modernist ethical position and assumptions under pressure and, a result of this pressure, the gaps, contradictions and problematic assumptions can be clearly seen in the paradigm's structure.

These texts are anti-theoretical, not because they have no theoretical presuppositions or positions – which would be impossible and locate them outside the world – but, more simply, because they locate themselves as defenders of the modernist critical paradigm, opposed to theory. These texts amalgamate a wide range of very different philosophical and critical positions into one category, theory, with which they can disagree. Theory, however, is not one united position: it is 'a combination of structuralism, deconstruction, psychoanalysis, philosophy, poetics, and cultural materialism'.[42] This process of amalgamation has three ramifications.

First, it leads to inaccuracies which reduce the debate to a simplistic binary opposition of 'criticism' versus 'theory'. For example, Warner Berthoff simply describes 'the newest criticism' which has its 'eye on something other than its proper objects'; Patrick Parrinder argues that 'literary theory has mainly been drawn from disciplines . . . which are quite separate from the experience and practice of poetry'. This both argues for theory's wide interdisciplinary genealogy but, at the same time, forces it into a unity as 'theory'.[43] In fact, 'theory', as some of these accounts themselves show, is a reductive catch-all name for a wide variety of different approaches, from different traditions and with different aims and politics.

Second, this tactic of amalgamation allows the anti-theorists to misrepresent the work of any one 'theorist' by allying him or her to others, forced into the same side of the false 'criticism/theory' opposition. By this process, the work of a very significant thinker – Derrida, for example – can be polemically 'defeated' by reference to a lesser thinker. Falck's work amalgamates the very different approaches of Miller, Bloom, Barthes, Foucault, de Man, Derrida and Northrop Frye into the 'deeply entrenched and interlocking structure of literary theoretical fallacy' which makes up 'post saussurian theory'.[44]

Third, the tactic of amalgamation allows the anti-theorists to set up straw figures which are easily brought down. Most often this involves ascribing political positions, when a thinker's politics are indistinct at best. Peter Washington amalgamates all literary 'theory' into one fictitious wave of 'Radical Literary Theory', which, riddled in 'obscure jargon' comes from 'the far left' and 'represents the worst, because the subtlest and most insidious, threat to intellectual honesty in the literary academy'.[45] Thurley writes that poststructuralist criticism is the neo-Marxist 'expression of a socio-political attitude'.[46] This is an over-simplistic approach to the issues they wish to address.[47]

These anti-theoretical critics and philosophers, unlike the wide range of theorists they amalgamate and oppose, do, however, form a relatively coherent group because they share the same paradigmatic view of the method and function of criticism. They all share the humanist ethics of modernist criticism and the assumptions which orient its methodology. Their work reveals not just the state of the modernist critical paradigm, but also its weaknesses, gaps and contradictions. Paradoxically, defending the paradigm shows up its frailty. Their defence usually works on two levels. First, these anti-theorists offer either an implicit or explicit defence of humanist ethics. This is done either by simple assertion, or by a very brief discussion. Second, and often at great length, they defend the methodological assumptions of the modernist paradigm against 'theory'.

HUMANISM AND CONTEMPORARY MODERNIST CRITICISM

These writers share a deep paradigmatic conviction that literature reveals humanity and that this is ethically good. This humanism is often understood and defined in a very vague manner. Patrick Grant, for example, suggests that it is the 'optimistic conviction of the power of human imagination and will', 'creative freedom' and the hope that a work of art might 'awaken a change of attitude'. Thurley argues for a universality based 'simply our humanness, our being-as-man'.[48]

This underlying humanism leads the anti-theoretical writers constantly to relate literature back to humanistic concerns, since their understanding of literature is a reflection of their own humanism. For them, humanist ethics lie in the very nature of literature as 'a human practice defining and serving human goals and purposes'.[49] Literary texts 'clarify the meaning of persons' since they are centred on the human as traditionally understood: by stressing the moral goods of 'autonomy and responsibility', 'great books tell us how to live'.[50] Siebers, in a Jamesian phrase, insists on literature's innate humanistic concerns: 'living and choosing in the human world are the only true subjects of literature . . . The finally human is literature'.[51] Poetry 'aims its wisdom at a vision of human behaviour, and so, implicitly, at ethics'.[52] All these writers explicitly link the ethical concerns of humanism with literary art.

Defenders of the humanist modernist critical paradigm believe that literary study must return to a 'truly humanist literary curriculum' and that the 'reconstruction of literary value . . . should be uppermost on the humanist's agenda'.[53] Siebers declares from the outset that the critic is in 'a special field of action: the field of human conduct and belief concerning the human'.[54] Ethics and criticism have a 'logical connection', because 'a concern for meaning and truth . . . is the basis of criticism'.[55] This position is most explicitly and strongly argued for by Freadman and Miller in their call for a 'philosophically toughened literary humanism' in opposition to what they understand as 'constructivist antihumanism' – another amalgamation of all 'theory'.[56] Concluding that de Man, a metonym for all theory, offers a 'worse than inadequate' account of ethics, they

> contend that language . . . is not wholly determinative . . . of ethics
> . . . the *actual* ethical realm is characterised by significant degrees of
> coherence and permanence . . . relatively consistent across time.
> Moreover, and most fundamentally, we maintain that the salient
> features of ethical life transcend particular cultural boundaries and are
> not reducible to culture specific social practices and ways of think-
> ing.[57]

Like the others opposed to theory, they maintain a universalising humanist and intuitionist position, which relies on contention and assertion. For them, a literary text unproblematically communicates value between author and reader and has transcendent aesthetic qualities. They argue for the 'demonstrable capability of fictional literature to communicate truth' and this links literature to ethics and 'render it a central form of human inquiry'.[58] For Freadman and Miller, it is only through this humanist understanding that criticism can continue.

If Freadman and Miller sum up the anti-theorists' humanist arguments, it is in the idea that 'criticism has a sort of *custodial* function to perform'.[59] This phrase contains ambiguities which cast light on some of the contradictions in the humanism of the modernist critical paradigm. Custody does not just mean a 'life-affirming' or 'sincere' approach to a text. Custody is also an idea which implies juridical control over something to prevent it escaping. Custody presupposes both a violent and disorderly force to be contained and so carries the implication that literature has exactly the qualities that custody tries to deny it – a capacity for deregulation or 'crime'. Literature, by being taken into custody as a criminal, shows itself to be immoral and unethical. By imposing 'custody' on literature, Freadman and Miller implicitly bestow on literature these qualities and so contradict their own understanding of literature as ethical.

Custody is also a feature of museums, where the objects exhibited are kept in custody, to prevent their decay or change through the passage of time or use, and the visitors are kept in a type of supervised custody to prevent them touching or interacting with the displays. Thus custody strips from objects their context, and offers them another context, the museum or the academy. It is an act which both changes the objects' meaning and denies a potential for uncontainable change and movement. This understanding of custody contradicts two modernist critical claims. First, it shows that the claim to objectivity is problematic, if not untenable:

'objectivity' – a place in the museum or the academy – is only one context amongst others. Secondly, the custodial academies, far from being the vital site of cultural and spiritual regeneration, turn into places that dispense degrees in curatorship and control. Criticism with a 'custodial function' is a way of controlling literature. For Freadman and Miller, the academies are able to resist change and to prevent the emancipation of the literature they claim is supposed to be liberating the minds of their students. Again, the humanist critical project seems to contradict itself.

Finally, custody has another, less obvious implication. It covers up its own power: a prisoner is created by custody. Custody hides its own violence towards the object it keeps. Far from the neutral, honest, 'objective' approach to literature that these texts claim to take, they disguise their own constricting power. They are as guilty of privileging their own discourse as the theorists they deride: they offer interpretations that claim not to be interpretations which change literature into a humanistic kerygma and demand that criticism should follow.

These anti-theoretical texts provide very little argument at a fundamental level, relying often on 'we contend' and 'I assert'. This contradicts their claim to be open and rational, in opposition to the 'irrational' claims of 'theory'. This remarkably unhumanist lack of argument has two possible causes. First, it may have been made impossible by the anti-theorists' rhetorical tactics, especially the tactic of 'amalgamation': it is impossible to do anything with a straw figure but knock it down. Second, it might be a sign of a genuine paradigm shift, over which it is impossible to argue: the different critical arguments might simply be incommensurable.[60] If this is the case, the very failure of their arguments, in defence of the modernist critical project, is itself a sign of the expiry of the modernist critical project. The inability of a rational humanist in good faith – and almost all of these accounts are well intentioned – to argue shows up the limits of rational humanism.[61]

DEFENDING THE PRESUPPOSITIONS
OF MODERNIST CRITICISM

In addition to defending the humanism core of their shared paradigm of modernist criticism, these anti-theoretical writers also defend, with more force, the methodological assumptions which stem from its humanist ethical basis.

Objectivity and the Disinterested Critic

A number of the anti-theorists argue that their criticism is objective, apolitical and value-free, whilst 'theory' is corrupting, political and manipulative. This claim is self-contradictory. An analysis of this inconsistency both vindicates the assertion that a value-free approach is impossible and illustrates the essential weakness that the assumption of objectivity introduces to the modernist critical paradigm.

Washington, arguing for objectivity, states that 'it is not our business as teachers [and critics] to transmit values of any kind' but to teach students skills and develop their 'mental capacities'.[62] This instrumentalist view of education and criticism is value-laden, stressing as it does certain practices over others and an illusory idea of impartiality. Moreover, it stands at odds with his statement that 'the literary academy will rediscover its sense of purpose' if it returns 'to the past, to the traditions of a truly humanist literary criticism'.[63] Humanism, here for Washington, is not a valueless creed. Thus, although Washington argues that no values should be taught, he contradicts himself by arguing that some values – humanist values – should be taught.

Thurley sums up several of these writers: there is

> no need for . . . assumptions and visions to be clearly articulated: in fact, one must suspect the critic who is able to do so. Critical praxis is far too complex and subtle to allow of very clear articulation . . . demands for a 'value system' or interpretation theory are likely to be more or less disingenuous.[64]

Critical presuppositions cannot be articulated, and, for Thurley, the values turn out to be invisible and inexpressible: 'the authentic act of criticism is recognisable by its violation of theoretical rules, by its reliance upon the value of the inexpressible'.[65] However, Thurley's position, like Washington's, contains self-contradictions. He argues 'value judgement is a necessary element of every authentic critical act' and value judgements do not occur in a vacuum.[66] Thurley's values are humanist, relying on the 'animal and chemical grounding of the species'.[67] This very vague statement of humanism is problematic not only because of its biological essentialism, but also because of the assumption that these 'essential' characteristics in some way guarantee the objectivity that Thurley claims.

To show how 'theory' is ideologically motivated, and to seek to defend their own objective practice as un-ideological or pure, many anti-theorists cite theorists' use of jargon as obscurantist and inappropriate. However, as Felperin points out, the plain speaking of, for example, Leavis, is a jargon itself: 'brittle', 'life-affirming' and 'sensibility' are not the straightforward English that modernist criticism claims, but a complex system of inter-related concepts. John Casey also makes the same point in a simple list of words 'associated with "life"' which also explicitly reveal modernist criticism's own jargon.[68] This way of viewing the language of modernist criticism makes its claim to be jargon-free and beyond any ideology look very weak. The apolitical ideal of objectivity and of disinterestedness it claims does not exist. It is a fiction created by the rhetoric of the particular humanist ethical concerns that motivate these critics' practice.

Practical Criticism

For a number of the anti-theorists, the heuristic power of offering a reading of a text is enough to justify the claims that they make. This is another contemporary version of Leavis's approach: the critic 'must be on his guard against abstracting improperly from what is in front of him' and limit himself or herself to a concrete engagement with texts.[69] Criticism should not make 'metacritical' points or engage with 'abstract ideas'. Berthoff's 'demonstrations', Cook's and Eldridge's range of readings, Thurley's demand for an 'empiricist criticism' and Grant's 'hermeneutic realism' all echo this.[70] Valentine Cunningham's *In the Reading Gaol* is almost totally made up of fascinating heuristic readings to make the same general point. Knapp and Michaels also argue for this: they suggest that theory is 'the attempt to govern interpretations by appealing to an account of interpreta-tion in general . . . with no direct bearing on the interpretation of individual works'. Any attempt to get outside of practice fails – 'no one can reach a position outside of practice' – and that, as a result, theory should stop.[71]

These positions are weak and self-contradictory. First, they all assume a rigorous distinction – a metacritical point itself – between types of writing, critical and literary. Second, they assume that 'criticism' can be a 'pure' act of interpretation, outside any influence or position. This interpretation is blind to its own method – it claims not to have a method – and thus is blind to the presuppositions which make up its theoretical base. It is impossible to be without a 'metacriticism', a series of assumptions that govern a critical approach. Third, their definitions do not hold up. Knapp's and Michaels's argument that 'no one can reach a position outside practice' means that what they call 'theory' is, in fact, as much 'practice' as a close reading of a poem. Thus, if 'theory' collapses into 'practice', there can be no 'metacriti-cism', no theory. This in turn means that the division between 'theory' and 'practice', on which their argument is based, disappears (and their article becomes self-contradictory). If there is no 'theory' as a contrast, a defining opposition, there is no category of 'practice'.

By offering demonstrations, these writers either appeal to the 'inexpressible' as a theoretical presupposition or to an unspoken set of assumptions that they refuse to make clear. This position correlates with the flawed idea of objectivity, which paradoxically stresses the individual responses to a text as 'pure', unmanipulated and thus, somehow, universal. Moreover, when the refusal to offer an 'abstract' set of presuppositions is avoided by offering 'concrete' practical criticism, that act of practical criticism has itself become an act of polemical metacriticism. When these critics comment on a literary object – offer 'practical criticism' – it is often in the interest of making a polemical metacritical point, ironically about the impossibility of making metacritical points.

The Literary Text as Aesthetic Object

For these anti-theoretical texts, the work of literature is 'phenomenally different . . . in constitution and operation', an 'inexpressible mystery', an indivisible 'constellation' which has an association 'with beauty or with sublimity' and is able to restore and 'remythologise our spiritual landscape'.[72] This aesthetic understanding immerses the reader in 'a community of feeling, thought and sensibility'.[73] Moreover, as Olsen argues, making explicit what Leavis keeps implicit, the 'appeal to aesthetic sensibility must thus be seen as logically prior to any directive argument, and the only criterion of validity for a directive argument is success in bringing about agreement in aesthetic perception'.[74] This appeal to intuition and to an unarguable understanding of the value of the literary work as a purely aesthetic object is, in many of these accounts, at the very basis of their critical epistemology.

There are three problems with this position. First, the individual sensibility, the personal reaction, would seem to be at odds with the assertion that an art work embodied universal values. If the aesthetic reaction recognised universal values, then those values would have to be recognised by everybody to be universal. If everybody recognised universal values, then the sensibility would not be personal at all. In addition, the personal response, sensibility, surely must be incommensurable with the idea of objectivity. A response to an art work cannot both be one's own – personal – and also objective – impersonal. Second, and significantly in direct opposition to Olsen's claim, it would be impossible to bring about agreement. If one reaction to an art work simply differed from another, this would be because of a difference in sensibility and not open to provable criteria or rational debate (unless sensibility is rational, which Olsen, Leavis and others deny). The idea of sensibility would seem to rule out free debate which humanism and modernist criticism claims to encourage. Third, this understanding of sensibility is very hard to maintain without a strong belief that the art work is separate from the world as an isolated aesthetic object. If this is the case, then the art work cannot be about, for example, the human condition, or humanist ethics in the world, precisely because it is separate from the world. Again, the modernist critical paradigm appears to be self-contradictory.

Modernist Criticism's Approach to Language

One of the key features of the modernist critical paradigm is its straightforward understanding of language and the problem of reference. Where critics like de Man, for example, problematise these issues, anti-theorists attempt to bypass them. Grant, for example, asserts that 'common sense and usage tell us enough about language for us to behave morally'.[75] Others attempt to ground language in the extra-linguistic. Tallis, for example, asserts that 'theorists' claim that there is no extra-linguistic reality and that language constructs reality: he responds by asserting that 'language does not construct anything. In so far as *speakers* construct "formations of words" they do so in reference to "patterns of reality"'.[76] It is clear here and throughout his argument that Tallis has conflated two very different ideas: he has made a very simplistic interpretation of Derrida's remark that there is nothing outside the text and Heidegger's assertion that it is language that speaks, not man. Tallis is not alone in coming to the extremely complex debates over language which have been central to Continental philosophy since (at least) the last century from an odd angle. These debates emerge from a different tradition from literary criticism and have different concerns.[77]

Cunningham, by using detailed close readings, aims to show that texts refer to 'the historico-worldly Other beyond the text, out there in the extra-linguistic, heterologic zones of that which is not merely textual'.[78] However, these references to the 'real world' are in language, and thus within a signifying system. This, in turn, implies these references are not an escape from language to reality, but rather still part of a signifying system.

Falck, rejecting Saussure, asserts that 'we have [meaning, *he* has] no philosophic choice but to insist . . . that language is not a prison house, or a closed "hermeneutic circle", or a labyrinth with no outlet'. In place of Saussurian theory, he argues that pre-linguistic 'underlying gestural relationships must continue to be present'. Gesture is pre-linguistic and speech is just gesture with sound so, following Collingwood's theory of language, Falck argues that 'every kind or order of language (speech, gesture, and so forth) was an offshoot from an original language of total bodily gesture'. For Falck, this is because of a biological essentialist humanism: 'we are animals before we are human beings, and primitive human beings before we are speakers and thinkers'.[79] It is hard to understand how this particular signifying system does not fall under the same understanding Saussure offers of general semiotic systems. Saussure's claim for semiology was that it would be 'a science which studies the role of signs in social life . . . It would investigate the nature of signs and laws governing them' which would obviously include what we call 'body language' or gesture. Moreover, in relation to spoken language, Saussure argues that linguistics would be 'only one branch of this general science'.[80] Spoken language is one example, not, as Tallis suggests, the master example, of how a semiotic system operates. Moreover, gesture and body language vary from culture to culture and from time to time, and thus surely cannot be as Falck demands, beyond interpretation, transhistorical or 'truly authentic'.[81] For Falck's assertions to hold true, they need to be secured against both a straightforward Saussurian analysis of gesture as a semiotic system and against a deconstructive suggestion of a 'nostalgia' for some sort of authentic meaning guaranteed by the body. Just as Cunningham tried to escape a semiotic system by referring to extra-linguistic objects, Falck relies on gesture, which also turns out to be within a semiotic system.

The Canon and the Problem of Authorship

The canon is central to the paradigm of modernist criticism, and almost all of the 'anti-theorists' defend it. René Girard defends the canon on the strictest of humanist grounds, arguing that 'the most perspicacious texts from the standpoint of human relations are the great texts of Western literature'.[82] Felperin states that without 'a canon, a corpus or a cynosure of exemplary texts, there can be no interpretive community, no more than there can be a faith community without a gospel'. Here his metaphor betrays not only a fundamental eurocentricity (not all faith communities have sacred books), but also the fact that he, and the others defending the canon, accept implicitly the idea that modernist criticism must offer a surrogate religious ethical healing of the fractured modern world. Indeed, for Felperin, the canon is central to this mission: it is 'the precondition for the institutional study of writing'. Felperin would exclude those attempts which, in his opinion, deform the canon because they do not pay heed to the humanistic mission of the university: feminist and ethnic minorities who demand that their own canonical works should be registered are 'special and sectarian, and hence, exclusive' and therefore to be themselves excluded from the formation of the canon.[83]

In association with the idea that certain canonical works are transhistorically valuable, some anti-theorists wish to reassert the primacy of authorial intention in criticism. This is slightly more exceptional: I. A. Richards, in *Practical Criticism*, excludes the author from his protocols and New Criticism found an 'incompatibility of authorial categories with immanent analysis' and made the author irrelevant.[84] In the light of this, when, for example, Berthoff claims that he opposes 'the exclusion of the concept of an author from textual analysis', he is opposing some part of the modernist critical paradigm.[85] However, it becomes clear that the author is often another site for the 'enigmatic sensibility' which modernist critics hold in such esteem. For example, Thurley discusses 'writer's susceptibility to certain feelings and thoughts'. Freadman and Miller argue for the 'experiential authenticity, the imaginative power of [the] author'.[86] This unargued assertion of the author and his or her intentions depends for its value as a claim on the interlocking array of modernist critical understandings which precede it.

The Mission of the University

For a number of anti-theoretical writers, 'theory' is inimical to the academies, and as a consequence, it is a threat to the teaching and learning institutions which are so central to modernist criticism. Ellis argues that deconstruction in particular is a false and destructive radicalism with its origins in the interaction of two very different educational cultures, the French and the American.[87] Fisher argues that instead of invigorating a new liberated academy, against the professionalisation of New Criticism, 'theory' has just produced a new clique of academics with a hierarchy and advancement based on secret knowledge decided upon by their peers, just like the previous generation. It is 'deeply conservative and cynical' with 'a sceptical disbelief in the possibility of improving things in any way'. He argues that the professionalism which dogged New Criticism remains and is made stronger by the jargon of the new orthodoxy. Fisher makes these claims because he follows Frye's humanistic (and Arnoldian) defence of the university and of education: 'the ethical purpose of a liberal education is to liberate, which can only mean to make one capable of conceiving a society as free, classless and urbane'.[88] Again, this illustrates the humanist belief that this position is both possible and objective. Moreover, it shows how important the idea of the university is for modernist criticism.

CONCLUSION: ETHICAL CRITICISM?

This chapter has argued that a modernist critical paradigm, which aimed to interpret works of literature in an ethical light, was inaugurated at the beginning of this century. The paradigm had and still has a theoretical infrastructure: it claims to be objective; to offer 'practical criticism'; to view the literary art work as separate from the world; to accept an unproblematic view on language; to place a canon of transhistorically great works at the core of criticism; it also considers the role of the university as central. All these assumptions rest on a humanist ethical position, and it is this that is thought to be threatened by 'theory'.

One of the key unspoken assertions for this critical paradigm is that it assumes that the realm of ethics is separate from the realm of the aesthetic, or from works of literature. In this, the paradigm insists on epi-reading, going through the text to a realm of ethics. Literary works, they argue, cannot avoid being about ethics, just as they may be about, for example, Dublin or the Second World War. This is one of the reasons that these anti-theorists are so concerned about the problem of reference. If language can only refer to language, then it can in no way refer to what they understand to be the separate realm of the ethical. This conception, however, presupposes that ethics is a realm or a 'thing', like a city or a horse race. It assumes the separation of ethics and language: ethics are a subject for discourse and the ethical is signified by language about ethics. It may well turn out that this conception of ethics, like the critical paradigm that depends on it, is no longer capable of providing the sort of grounding these critics and thinkers argue criticism needs.

The modernist critical paradigm has become frail, inconsistent and self-contradictory. Moreover, it is unable to answer questions put to it from a variety of positions. As a consequence, it cannot maintain itself in its current form. This critical paradigm is reaching its end because there is, as these anti-theorists show, a problem at the underlying level of critical thought, the level of ethics. The modernist critical paradigm, riddled with contradictions and problematic claims, is no longer able to offer an ethical criticism.

In response to this, lines of opposition have been drawn up between two parties. On the one hand are those who would renegotiate the modernist, humanist critical paradigm demanding a 'philosophically toughened literary humanism'.[89] These, seeking ethics beyond the text, in a world reached through that text, can be generally characterised as epi-readers. On the other hand, those critics who can be characterised as graphi-readers because they do not envisage anything beyond the language of text. Chapter 2 will explore the neo-Aristotelian thought of Martha Nussbaum, as a significant example of a literary critical modernist, in her attempts to renegotiate a humanist criticism. In contrast, Chapter 3 will analyse the ethical claims of graphi-reading, as exemplified in the deconstructive criticism of J. Hillis Miller.

NOTES

1. Chris Baldick, *The Social Mission of English Criticism* (Oxford: Clarendon Press, 1983), pp. 4–5.
2. Hayden White, *Metahistory: The Historical Imagination in Nineteenth Century Europe* (Baltimore: Johns Hopkins University Press, 1973), p. x.
3. Dominick Lacapra, *History and Criticism* (London: Cornell University Press, 1985), p. 100.
4. William Wimsatt and Cleanth Brooks, *Literary Criticism: A Short Introduction* (London: Routledge and Kegan Paul, 1957), p. 755.
5. Harry Blamires, *A History of Literary Criticism* (London: Macmillan, 1991).
6. On this process of historical decontextualisation, see Paul Ricoeur, *Time and Narrative*, trans. Kathleen McLaughlin and David Pellauer (Chicago: University of Chicago Press, 1988), vol. 3.
7. Terry Eagleton, *The Function of Criticism* (London: Verso, 1984), p. 13, p. 9.
8. Eagleton, *The Function of Criticism*, p. 107.
9. H. Nettleship, *The Moral Influence of Literature: Classical Education in the Past and Present: Two Popular Addresses* (London: Percival, 1890).
10. I. A. Richards, *Practical Criticism* (London: Routledge and Kegan Paul, 1973), pp. 350–1.
11. See D. J. Palmer, *The Rise of English Studies* (London: University of Hull Press/Oxford University Press, 1965) for an account of this debate in the UK: for the US parallel, see *The Origins of Literary Studies in America*, eds Gerald Graff and Michael Warner (London: Routledge, 1989).
12. H. Nettleship, *The Study of Modern European Languages and Literatures in the University of Oxford* (Oxford: Parker, 1887), p. 6.
13. Nettleship, *The Study of Modern European Languages*, p. 14–15.
14. See Palmer, *The Rise of English Studies*; Baldick, *The Social Mission of English Criticism*, pp. 59–85.
15. E. M. W. Tillyard, *The Muse Unchained: An Intimate Account of the Revolution in English Studies at Cambridge* (London: Bowes and Bowes, 1958), p. 84; Graff and Warner, *The Origins of Literary Studies in America*, p. 4.
16. Edward Said, *Culture and Imperialism* (London: Vintage, 1994), p. 48.
17. Gauri Viswanathan, *Masks of Conquest: Literary Studies and British Rule in India* (New York: Columbia University Press, 1989), p. 199.
18. Viswanathan, *Masks of Conquest*, p. 93.
19. Matthew Arnold, *Culture and Anarchy*, ed. J. Dover Wilson (Cambridge: Cambridge University Press, 1960), pp. 69–70.
20. Palmer, *The Rise of English Studies*, p. 78.
21. Tillyard, *The Muse Unchained*, p. 11.
22. See also Baldick, *The Social Mission of English Criticism*, pp. 86–108 and 134–61. Cornford's work is mentioned, rather coyly, in Tillyard, *The Muse Unchained*, p. 77. See F. N. Cornford (originally anonymous), *Microcosmographia Academica: Being a Guide for the Young Academic Politician* (Cambridge: Bowes and Bowes, 1908).
23. See, for some examples, Perry Anderson, 'Components of the National Culture', *New Left Review*, Vol. 50 (1968), pp. 3–57; Michael Bell, *F. R. Leavis* (London: Routledge, 1988); Inglis, *Radical Earnestness*; Baldick, *The Social Mission of English Criticism*; Terry Eagleton, *Literary Theory* (Oxford: Blackwell, 1983); Bernard Bergonzi, *Exploding English: Criticism, Theory, Culture* (Oxford: Clarendon Press, 1990); *The British Critical Tradition*, ed. Gary Day (Basingstoke: Macmillan, 1993); Francis Mulhern, *The Moment of Scrutiny* (London: New Left Books, 1979); *Re-reading English*, ed. Peter Widdowson (London: Methuen, 1982). On its development in America, see Paul Bové, *Mastering Discourse: The Politics of Intellectual Culture*, (London: Duke University Press, 1992); Frank Lentricchia, *After the New Criticism* (London: Methuen, 1983).
24. In *The Intellectuals and the Masses* (London: Faber and Faber, 1992), for example, John Carey

places both the Leavises very much on the side of 'proud' and 'prejudiced' modernist intellectuals like Eliot.

25. Selya Benhabib, *Critique, Norm and Utopia* (New York: Columbia University Press, 1986), p. 259.
26. Benhabib, *Critique, Norm and Utopia*, p. 259.
27. Rudolf Bultmann, 'Is Exegesis Without Presuppositions Possible?', in *The Hermeneutics Reader*, ed. Kurt Mueller-Vollmer (Oxford: Blackwell, 1985), pp. 242–8 (p. 242).
28. For a parallel reading of the presuppositions of the modernist 'paradigm', see Anthony Easthope 'Paradigm Lost and Paradigm Regained', in *The State of Theory*, ed. Richard Bradford (London: Routledge, 1993), pp. 90–104. He lists five features of this paradigm: epistemological empiricism; a method of modernist reading; the high cultural canon; the idea of the literary object; a self-sufficient textual unity.
29. With Eliot, the concern for ethics is double-edged. His concerns twist into a vicious anti-semitism, elitism and aggressive reaction against social change. His series of lectures, *After Strange Gods: A Primer of Modern Heresy* (London: Faber and Faber, 1934), shows up more than the casual anti-semitism of 1930s British society. It is a piece of premeditated rabble-rousing, much more pernicious than, for example, Paul de Man's wartime journalism. Eliot's views in this text, not only on race but also on other subjects, compare with Heidegger's 'Rectorial Address'. See Anthony Julius, *T. S. Eliot: Anti-Semitism and Literary Form* (Cambridge: Cambridge University Press, 1996).
30. Tillyard, *The Muse Unchained*, p. 97.
31. Richards, *Practical Criticism*, p. 1.
32. *Writing Englishness 1900–1950*, eds Judy Giles and Tim Middleton (London: Routledge, 1995), pp. 149–60 (p. 159, p. 158).
33. Although Marxist criticism seemed to offer a challenge to the consensus, in fact it remained very much within the modernist paradigm, hoping to restore an ethical unity to the fragmented world of modernity not by appeals to 'Englishness' or 'Morality' but to an 'ethics' developed from a totalising meta-narrative of a socialist utopia. Most Marxist critics are best understood as 'left Leavisites' maintaining the same understanding as modernist critics of the ethical role of criticism.
34. Michael Payne and Harold Schweizer, 'The General Preface to The Bucknell Lectures in Literary Theory', in Terry Eagleton, *The Significance of Theory* (Oxford: Blackwell, 1990), p. vi.
35. Linda Nicholson, 'Introduction', *Feminism/Postmodernism*, ed. Linda Nicholson (London: Routledge, 1990), pp. 1–16 (p. 4).
36. Baldick, *The Social Mission of English Criticism*, p. 1.
37. Howard Felperin, 'The Anxiety of Deconstruction', *Yale French Studies*, Vol. 69 (1984), pp. 254–66; Eugene Goodheart, *The Sceptic Disposition in Contemporary Criticism* (Princeton: Princeton University Press, 1984), p. 14.
38. Tobin Siebers, *The Ethics of Criticism* (London: Cornell University Press, 1988), p. 41. Michael Fisher, *Does Deconstruction make any Difference?: Poststructuralism and the Defense of Poetry in Modern Criticism* (Bloomington: Indiana University Press, 1985), p. xi, p. xiii.
39. David Kaufmann 'The Profession of Theory', *PMLA*, Vol. 105 (1990), pp. 519–30, (p. 519); M. Schiralli, 'Reconstructing Literary Value', *Journal of Aesthetic Education*, Vol. 25 (1991), pp. 115–19 (p. 115).
40. Patrick Parrinder, *The Failure of Theory* (Brighton: Harvester Press, 1987) p. ix; Easthope, 'Paradigm Lost and Paradigm Regained', p. 93. LaCapra, *Criticism and History*, p. 96; Warner Berthoff, *Literature and the Continuances of Virtue* (Princeton: Princeton University Press, 1986), p. 30.
41. Peter Washington, *Fraud: Literary Theory and the End of English* (London: Fontana, 1989). "Hackademe" is a recurring pun from Raymond Tallis, *Not Saussure: A critique of Post-Saussurian Literary Theory* (London: Macmillan, 1988).
42. Barbara Johnson, *The Wake of Deconstruction* (Oxford: Blackwell, 1994), p. 79.
43. Berthoff, *Literature and the Continuances of Virtue*, p. 30; Parrinder, *The Failure of Theory*, p. 14.
44. Colin Falck, *Myth, Truth and Literature: Towards a True Postmodernism* (Cambridge: Cambridge University Press, 1989), p. 24.
45. Washington, *Fraud*, pp. 12–13.
46. Geoffrey Thurley, *Counter-modernism in Current Literary Theory* (London: Macmillan 1983), p. 228.
47. In fact, thinkers on the left often oppose 'theory', especially deconstruction: Eagleton writes that it is not at all obvious that 'theory is an inherently radical affair' ('Discourse and Discos: Theory in the Space between Culture and Capitalism', *Times Literary Supplement*, 15 July 1994, pp. 3–4 (p.

3). See also Terry Eagleton, *Against the Grain* (London: Verso, 1986); Christopher Norris *What's Wrong with Postmodernism* (London: Harvester Wheatsheaf, 1990); Christopher Norris, *Uncritical Theory: Postmodernism, Intellectuals and the Gulf War* (London: Lawrence and Wishart, 1992); Christopher Norris, *Truth and the Ethics of Criticism* (Manchester: Manchester University Press, 1994); Peter Dews, *Logics of Disintegration* (London: Verso, 1987). The best work on these issues is Gillian Rose, *The Broken Middle* (Oxford: Blackwell, 1992).

48. Patrick Grant, *Literature and Personal Values* (Basingstoke: Macmillan, 1992), p. 133; Thurley, *Counter-modernism in Current Literary Theory*, p. 235.

49. Stein Haugom Olsen, *The End of Literary Theory* (Cambridge: Cambridge University Press, 1987), p. 155.

50. Grant, *Literature and Personal Values*, p. 217, p. 221.

51. Siebers, *The Ethics of Criticism*, p. 13, p. 240.

52. Albert Cook, *Canons and Wisdoms* (Philadelphia: University of Pennsylvania Press, 1993), p. 131.

53. Washington, *Fraud*, p. 177; Schiralli, 'Reconstructing Literary Value', p. 119.

54. Siebers, *The Ethics of Criticism*, p. 1.

55. Fisher, *Does Deconstruction make any Difference?*, p. 26; Palmer, *Literature and Moral Understanding*, p. 58.

56. Richard Freadman and Seamus Miller, *Re-thinking Theory* (Cambridge: Cambridge University Press, 1992), p. 4.

57. Freadman and Miller, *Re-thinking Theory*, p. 67.

58. Freadman and Miller, *Re-thinking Theory*, p. 229, p. 231.

59. Freadman and Miller, *Re-thinking Theory*, p. 163.

60. On incommensurability between different paradigms of thought, see Alastair MacIntyre, *Three Rival Versions of Moral Enquiry* (London: Duckworth, 1990).

61. For relevant discussions of humanism specifically, see Martin Heidegger, 'Letter on Humanism', in *Basic Writings*, ed. David Farrell Krell (London: Harper Row, 1977), pp. 189–242: humanism 'is opposed because it does not set the humanitas of man high enough' (p. 210); Emmanuel Levinas, *Otherwise than Being: or, Beyond Essence*, trans. Alphonso Lingis (The Hague: Martinus Nijhoff, 1981): humanism 'has to be denounced because it is not sufficiently human' (p. 128).

62. Washington, *Fraud*, p. 12.

63. Washington, *Fraud*, p. 177.

64. Thurley, *Counter-modernism in Current Literary Theory*, p. 123.

65. Thurley, *Counter-modernism in Current Literary Theory*, p. 98.

66. Thurley, *Counter-modernism in Current Literary Theory*, p. 101.

67. Thurley, *Counter-modernism in Current Literary Theory*, p. 235.

68. Howard Felperin, *Beyond Deconstruction* (Oxford: Clarendon Press, 1985), ch. 1, 'Leavisism revisited'; John Casey, *The Language of Criticism* (London: Methuen, 1966), pp. 177–8.

69. F. R. Leavis, *The Common Pursuit* (London: Chatto and Windus, 1952), p. 213.

70. Berthoff, *Literature and the Continuances of Virtue*, p. 4; Cook, *Canons and Wisdoms*; Richard Eldridge, *On Moral Personhood* (London: University of Chicago Press, 1989); Thurley, *Counter-modernism in Current Literary Theory*, p. 5; Grant, *Literature and Personal Values*, p. 222.

71. Steven Knapp and Walter Benn Michaels, 'Against Theory', in *Against Theory*, ed. W. J. T. Mitchell (London: Chicago University Press, 1985), pp. 11–30 (p. 11, p. 30).

72. Berthoff, *Literature and the Continuances of Virtue*, p. 5; Tallis, *Not Saussure*, p. 127; Olsen, *The End of Literary Theory*, p. 3; Falck, *Myth Truth and Literature*, p. 135; Cook, *Canons and Wisdoms*, p. 21.

73. Palmer, *Literature and Moral Understanding*, p. 58.

74. Olsen, *The End of Literary Theory*, p. 7.

75. Grant, *Literature and Personal Values*, p. 133.

76. Tallis, *Not Saussure*, p. 60, p. 76.

77. For this argument in detail, see Rudolphe Gasché, 'Deconstruction as Criticism', in *Glyph 6* (London: Johns Hopkins University Press, 1979), pp. 177–216; Rudolphe Gasché, *The Tain of the Mirror* (London: Harvard University Press, 1986).

78. Valentine Cunningham, *In the Reading Gaol* (Oxford: Blackwell, 1994), p. 61.

79. Falck, *Myth, Truth and Literature*, pp. 17– 43.

80. Ferdinand de Saussure, *Course in General Linguistics*, trans. Roy Harris (London: Duckworth, 1983), p. 15, p. 16.

81. For body language and gesture varying over cultural and temporal space, see, for one example, in relation to the face, *The Challenge of Facework: Cross-Cultural and Interpersonal Issues*, ed. Stella

Ting-Toomey (Albany: State University of New York Press, 1994). Thanks to Susan Brown for this reference.

82. Girard, 'Theory and its Terrors', in *The Limits of Theory*, ed. T. Kavanagh, pp. 225–55 (p. 253).
83. Felperin, *Beyond Deconstruction*, p. 46, p. 48, p. 48.
84. Seàn Burke, *The Death and Return of the Author: Criticism and Subjectivity in Barthes, Foucault and Derrida* (Edinburgh: Edinburgh University Press, 1992), p. 16.
85. Berthoff, *Literature and the Continuances of Virtue*, p. 6.
86. Thurley, *Counter-modernism in Current Literary Theory*, p. 235; Freadman and Miller, *Re-thinking Theory*, p. 163.
87. Ellis argues that, in contrast to Anglo-American universities, French universities follow a rigid system. The Anglophone critical world has been used to theoretical debate about literature since the 1930s, whereas in France literary study was a question of literary history and biography until the 1960s – there is no equivalent to the biblical learnt-by-rote *Literary History of France* by Gustav Lanson in the Anglo-american tradition. Ellis argues that Saussure's work, which only re-emerged through Lévi-Strauss and structural anthropology in the 1950s in France, was certainly known, if not widely read, by philosophers of language in Britain: his insights came as no surprise and, in some cases, had already been reached by different routes. From discussing these and other oppositions, Ellis concludes that although deconstruction may have been a radical thing in France, it was not so for America. As a result of this, the 'prevailing climate of American criticism, whose watchword was pluralism, scarcely provided a well-guarded citadel that deconstruction needed to conquer by force' (Ellis, *Against Deconstruction* (Princeton: Princeton University Press, 1989) p. 157).
88. Fisher, *Does Deconstruction make any Difference?*, p. 109, p. xiv.
89. Freadman and Miller, *Re-thinking Theory*, p. 4.

2

———— • ————

THE DIALOGUE BETWEEN PERCEPTION
AND RULE: MARTHA NUSSBAUM

I imagine . . . a future in which our talk about literature will return,
increasingly, to a concern with the practical – to the ethical and social
questions that give literature its high importance in our lives . . . a
future in which literary theory . . . will join with ethical theory in
pursuit of the question 'how should one live?'. Join, I mean, not as
didactic moralist but both as devious ally and subversive critic.

Martha Nussbaum

When a person happens to have a professional activity that is or
becomes relevant to major ends of human life – how exhilarating that
activity then is, and how deep, I think, the obligations it then imposes.

Martha Nussbaum[1]

LITERATURE, PHILOSOPHY AND
`ETHICAL THEORISING´

The previous chapter argued that the dominant literary critical paradigm
was no longer able to offer a convincing ethical criticism because it could no
longer justify either its ethical position or its methodology. The humanist
ethical position on which it was grounded – fully thought out or not by the
defenders of the model – was not a solid foundation for criticism. In the
traditional model of ethical criticism both 'ethical' and 'criticism' are
problematic.

However, this is not in itself reason enough simply to dispose of this
critical paradigm and seek others. Gillian Rose, using friendship as a
metaphor for reason, argues that if a 'friend whom you trust more than any
other . . . lets you down suddenly . . . [and] ceases to fulfil expectations
which . . . you have come to take for granted' the correct, responsible
reaction, is not to give up friendship altogether but to renegotiate that
friendship.[2] In the same way, Freadman and Miller argued not for a new

paradigm, but for a rethinking of the old, for a 'philosophically toughened humanism'.[3] In response to these demands, this chapter explores a wide-ranging renegotiation of modernist ethical criticism in the work of the neo-Aristotelian thinker Martha Nussbaum.

Nussbaum offers a fully explored and well-defined ethical position and applies this to the relationships between ethics, literature and criticism. Indeed, her work can be seen as the most sophisticated evolution of attempts by neo-Aristotelians, like Wayne Booth and the Chicago critics, to explore these issues. As an Aristotelian, her view is that 'ethical theorizing proceeds by way of a reflective dialogue between the intuitions and beliefs of the interlocutor, or reader, and a series of complex ethical conceptions, presented for exploration'.[4]

For Nussbaum, literature has an absolutely central role to play in 'ethical theorizing'. She writes that 'moral attention and moral vision finds in novels its most appropriate articulation . . . the novel itself is a moral achievement, and the well lived life is a work of literary art' (*LK*, p. 148). As Nussbaum argues in her essay 'Perceptive Equilibrium', this is because literature

> speaks *about us* . . . As Aristotle observed, it is deep and conducive to
> our inquiry about how to live because it does not simply . . . record
> that this or that event happened; it searches for patterns of possibility –
> of choice and circumstance, and the interaction between choice and
> circumstance – that turn up in human lives with such a persistence that
> they must be regarded as *our* possibilities. (*LK* p. 171)

Nussbaum's work seems to question the boundary between philosophy and literature by claiming to uncover complementary qualities of 'ethical theorizing' in both.

Nussbaum's argument is clear in her work on the essential vulnerability of human goodness in classical antiquity, *The Fragility of Goodness*. In antiquity, the division between literary works and philosophical works simply did not exist:

> for them, there were human lives and problems, and various genres in
> both prose and poetry in which one could reflect about those
> problems. Indeed, epic and tragic poets were widely assumed to be
> the central ethical thinkers and teachers of Greece; nobody thought of
> their work as less serious, less aimed at truth, than the speculative
> prose treatises of historians and philosophers. (*FG*, p. 12)

Plato exiled the poets from his republic because he saw them as 'dangerous rivals' (*FG*, p. 12): his philosophy about the good life and the human soul demanded a specific comprehension of writing.[5] According to

Nussbaum, this does not mean that for the ancient Greeks 'literary works are dispensable in an inquiry that aims at ethical truth' (*FG*, p. 12). For Nussbaum, literature is of key importance not just as cultural background to Plato and Aristotle, or as an illustration of the popular ideas these philosophers may have been working against. Instead, literary works are 'an ethical reflection in their own right' (p. 13). This is because these works 'are likely to confront and explore problems about human beings . . . that a philosophical text might be able to omit or avoid' (p. 13), which in itself makes them worthy of study as philosophy. More importantly, however, and central to Nussbaum's argument here and elsewhere, literature offers not simply clear examples of ethical difficulties to be drawn out by a philosopher or critic, but rather a *heuristic* working through of the issues involved. She writes:

> a tragedy does not display the dilemmas of its characters as pre-articulated; it shows them searching for the morally salient; and it forces us, as interpreters, to be similarly active. Interpreting a tragedy is messier . . . than assessing a philosophical example . . . To invite such material into the centre of an ethical inquiry concerning these problems of practical reason is . . . to add to its content a picture of reason's procedures and problems that could not be readily conveyed in any other form. (*FG*, p. 14)

Here literature plays a key methodological role, bridging 'the gap between belief and theory' to help the 'elucidation and assessment of someone else's complex position' (*FG*, p. 11). This heuristic working through of a particular set of moral problems in literature is, she claims, an experience open to everybody. In this, also, literature furthers the Aristotelian project, 'whose aims are ultimately defined in terms of a 'we', of people who wish to live together and share a conception of virtue' (*FG*, p. 14): literature becomes part of a community's experience. Stylistic conceptions, too, are bound up with ethical inquiry, and choices of style not open to philosophy are open to literature. Parallel to a point made by Wayne Booth, she argues that style 'itself makes its claims, expresses its own sense of what matters. Literary form is not separable from philosophic content, but is, itself, part of content – an integral part, then, of the search for and the statement of truth' (*LK*, p. 3).[6] Finally, Nussbaum argues that philosophy appeals only to the intellect: literature, however, 'centrally involves emotional response' and as such can involve the whole person in the sort of heuristic self-reading and development Nussbaum sees as the base of the Aristotelian project (*FG*, p. 15).

Nussbaum takes these considerations from classical Greece into modern debates about literature. Whilst discussing Aristotle, she writes that 'we could exemplify Aristotelian perception using texts of many different sorts. I think above all, of the novels of Henry James' (*FG*, p. 313). It is chiefly through her understanding of James, and *The Golden Bowl* in particular, that Nussbaum makes explicit her understanding of the relationship between ethics and literature by developing a concept she names 'perceptive equilibrium'.

PERCEPTIVE EQUILIBRIUM

For Nussbaum, as for James,

> [O]btuseness and refusal of vision are our besetting vices. Responsible lucidity can be wrested from that darkness only by painful, vigilant effort, the intense scrutiny of particulars. Our highest and hardest task is to make ourselves people 'on whom nothing is lost'. (*LK*, p. 148)[7]

This task is, for Nussbaum, an essentially practical one to be achieved through perceptive equilibrium, a concept adapted from John Rawls's influential work of political theory, *A Theory of Justice*. Rawls, in order to maintain his theory of social justice, introduces the concept of 'reflexive equilibrium'. The key question for Rawls is neither the Kantian 'what is my moral duty?' nor the Utilitarian 'how shall I maximise my utility?' but rather a more general one about how one should live in society. The aim of any inquiry is not to reveal immutable moral laws, such as Kant's Categorical Imperative, but rather to respond to human experience and make effective changes. Theoretical inquiry is useful to revise goals, improve self-understanding and to attune oneself to the community, but the aim is essentially practical: the results must be coherent and shareable with everybody. The point of reflective equilibrium 'is reached after a person has weighed proposed conceptions and he has either revised his judgements to accord with one of them or held fast to his initial convictions (and the corresponding conception)'.[8] It achieves 'considered judgements', trusting some conclusions and rejecting others: any conclusions must be general in form, universal in application, public, order conflicting claims and regard themselves as final and conclusive.

Nussbaum modifies this concept. She accepts the vital importance of practical application but insists that the capability to perceive, the 'effort to see', is of primary ethical significance (*LK*, p. 185). Lack of awareness is immoral, 'obtuseness is a moral failing' (*LK*, p. 156). Nussbaum considers that any universalising principles – even those of Rawls, for example – are always capable of missing something, of 'blindness', in a specific situation.

To supplement this central weakness of rule-based moral systems, she argues that narratives

> cultivate our ability to see and care for particulars, not as representa-
> tives of the law, but as what they themselves are: to respond vigorously
> with senses and emotions before the new; to care deeply about chance
> happenings in the world, rather than to fortify ourselves against them;
> to wait for the outcome, and to be bewildered – to wait and float and
> to be actively passive. (*LK*, p. 184)

For Nussbaum it is the working through of ethical difficulties through the practical heuristic situation of literature that best embodies an Aristotelian conception of the ethical. Literature offers an experience through which our ethical intuitions and moral outlines can be tested, explored and modified. Perceptive equilibrium is always making the effort to see, not only in terms of a universalising rule, but as a constant 'dialogue between perception and rule' (*LK*, p. 157). As such, in a constant dialectic, it can never reach a fixed conclusion, but rather is forced to explore different particularities over and over again, in an open-ended inquiry. Throughout this process 'we will need to maintain as much self-consciousness as possible about our method and our implicit ends, asking what evaluative content they themselves express' (*LK*, p. 186).

Inherent in Nussbaum's argument is the understanding that a universal law must be explored through practical, heuristic examples: without 'the abilities of perception' she argues, 'duty is blind and therefore powerless' (*LK*, p. 156) To avoid failing by the standards of her own argument she offers two readings of *The Golden Bowl*.

PERCEPTIVE EQUILIBRIUM IN ACTION:
NUSSBAUM´S READINGS OF *THE GOLDEN BOWL*

Viewing Imperfect Fidelity

In her first essay specifically on *The Golden Bowl*, 'Flawed Crystals: James's *The Golden Bowl* and Literature as Moral Philosophy', Nussbaum argues that Maggie Verver aims at 'moral perfection' (*LK*, p. 125) and has an 'extreme emphasis on flawless living', in which harmony and guiltlessness are the highest good (*LK*, p. 131). This childlike 'attachment to moral simplicity' (*LK*, p. 128), which Nussbaum illustrates by emphasising Maggie's metaphor of life as a watertight ship, becomes the motivating narrative force in the first part of *The Golden Bowl* as Maggie tries to combine the conflicting relationships between her husband, her father and her friend Charlotte. Nussbaum argues that this approach to life has a number of consequences. First, it prevents Maggie from resolving her own conflict (essentially, perhaps, a sexual conflict) between her role as wife and her role as daughter because a resolution would involve the guilt and betrayal inherent in giving one intimate relationship priority over another. Second, it means that it is impossible for Maggie to see 'values, including persons, emerge as distinct ends in their own right' (*LK*, p. 130) since all human particularities disappear under her overarching aim of moral perfection. Nussbaum embodies this by examining the way in which the angular pagoda at the start of the second part of the novel is used as a metaphor to represent the irregular shape of personal relationships which contrast with the smooth, well-rounded approach to life that Maggie wishes to follow. She suggests that the smoothness of the bowl, contrasted with the jagged, angular crack which is the flaw in the crystal, is another version of this motif. Third, Maggie's moral simplicity leads her and her father to believe in the separateness of persons: a human being is, for the Ververs, a thing in itself, isolated from a network of moral responsibilities. The Ververs perceive people, and the Prince in particular, as *objets d'art*, to be looked at and admired, but in relation to which one accrues no responsibility. Nussbaum suggests, as an analogy, that if 'one day I spend my entire museum visit gazing at the Turners, I have not incurred a guilt against the Blakes in the next room' (*LK*, p.132). Treating people as things allows a harmony impossible if each person is a particular, and, Nussbaum argues, this is symptomatic of Maggie's approach to life. This ideal, writes Nussbaum, 'followed out to its strictest conclusion, generates an extraordinary blindness to values and ends by subordinating the particular claim of each commitment and love to the claims of harmony' (*LK*, p. 132).

For Nussbaum, *The Golden Bowl* shows 'a human being's relation to value in the world to be, fundamentally and of contingent necessity, one of imperfect fidelity and therefore of guilt' (*LK*, p. 133). We are always already involved in a network of relationships that involve choice and conflict, and to aim blindly at a moral purity risks immoral obtuseness. For Nussbaum, Maggie responds to this in the second part of the novel: Maggie realizes that 'meaningful commitment to a love in the world requires the sacrifice of one's own moral purity' (*LK*, p. 134). She argues that in the face of the actual situation in which the four central characters find themselves, Maggie reaches adulthood by her resolution to act, which shatters the harmony of the group and involves difficult moral choices: her cruelty to Charlotte and her effective exile of her father are the two key moments in this process of reaching maturity.

Nussbaum draws a number of conclusions from this reading. She argues that *The Golden Bowl* has profound moral content which makes specific moral demands on the reader and interpreter. She suggests that 'a philosophical text would have a hard time mounting a direct argument' for the claim she finds central to *The Golden Bowl*, that 'our loves and commitments are so related that infidelity and failure of response are more or less inevitable features even of the best examples of loving,' (*LK*, pp. 139–40). As a way of dealing concretely with issues such as these, the novel is an indispensable tool. Moreover, Nussbaum suggests that these possibilities for moral response were put there by the 'high and fine mind' (*LK*, p. 141) of Henry James. By his manipulation of plot and language, James is able to draw out moral significance unobtainable to others. Finally, her key point again concerns perception. Her reading of James's novel, based on the testing of a rule (Maggie's insistence on harmony) against a particular situation, provides an invaluable corrective to philosophy's more usual move from particulars to universals and thus an example of perceptive equilibrium. The 'primacy of intuitive perception' argues that although universal conclusions are to be drawn from particulars, these conclusions must be constantly tested against the particulars which continually recur. Nussbaum concludes, therefore, that the moral content of the novel offers the

> idea that human deliberation is a constant adventure of the personality, undertaken against terrific odds and among frightening mysteries, *and* that this is . . . the source of much of its beauty and richness, that texts written in a traditional philosophical style have the most insuperable difficulty conveying to us. (*LK*, p. 142)

This 'adventure' implies that the novel also makes demands on and puts questions to the reader's abilities of moral perception. The reader is involved in an heuristic adventure exploring and working through the particular difficulties of the novel. This sort of questioning, active involvement itself supplements and completes the aims of the Socratic enterprise. In addition, and perhaps more significantly in this case, Nussbaum argues that the text itself acknowledges our flawed attention, our inability to see, and our own destructive purity of aims as readers. The novel's stylistic subtlety, the frequent and delicate use of easily missed nuances and the limitations of the narrative voice remind the reader of his or her own fallible attention, partial view and the need for interpretation. Indeed, for Nussbaum, the voice of the narrator (she unproblematically names this voice James's own) is an implicit critique of the way in which nineteenth-century literature frequently made use of the omniscient narrator. Moreover, Nussbaum argues that the identification with Maggie always limits the reader's comprehension, and that, having made this identification – 'seeing this world through her intelligent eyes' (*LK*, p. 145) – it is the reader who is revealed with Maggie to be 'superficial and impoverished' (*LK*, p. 145). Maggie, the authorial voice and the subtlety of the writing style all combine to reproduce in the activity of writing exactly the same moral flaws that the book's narrative illustrates.

Literary Imagination/Moral Imagination

In Nussbaum's second essay specifically on *The Golden Bowl*, '"Finely Aware and Richly Responsible": Literature and the Moral Imagination', her aim is to argue that 'the work of the moral imagination is . . . like the work of the creative imagination, especially that of the novelist' (*LK*, p. 148). Instead of covering the whole narrative of the novel, she concentrates on Chapter 37, in which Adam and Maggie Verver are reconciled to each other by their decision to separate. Nussbaum sees this moment as a 'moral achievement of deep significance' in which Maggie makes the transition from child to woman (*LK*, p. 151). Perception here is crucial since, Nussbaum argues, this moment occurs precisely because both Adam and Maggie are able to see each other in new ways. Nussbaum explores a long passage, heavy with sexual imagery, in which Adam sees Maggie as a sea creature imbued with independence and an almost playful arrogance. Maggie is no longer his nun-like daughter and travelling companion, but a person in her own right. In turn, Maggie suddenly comes to the realisation that Adam in himself is more precious than all his expensive works of art: he becomes simultaneously small and limited, only a particular person, and at the same time 'great and deep' for precisely the same reason, valuable in his very personhood.

This moment of a mutual change of perception marks, for Nussbaum, the central shift in the novel. However, as she takes pains to point out, moral action, although it may be based on and motivated by perception, also makes more concrete demands and calls to responsibility. Nussbaum writes that James 'shows us how perception without responsibility is dangerously free-floating, even as duty without perception is blunt and blind' (*LK*, p. 155). It is this that leads her to consider the duties of the artist: following James, she argues that he or she must render the world accurately, and yet have room for new perceptions. She finds in the figure of Maggie, who often thinks of herself as an actress forced to improvise, a key symbol of this. Improvisation depends on an acutely aware perception of both historical contexts and of shifting, changing patterns of responsibility and commitment. Concrete perceptions, then, are crucial for the improvisation which underlies both the artistic and the moral imaginations.

General rules, both of moral behaviour and artistic creation, are 'insufficiently equipped' (*LK*, p. 156) for practical events in the world and by 'themselves, trusted for and in themselves, the standing terms are a recipe for obtuseness' (*LK*, p. 156). There will always be good actions for which there cannot be a preceding principle, because actions take place in constantly developing, new contexts. For Nussbaum, and, she claims, for James, the moral actor and the aesthetic perceiver employ universal terms 'in an open-ended, evolving way' (*LK*, p. 157).

Nussbaum goes on to claim that moral rules themselves can only be shown in a narrative in their correct relation to perceptions. She writes that if

> we are to assess the claim that correct judgement is the outcome of a dialogue between antecedent principle and new vision, we need to see the view embodied in prose that does not take away the very complexity and indeterminacy of choice that gives substance to the view. (*LK*, p. 160)

A principle cannot just be stated; rather any principle must be embodied in a text and that text in turn will question that principle by offering new perceptions. An abstract philosophical text is not able fully to express a principle, unless that principle itself can be seen in a practical context which reflects the difficulties and confusions of the real world.

This raises again the issue of the status of the distinction between philosophic texts and literary texts. Nussbaum argues again that the literary text is the 'ally' (*LK*, p. 161) of a philosophical text: the two sorts of texts interact and supplement each other, the one – following Aristotle – offering abstract philosophical 'outlines' of rules, the other offering complex moments of interaction between the rules and particular situations, and thus both new perceptions and a space for dialogue.

It is because of this interaction that Nussbaum can make the concluding claim of her article, that there is an overlapping relationship – 'more than an analogy' (*LK*, p. 162) – between moral attention and aesthetic attention, and between artistic creation and moral achievements. Her argument suggests that reading a novel is the same as 'reading' one's own life:

> a novel, just because it is not our life, places us in a moral position that is favourable for perception and it shows us what it would be like to take up that position in life. We find here love without possessiveness, attention without bias, involvement without panic. (*LK*, p. 162)

Precisely because Nussbaum understands moral experience as a lucid apprehension, the skills involved in reading a novel are applicable to the skills involved in perceiving and acting on moral demands in the world: novels are a 'dry run' for reality. The logic of this argument leads Nussbaum to conclude that some people, in this case James, 'who have developed their faculties more finely . . . can make discriminations . . . that are unavailable to the rest of us' (*LK*, p. 164). She writes that in 'the war against moral obtuseness, the artist is our fellow fighter, frequently our guide' (*LK*, p. 164). It follows from this that reading in a clear, attentive way will make each of us more attentive, more perceptive to our world, and that 'these alert winged books are not just irreplaceably fine representations of moral achievement, they are moral achievements on behalf of the community' (*LK*, p. 165).

NUSSBAUM'S APPROACH AND MODERNIST CRITICISM

This belief in the communal role of the literary work, what James called 'the civic use of the imagination', is not the only similarity between Nussbaum's approach and modernist critical paradigm. She writes that her approach is 'implicitly' linked to the work of F. R. Leavis and Lionel Trilling, and indeed, there are many similarities (*LK*, p. 190). For Nussbaum, as for Leavis, Trilling and others, literature 'speaks about us' and deals with 'human lives': she is, as they were, centrally concerned with the ethical significance of literature (*LK*, p. 171). Leavis's 'maturity' and 'sensibility' correlate to Nussbaum's 'keen vision and alert feelings' (*LK*, p. 141): Leavis writes that the 'critic's aim is . . . to realize as sensitively as possible this or that which claims his attention'. For Nussbaum, as for these critics, 'epic and tragic poets' are the 'central ethical thinkers and teachers' (*FG*, p. 12). She supports 'practical criticism', 'the intense scrutiny of particulars' in texts (*LK*, p. 148). Like Leavis – author of *The Critic as Anti-philosopher* – Nussbaum claims that literature cannot be reduced to philosophical explanations: 'interpreting a tragedy is messier. . . than assessing a philosophical example' (*FG*, p. 14). Literature, and especially the authorial voice, has access to finer moral perceptions – to which others are blind – and these distinctions are weapons in the 'war' against obtuseness: literature, for the traditional critics as well as for Nussbaum, is an ethical tool whith which to improve humanity. Again, for Nussbaum as for Leavis, Trilling and others, literature also fosters a spirit of communal identity: great works 'are moral achievements on behalf of the community' (*LK*, p. 167): their aims are 'ultimately defined in terms of a 'we', of people who wish to live together and share a conception of virtue' (*FG*, p. 14). This echoes precisely the ways in which more traditional criticism sought to use literature as a way of fostering a unifying nationalistic ideal in a fissiparous state: as Leavis suggested, literature is 'an essential means of continuity'.[10]

It is in these ways that Nussbaum is restating the central precepts and the ethical ideals of the modernist criticism. However, she is offering a renegotiation of these ideas, a 'toughened literary humanism', because of her clear commitment to a neo-Aristotelian ethical framework. She explicitly places literary texts in a specifically ethical context, and literature is understood as a heuristic device, in which 'the dialogue between perception and rule' is enacted (*LK*, p. 157). Where the ethics of criticism examined in Chapter 1 was unstated, or too vague to provide a solid grounding, Nussbaum provides a fully worked out philosophic grounding for her literary analysis and defence of reading. However it is precisely this firm commitment to an ethical programme which opens her methodology to critique. Despite her claim that she intends to 'maintain as much self-consciousness as possible about . . . method and . . . implicit ends' (*LK*, p. 186), her ethical commitments makes her blind to a number of extremely problematic assertions and presuppositions which inform her critical practice. If the 'ethical' in her ethical criticism is fully laid out, the 'criticism' is not.

PROBLEMS WITH NUSSBAUM'S APPROACH

Nussbaum's approach to these issues is open to question on three levels. First, it can be shown that she offers poor and sometimes inaccurate readings of the literary texts on which she concentrates. Second, her conception of the act of reading contains a number of problematical assumptions. Third, her understanding of the issues which surround this practice, her metacritical position, has a number of crucial blindnesses and contradictions, not least in the way her view of literature reaffirms precisely the binary opposition of philosophy against literature that her texts claim to challenge.

NUSSBAUM'S CRITICISM

Nussbaum's actual reading of texts is very often quite reductive. This is perhaps best shown briefly by looking at her readings of *The Golden Bowl*. The key claim that Maggie is in pursuit of moral purity, for example, Nussbaum takes verbatim from the lips of Fanny Assingham.[11] Fanny Assingham, amongst other things, lies throughout the novel, breaks the symbolic golden bowl to cover up her deceptions (p. 448), admits that she is no more than a high class pander (p. 412) and anyway has only become involved out of her desire to win a victory in her never-ending war of words with her husband. She is not in any way an objective or neutral observer, and what she says simply cannot be taken at face value. Maggie can equally well (and on her own admission) be seen as selfish and acquisitive (p. 506). There are a number of such examples of over-determination in Nussbaum's analyses. However, this in itself does not discredit her philosophical approach. What does cause problems for it are, however, a number of deep and unquestioned assumptions about the nature of reading itself.

In order to maintain her claims for the importance of literature as a heuristic tool, Nussbaum is forced to offer a reductive and over-simplified understanding of the act of reading which is open to a wide-ranging critique.

Nussbaum as 'Epi-reader'

Nussbaum continually passes over the textual nature of a literary work and it is this which forms her crucial blindness. She understands a text as a surface behind which there are real situations and real events. Denis Donoghue describes this as 'epi-reading', 'not willing to leave written words as it finds them on the page . . . [epi-reading] wants to restore the words to a source, a human situation involving speech, character, personality and destiny construed as having a personal form'.[12] This is precisely what Nussbaum's approach does. Indeed, she claims that literature '*speaks* about us' (*LK*, p. 171, italics added) and her texts are full of similar phonologocentric assumptions. The assumption that literary texts are 'real' presentations of people and situations actually present in some way, and not just linguistic artifacts, is essential for her central claim that literature offers a particular real situation as a heuristic working through of ethical principles.

There are a number of problems with this version of epi-reading. First, as much of Derrida's work (amongst others) argues, this phonologocentric assumption is unwarranted. Nussbaum assumes real presence in texts, ignoring the fact that the text's very existence is based on absence and that representation comes into existence in order to represent what is absent. She has passed over the very textuality of texts because her ethical project demands that she uses texts as heuristic balances for philosophical positions. For Nussbaum, texts become no more than glass panes behind which events occur. Derrida, in relation to a reading of Mallarmé, writes that it is necessary to 'take into account the process of vitrification and not discount the 'production' of the glass. This production does not consist . . . simply in unveiling, revealing, presenting; nor in concealing or causing to disappear all at once . . . The glass must be read as a text.'[13] This is precisely what Nussbaum does not do.[14] In addition to being deeply problematic and unsatisfactory in itself, this failure to engage with the text as text has a number of profound ramifications.

To assume presence in a literary text in this way implies that any interpretation will take as its object the meaning of the events rather than the representation of events. The medium, the text itself, is beyond interpretation. Even the obscure and elliptical style of *The Golden Bowl* is, for Nussbaum, a narrative event, for example. As classical Greek tragic theatre forms the basis of her poetics, this is perhaps not surprising. However, as Paul de Man, following Derrida, argues, the act of reading itself implies that 'literature is not a transparent message in which it can be taken for granted that the distinction between the message and the means of communication is clearly established'.[15] Nussbaum, in contrast, does take this distinction for granted. As a result of this assumption that the narrative events stand out as separate from their representation, Nussbaum rejects any suggestion that the meanings of texts are the result of certain historically variable understandings, or, as Stanley Fish argues, interpretative communities. Indeed, it is in response to an article by Fish, that she writes, 'literature can show us . . . what it is like to live in a certain way'.[16] In fact, literature does not 'show' its readers, constructed by Nussbaum as passive spectators; rather, it is actively read. It is her unquestioning acceptance of the idea that literature is to be read through to a 'life beyond the text' which underlies Nussbaum's critical approach and leads her to a reductive understanding of reading.

This in turn means that Nussbaum is blind to a wide range of ambiguities and indeterminate conclusions that result from the 'textual surface', the words on the page. Although her practice can deal with indeterminate meanings of actions and events, it cannot accept and, indeed, it must ignore, indeterminate meanings in a literary text. It also illustrates that Nussbaum is not fully self-conscious in her reading of texts, nor of the crucial importance of her own methodology – her critical practice – in actively producing readings. Finally, her failure to deal with this issue of textuality helps to maintain the very binary philosophy/literature distinction she wishes to elide by suggesting that a philosophical argument is in fact there on the page, a textual thing in itself, in contrast to an act of literature in which the writing is passed through to 'a human situation'.

Emotional Response

Nussbaum's argument also depends on the assumption that reading works of literature principally evokes only emotional responses. She writes that our 'cognitive activity, as we explore the ethical conception embodied in the text, centrally involves emotional response. We discover what we think about these events partly by noticing how we feel' (*FG*, p. 15). Later she writes that we must 'acknowledge in our writing and reading the emotions that it is its [literature's] function to summon' (*FG*, p. 394). The reason for this, as she makes clear in a number of places, is that both consideration of the emotions and an admission of their importance 'add to . . . a picture of reason's procedures and problems' (*FG*, p. 14).

However, this claim, vital for her understanding of the heuristic nature of literature, is problematic. The understanding of an 'emotional response' is itself rather vague. Indeed, some literary texts – the high modernist avant-garde, for example – try to avoid the very idea of an 'emotional' response. What, if any, emotional responses are called for by Wallace Steven's 'Jar in Tennessee'? Again, her understanding of literary texts seems to have its model in Aristotle's *Poetics* and in classical Greek tragedy, aiming to evoke pity and awe. At a more profound level, Nussbaum's binary opposition of intellect and emotion can be questioned. Having made this not unproblematic binary division, it is clear that an emotional response is only an emotional response in distinction from an intellectual one: the two categories always already define and delimit each other. However, if the emotional response from literature is being used to further moral inquiry as Nussbaum argues, it becomes part of a wider intellectual response, rather than a thing in its own right: the intellectual subsumes the emotional which is no longer, then, a reaction in its own right. Finally, it is clear that for Nussbaum, the origins of an emotional response lie in a straightforward idea of identification, an idea which both illustrates and leads to a reductive understanding of reading.

Identification

Nussbaum's approach demands that the reader identifies with the characters in order to enact their stories and it is this enactment which generates the emotional response. The text is an 'adventure of the reader', almost as if a text were an educational or therapeutic role-playing exercise (*LK*, p. 143). This is apparent in Nussbaum's reading of Euripides' *Hecuba* and is even more evident in her readings of *The Golden Bowl*. The concluding chapter of *The Fragility of Goodness* discusses *Hecuba* (*FG*, pp. 397–421) and is, at first, taken from the audience's perspective: 'we see a child approaching' (*FG*, p. 397). However, as Nussbaum's account continues, the audience and Hecuba – that is, we, the readers of *The Fragility of Goodness* constructed in Nussbaum's account as the audience of *Hecuba*, and Hecuba – become more and more involved and identified with each other both in and as a result of Nussbaum's rhetoric: 'at first, Hecuba is merely unhappy' (*FG*, p. 399); 'she clearly holds our ethical values' (*FG*, p. 403); 'we make distinctions, Hecuba had said, we cut up the world' (*FG*, p. 408). Finally, in a key moment of Nussbaum's retelling and her argument, where both texts (*Hecuba* and *The Fragility of Goodness*) and various characters (Hecuba and the narrator of *The Fragility of Goodness*) develop a fascination with eyes and looking (the key moment of the play and of Nussbaum's argument about perception), we become identified fully with Hecuba as Nussbaum writes: '*we* take Hecuba's refusal, first as a retributive denial; *you* abused *my* offers of love, so *I* shall abuse *yours* in return' (*FG*, p. 411, italics added): the audience (the readers of the book constructed as the audience of the play) has spoken in Hecuba's voice in an act of total rhetorical identification. At the end of 'Flawed Crystals', Nussbaum suggests, in a similar but more explicit way, that as 'we carefully follow Maggie, seeing the world through her intelligent eyes, we hardly notice that we ourselves are rapidly becoming as distant from Charlotte, and as blind to the inner pain of her life, as Maggie herself' (*LK*, pp. 144–5). Indeed, Nussbaum suggests that it is in no small part through this process of personal identification that literature becomes ethically significant. Maggie and Hecuba, for Nussbaum are not simply textually created figures, but rather ourselves living in the text.

This idea of emotional response through identification and enactment is open to question on both a critical and a philosophical level, and also contradicts another part of her understanding of reading, the idea of surprise. First, Nussbaum's straightforward idea of identification again betrays her phonologocentric assumptions of presence because it assumes that textual characters are just the same as 'real' people actually present. Second, while some texts certainly demand a level of identification, it is possible to resist this demand. It is easily possible to imagine reading *The Golden Bowl* and identifying not with Maggie, but with any one of the other characters, or some or other in turn, or none of the characters.[17] In his reply to Nussbaum's essay, Richard Wollheim argues that 'specific patterns of changing viewpoints, of shifting identifications are not just contingent but are essential features of novels'.[18] This view has parallels with the views of a number of other thinkers on the novel, perhaps most notably Bakhtin.[19]

At a deeper level, Nussbaum's insistence on identification and heuristic enactment seems to contradict her own argument. Nussbaum's demand that the reader makes a straightforward imaginative identification with the characters to 're-enact' the particular ethical situation of the novel. Once the reader has identified with a character, the novel becomes 'mine', that is, it becomes a role-play enactment of the reader's moral dilemmas. However, the whole thrust of Nussbaum's argument relies on the novel as offering an *other* approach to understanding the world, a surprising new and challenging perspective, *that cannot be identified as one's own but with which one enacts a dialogue.* 'To enact' in itself implies that one is enacting something different from oneself, and thus reaffirms the otherness of the text. To identify with a character means that the text can no longer offer a surprise or a challenge to one's normative set of rules, in exactly the way that Nussbaum's argument crucially demands that it does.

This idea of enactment has a corollary in the way that Nussbaum identifies the narrative voice (and occasionally other voices) unproblematically with the author, who in turn becomes identified as an ethical guiding presence. For example, she describes Bob Assingham's conversation with Fanny in *The Golden Bowl as* 'James' talk (or Bob's talk)' (*LK*, p. 160), assimilating a character with James. Despite her awareness of the fallibility of the narrator, Nussbaum seems to argue that the narrative voice becomes a moral Virgil, fully present 'beyond' the text, offering a meta-narrative beyond the narrative of the text. Just as the reader identifies with a character, the reader also understands the 'author as our guide and accomplice' (*LK*, p. 145). Nussbaum considers the writer himself or herself as a moral guiding force. This assumption, too, is problematic.

In a contradictory passage in the introduction to *Love's Knowledge*, Nussbaum follows Booth in dividing the author into narrator, authorial presence and real person.[20] She is concerned with the first two aspects of the author's role and claims that

> nothing I say about the author here implies that critical statements made by the writer have any particular authority in the interpretation of the text . . . I am interested . . . in all and only those thoughts, feelings, wishes, movements and other processes that are actually there to be seen in the text. (*LK*, p. 9)

This statement, however, contradicts her work on James. She goes on to argue that in reading a literary text 'there is a standard of correctness set by the author's sense of life, as it finds its way into the work. And the text, approached as the creation of human intentions, is some fraction or element of a real human being' (*LK*, pp. 9–10). Thus, although the writer's criticism may have no bearing on the interpretation, his or her shade, like Virgil's, directs and delimits the reading of the work by an unspecified 'standard of correctness'; again, beyond the text itself (to which she claims to be solely attentive), Nussbaum relies on the real presence of the author and the literary text is a nearly corporeal 'fraction' of a real human being.

This reliance on the presence of the author as a guide to interpretation is perhaps clearest in her use of James's preface as part of the authoritative meta-text of *The Golden Bowl*. Nussbaum is aware that the prefaces are 'not . . . infallible' and remain only 'perceptive and helpful guides to the novels' (*LK*, p. 10). Unfortunately, this claim is contradicted, as she often uses the preface to *The Golden Bowl* as an authoritative guide to interpretation. Moreover, she then argues that the prefaces to James's novels form part of the novels themselves, 'combining commentary and narration' (*LK*, p. 10). This seems to raise the question of where such 'combining' stops. Does editing count as part of the process? Do other acts of commentary become part of the novel as well? For Nussbaum, the coherency of James's work is maintained again through the same assumptions of presence which inform the rest of her work. To make the unwarranted leap from 'thoughts, feelings, wishes, movements and other processes that are actually there to be seen in the text' (*LK*, p. 9) to the assumption of authorial intention and a 'standard of correctness set by an author's sense of life' (*LK*, p. 9) is the result of the need for Nussbaum's ethical criticism to ground itself in the actual presence of an author beyond the text.

Surprise and Identification

The difficulties inherent in understanding identification and surprise as so important in literature also become clear in relation to Nussbaum's understanding of the universal appeal of literature. Nussbaum argues that the ethically minded reader must be open to surprise and avoid any preordained approach. This means, she suggests, that a work of literature 'is equally available to all readers' (*FG*, p. 14). Ignoring the sociological, institutional and historical inaccuracies of this claim, it presupposes a certain approach to reading. To appreciate the moral significance of surprise, the reader must put aside preconceived political, social and personal ideas and respond only to the text. This involves a number of difficulties. First, this ideal reader is impossible: we are all rooted in the world. Second, surprise, a moment in the heuristic process of reading which involves a suspension of one's own character traits, and identification, which involves putting one's own character into the shoes of another because there is a spark of recognition, seem to be at odds in Nussbaum's thought. Nussbaum wants literature to be surprising – not like oneself – and identifiable – like oneself – at one and the same time. Third, both to identify with a character (to bracket off one's own position and personality) and to use that character as a reflection on our own position seems to be contradictory. If the reader *is* the character – as the audience becomes Hecuba, for example – this surely limits the amount of reflection the reader can have by denying access to a wide and shifting range of viewpoints.

Finally, Nussbaum's work lacks any political dimension (although, of course, this absence is itself political). This is because the ideal of surprise also removes from Nussbaum's account of reading any other ways of approaching a text, save a continual awareness of surprise itself. Further, this rules out other, equally ethically motivated readings based on, for example, ideas of gender or social justice: to read *The Frogs* in terms of gender difference would automatically, for Nussbaum, cancel out the central idea of surprise. Despite her claims to the contrary, her argument forms a self-enclosing circle by defining what to look for in a text – the surprising – which in turn justifies itself by its own search. Nussbaum, in her 'war on obtuseness' overlooks other ethical or political implications, looking only to be surprised by a text.

Nussbaum's understanding of reading is simplistic and reductive for a number of reasons. First, it relies on an assumption of presence beyond the text. This assumes the disappearance of the very idea of text itself: the actual text, the 'words on the page', become a pane of glass. Second, she unproblematically assumes that readers have an 'emotional response' to a literary text and also presupposes a model of the persona split between intellectual and emotional. Third, she demands an intense and highly problematic identification with characters, which her rhetoric reinforces. Fourth, she locates the author as a meta-textual presence, guiding an ethical interpretation. Fifth, she argues for an inconsistent principle of surprise. All these are flaws in her conception of reading and have two combined sources: her ethical position and the way in which she understands criticism and reading itself. She wishes to eschew any claim that her critical position is, in fact, a critical position.

NUSSBAUM AND THE CONCEPT OF CRITICISM

Nussbaum's Understanding of Criticism and Theory

Nussbaum's view of the activity and history of literary criticism and theory is, in many respects, limited. Particularly relevant is her argument, made in her essay on perceptive equilibrium, that moral and ethical concerns have disappeared from criticism. While it is true that a number of significant critics who had strong and overt moral commitments, and are admired by Nussbaum, are now regarded as problematic in the extreme, to suggest that ethics have fallen out of criticism is an overstatement. As one of Nussbaum's supporters, Richard Freadman, writes, there can be no suggestion that contemporary literary theory has simply neglected ethical concerns . . . the various emancipatory and advocative forms of theory – Marxism, feminism and most recently post-colonial studies are nothing if not *moral projects*: they seek various forms of political, moral and cultural redress and change in the light of particular moral commitments.[21]

It is clear that Nussbaum is not concerned with these critical projects. Indeed, in a footnote she specifically discounts feminism and Marxism, suggesting that they 'are major exceptions . . . [that] in their difference from and frequent opposition to what surrounded them . . . prove the rule' (*LK*, p. 171n.). Rather, Nussbaum is offering an ethics of criticism in opposition to poststructuralist and deconstructive approaches to literature. Crucially, however, she refuses to engage in recent thought on, for example, textuality or identification (*LK*, p. 12, p. 21). Although she concedes that 'literary theorists allied to deconstruction have taken a marked turn towards the ethical', this work is 'not . . . the rigorous engagement with ethical thought characteristic of the best work in moral philosophy' (*LK*, p. 29). Her philosophical approach relies on highly contentious and problematic assumptions about literary texts which are shared by critics like Leavis and Trilling. Most significantly perhaps, she seems not to accept that she is, herself, engaged in a certain act of criticism that depends on certain preconceptions. Nussbaum is blind to her own presuppositions about her criticism. This in turn hampers her critical practice.

Defining and Defined by Canons

One example of this is her unspoken concept of 'canon'. Her viewpoint demands that there must be canonical great works: she argues that some authors themselves offer clearer and more refined moral distinctions than others. This must imply that other works do not: authors more brutish, perhaps, or texts that simply repeat platitudinous truths. Thus Nussbaum's approach implicitly sets up a theoretical basis that demands a canon, and the theoretical demand for, and practical selection of, a canon have profound ramifications for any understanding of literature. As Hartman remarks,

every literary theory is based on the experience of a limited canon or generalises strongly from a text-milieu. To take the metaphysical poets as one's base or touchstone, and to 'extend' their poetics toward modern poetry and then to all poetry, will produce a very different result from working from Cervantes toward Pynchon, or from Hölderlin.[22]

Nussbaum's canon takes its basis from antiquity – tragic plays and philosophic texts – and projects forward until it encounters James, Beckett and Proust. As a result, as Hartman makes clear, her literary methodology is shaped by the texts in her canon – her way of reading arises from these texts and then reaffirms itself by reading these texts. The influence of a particular canon is also clear in Nussbaum's constant elision of 'this novel', 'novels', 'the novel' (see, for example, *LK*, p. 138, p. 148, p. 157). A reading of one novel or one author's corpus should not, perhaps, be the grounding of a criticism. It is impossible for Nussbaum to draw out universal laws of literature from a limited canon. The complete lack of consideration of poetry, or less narrative forms, is a result of this 'canonicity' and would present possibly insuperable problems for Nussbaum. (For example, is it always clear in a poem with whom one should identify? Not all poems have 'persons' in them.) When Nussbaum discusses literature, it seem clear that she means narrative texts which make claims to be realistic, texts most sympathetic to epi-reading. Again (and this critique is one often made at exactly the 'theoretical' sorts of reading Nussbaum is trying to counteract), her reading of James makes a metacritical point concerning the relationship of all novels to perception. For Nussbaum, all great texts properly read echo the same Aristotelian moral points, about perception, about community and about identity. However, this would seem to contradict her claim that texts offer radically new perceptions. Again, her argument forms a self-enclosing circle by defining what to look for in a text which in turn is justified by what it finds during its search.

Philosophy and Criticism

Nussbaum covers up her implicit critical methodology. She argues that responses to literary works cannot be reduced to schematic readings and do not need to be drawn out, but simply happen. In her essay 'Finely Aware' she discusses 'a philosophical criticism of literature' (*LK*, p. 161) but argues that the text itself 'displays, and is, a high kind of moral activity' (*LK*, p. 161): the 'philosophical explanation acts . . . as an ally of the literary text' (*LK*, p. 161). The explanation is in tandem with the text and certainly does not interpret or shape the understanding of the text. Wollheim responds by suggesting that

> even the truths of moral philosophy . . . follow from the text of *The Golden Bowl* in conjunction with some commentary . . . In fact it seems to me that the most powerful considerations for thinking that

literature is an essential element in the formation of moral philosophy also shows how crucial it is to have commentary as well.[24]

Putnam argues that the 'work of fiction must not be confused with the 'commentary' and it is the commentary that is (or can be) a work of moral philosophy'.[25] Both responses make it clear that Nussbaum has, despite her claims, an interpretative approach. It is the commentary, not the literary text itself, which can be moral philosophy. Moreover, they make it clear that she has interpreted the text using a particular philosophical schema in exactly the way she claimed not to do. In an Endnote to her essay 'Flawed Crystals', written some later, Nussbaum agrees with Wollheim's insistence on the importance of commentary in the philosophical analysis of texts. However, despite this, she still understands her writing on literature as 'degree-zero', neutral, objective 'commentary', rather than a view coming from a certain subject position. The moral truths she finds in texts are directly available, mediated only by the keen sight of the critic and are not the result of any act of interpretation. This is the significance of her term 'commentary' – it seems to suggest a neutral, passive 'explaining' of a text, rather than an active interpretation.

Nussbaum has to hold this position because of her insistence that literary texts – emotional, irregular, particular – supplement philosophical discourse. She writes that philosophy, as 'the pursuit of truth . . . must become various and mysterious and unsystematic if, and in so far as, the truth is so' (*LK*, p. 29). The supplement literature offers to philosophy, as a dry-run for life and a site to explore philosophical situations, would not be tenable if it were suggested that the 'mysterious and unsystematic' content was imported into the text by a way of reading. For Nussbaum, although debate can occur at a philosophical level ('was Maggie right to behave in such and such a way?', for example), it cannot be allowed to occur at the level of textual meaning; the question of what Amerigo and Charlotte actually did, left very vague in James's text, for example, is not open to Nussbaum. Simply, although indeterminacy can exist at the level of philosophical debate, it cannot exist at the level of textual interpretation.

Nussbaum provides readings of texts that disavow their very nature as 'readings' – acts of criticism – and claim to allow the literary text to be an ally of, or supplement to, philosophy. She wants to practise a meta-criticism (in her terms, a 'philosophic criticism' or simply a 'moral inquiry') which has done away with interpretation and relies on an innocuous commentary on the events of the narrative. This in itself follows on from her position as an epi-reader, wishing to abolish the very textuality upon which reading depends. This meta-criticism takes its value, as she makes clear, precisely from the 'messy' and specific nature of a literary text – that is, from the impossibility of making a 'literary' text into simply an 'example' for philosophy. However, it is precisely this impossibility of fitting a text into a simple schema for analysis which opens up a text to criticism and a variety of contending interpretations. For her claims for the relationship between philosophy and literature to hold, she must argue that a literary text has a clear and determinate application to philosophical issues, which would mean that it was no longer a specific particular thing in itself but precisely what Nussbaum wishes to avoid, an example of philosophy. Paradoxically then, the very fact that a 'literary text' is not a work of philosophy, for Nussbaum, gives it status as a work of philosophy. This process can only take place, in Nussbaum's work, if a variety of different interpretations – the results of acts of criticism – are disallowed and one view of criticism, a view that takes a literary text as a philosophical one, is taken as true. Nussbaum creates a neo-Aristotelian criticism which is flawed because it denies its status as criticism and is unable to come to terms with textuality. Nussbaum's criticism simply assumes the events in a literary text are real and delivers up the narrative – and for Nussbaum, even the style is part of the narrative – for an analytical philosophical analysis. To incorporate literary texts into philosophical texts, it is necessary to eliminate any other readings, except, perhaps, formalistic ones.

An illustration which both brings the subversive power of textuality to light and exposes this key flaw in Nussbaum's argument occurs in her analysis of Chapter 37 of *The Golden Bowl*. In Nussbaum's reading Adam Verver has seen Maggie anew as an autonomous person for the first time and Maggie – for Nussbaum the central character with whom the reader is supposed to identify – sees her father anew.

> Like an artist whose labour produces, at last, a wonderful achieved form, she finds . . . a thought of her father 'that placed him in her eyes as no precious work of art probably had ever been placed in his own'. To see Adam as a being more precious than his precious work of art becomes, for her, after a moment, to see him as 'a great and deep and high little man'. (*LK*, pp. 152–3)

This moment represents Maggie's moral achievement for Nussbaum. Maggie no longer sees people as separate, as generalities, as works of art uninvolved in a network of relationships but rather as particular individuals: the idea of person-as-art-object is broken through and understood as person-as-person. However, the passage can be read in a totally different way. Maggie's moral blindness comes from judging people as if they were works of art. She changes her viewpoint as 'an artist produces': her metaphor is one of art. Her father's new value, in direct contrast to Nussbaum's reading, is still in relation to art works. He is 'placed' in her eyes as he has 'placed' art works in his own vision.[26] His value has increased, not in transcending the value of an art work, as Nussbaum argues, but in relation to it: he has become 'more precious than' an art work, still understood in that scale but now at the top, as the most expensive. His materiality, expressed by his littleness, is now no longer an issue, as his revaluation as the most expensive art work gives him other qualities – greatness, depth, height – just like a painting, not imposing in size, perhaps, but in value. Maggie, in this reading, has not changed her view of human life as Nussbaum suggests, but rather simply re-evaluated her father's worth using the same destructive metaphor of people-as-art-object that created the moral blindness in the first place. Her father is still understood as an art work, but now as a more valuable art work.

This reading of the passage can also be read against Nussbaum's argument to show up the 'blindness' in her general account. Nussbaum suggests that texts can interrogate our own rules and, through perception, alter them for the better, in a continuing dialogue. Maggie is claimed as an example of this process: she sees people as art works and through a specific experience changes to see people as real people. However, if Maggie is read not as breaking free from her art/value metaphor but reorganising the values within it, she never comes to see people as people in their own right, because an adjustment of her relative (financial) values has resolved the situation. The same holds true for Nussbaum but in reverse: Nussbaum reads art works as people, made real through enactment and emotional involvement, but she is never able to admit that they are just art works. Nussbaum and Maggie are both able to re-evaluate but only within a preconceived system of evaluation that neither of them questions at a deep enough level: Maggie has a system of art/financial value, Nussbaum a system of unquestioned presence.

Philosophy and Literature

These difficulties stem from the very assumptions that Nussbaum makes about the distinction between philosophy and literature. Instead of removing the distinction between the two, which is what she intends, she offers literature *as* moral philosophy. Nussbaum's work aims to abolish the strict opposition between philosophy and literature, and to allow the two to complement each other in the realm of ethical inquiry. However, within Nussbaum's own conceptions of the two categories this proves to be impossible. Nussbaum draws the two categories of text into a series of binary oppositions.[27] Philosophy is rational, abstract, universal, fully present on the page as argument. Literature is emotional, specific, contingent, not present as text but as 'real life' situations.[28] Nussbaum wants to use the second category to supplement the first, just as the emotional response became part of the wider intellectual response. Literature offers another picture of 'reason's procedures and problems', another part of practical reason (*FG*, p. 14). To use her own military metaphor, philosophy has become the 'ally' of literature in 'the war against moral obtuseness': the artist 'is our fellow fighter, frequently our guide' (*LK*, p. 161, p. 164). The alliance is not, as her rhetoric suggests, one offering complementary strength to each side, but rather an allegiance of literature to the overriding aims of philosophy. The only reason to use literary texts is to help the work of philosophy: reasoning, understood in a broader sense, has subsumed literature. She writes that the 'very qualities that make the novel so unlike dogmatic abstract treatises are, for us, the source of their *philosophical* interest' (*LK*, p. 29). Literature is a source of philosophic interest because what it offers, to an epi-reader like Nussbaum, is a series of heuristic exercises for philosophy, sharpening up the tools of perception, just as a military guide does not fight, as such, but simply shows the way for the main force of the army. Paradoxically, literature has become exactly what Nussbaum claims she thinks it cannot be, examples for philosophy, exploring reason. Since literature has become a branch of philosophy, it can logically no longer maintain any of the claims she wishes to make for it. This is because these claims depend on the difference between philosophy and literature, the binary oppositions, which can no longer have any value for argument when one side is subsumed in the other. Nussbaum's argument is limited by the very presuppositions that she wishes to challenge, and instead of offering an equal alliance of literature and philosophy, she turns literature into philosophy. In her attempt to get beyond Plato's banishment of the poets and imply that both forms of writing are equal, she simple reinforces the idea of philosophy's superiority to literature.

CONCLUSION: LITERATURE AS MORAL PHILOSOPHY

Nussbaum's argument is that literature can be understood as moral philosophy and be ethically significant in its own right because of its unique 'unphilosophical characteristics'. It is through readings, based on an implicit and unanalysed neo-Aristotelian ethical criticism, that she attempts this. However, it is her readings of literary texts based on her philosophically motivated criticism that provide her philosophical arguments. She is not writing then about literature but about the result of her readings. She offers an interpretation which denies its nature as interpretation. It is because of its lack of self-reflexivity that it is flawed at a fundamental level. It makes a number of highly problematic presuppositions which it cannot support and does not examine, and which in turn debilitate its critical practice and ethical conclusions.

Martha Nussbaum is offering an 'ethical criticism', even though she passes over the term. However, it is also a criticism which seems to be so concerned with the 'ethical' that it ignores and subsumes 'criticism': it covers up and ignores the difficulties inherent in reading and interpreting a text. In order to achieve a properly ethical criticism, both terms need to be fully explored. Nussbaum's ethically aware renegotiation of positions taken by Leavis, Trilling and others refuses to explore its own critical practice. The next chapter offers an analysis of the radically different work of J. Hillis Miller – the emphasis for Miller falls on the 'criticism' rather than the 'ethical'. Where Nussbaum reads literature as moral philosophy, Miller reads moral philosophy as literature.

NOTES

1. Martha Nussbaum, *Love's Knowledge: Essays on Philosophy and Literature* (Oxford University Press: Oxford, 1990), p. 168, p. 192. Further references to *Love's Knowledge* will be given in the text with the abbreviation *LK*.
2. Gillian Rose, *Judaism and Modernity: Philosophical Essays* (Oxford: Blackwell, 1993), p. 2.
3. Richard Freadman and Seamus Miller, *Rethinking Theory* (Cambridge: Cambridge University Press, 1992), p. 4.
4. Martha Nussbaum, *The Fragility of Goodness: Luck and Ethics in Greek Tragedy and Philosophy* (Cambridge: Cambridge University Press, 1986), p. 10. Further references to *The Fragility of Goodness* will be given in the text with the abbreviation *FG*. As with all Aristotelian-influenced thought, Nussbaum presupposes a unified human agent and the ability of that agent to act rationally, or at least as able to negotiate both with and in terms of reason.
5. Nussbaum deals with this particular issue in *The Fragility of Goodness*, pp. 122–35. She argues that Plato does not disapprove of the intrinsic nature of poetry or tragedy, but that because poetry and tragedy appeal to the emotions, they are unsuitable for Plato's form of moral enquiry. Plato's conception of ethical improvement 'teaches by appeal to intellect alone; learning takes place when the interlocutor is enmeshed in logical contradiction . . . No jarring event, no experience that directly awakens feeling should play any role in the interlocutor's learning' (*FG*, p. 133). It is the use of rhetoric designed to teach through emotion and irrationality, as opposed to reason and an appeal to the intellect, which leads Plato to banish the poets.
6. See Wayne Booth, *The Company We Keep* (Berkeley: University of California Press, 1988) pp. 217–20.
7. Nussbaum is both referring to and citing from Henry James, *The Art of the Novel* (New York: Scribner, 1934), p. 149.
8. John Rawls, *A Theory of Justice* (Oxford: Clarendon Press, 1972), p. 48.
9. F. R. Leavis, *The Common Pursuit* (London: Chatto and Windus, 1952), p. 213.
10. F. R. Leavis, *The Critic as Anti-philosopher*, ed. G. Singh (London: Chatto and Windus, 1982), p. 128.
11. Henry James, *The Golden Bowl* (Harmondsworth: Penguin, 1985), pp. 316–17.
12. Denis Donoghue, *Ferocious Alphabets* (London: Faber & Faber, 1981), p. 99.

13. Jacques Derrida, *Dissemination*, trans. Barbara Johnson (London: The Athlone Press, 1981), p. 233.

14. As if to make this point even more clearly, when Nussbaum dismisses Derrida's work on literature, she chooses a corporeal image, a metaphor for the body really present: citing Zarathustra/ Nietzsche's remark that he loves only what a man has written with his blood, she writes that after 'reading Derrida, and not Derrida alone, I feel a certain hunger for blood; for, that is, writing about literature that talks of human lives and choices' (*LK*, p. 171). To write in blood is to guarantee presence by actual corporeal substance, to hunger for blood is to hunger for that actual living presence. It is this assumption of presence that Derrida's work reacts against and deconstructs: in contrast, it is precisely this presence, as 'speech, character, personality . . . construed as having a personal form' that Nussbaum's thought presupposes and needs in order to work (Donoghue, *Ferocious Alphabets*, p. 99). Her ethical approach to texts is based on the hunger for presence always already having being assuaged, or its absence forgotten.

15. Paul de Man, *The Resistance to Theory* (Minneapolis: University of Minnesota Press, 1986), p. 15.

16. Martha Nussbaum, 'Sophistry about Conventions', *New Literary History*, Vol. 17 (1985–6), pp. 129–40 (p. 137). It is a reply to Stanley Fish, 'Anti-professionalism', *New Literary History*, vol. 17 (1985–6), pp. 89–108.

17. Gore Vidal, for example, in his introduction to the Penguin edition, finds Amerigo, not Maggie, the 'most sympathetic' character: James, *The Golden Bowl*, p. 11.

18. Richard Wollheim, 'Flawed Crystals: James's *The Golden Bowl* and the Plausibility of Literature as Moral Philosophy', *New Literary History*, vol. 15 (1983), pp. 185–91 (p. 188).

19. M. M. Bakhtin, *The Dialogic Imagination: Four Essays*, trans. Caryl Emerson and Michael Holquist, ed. Michael Holquist (Austin: University of Texas Press, 1981), pp. 259–422. Indeed, following Bakhtin it is possible to expand this point from a literary to a political arena. Bakhtin discusses Aristotelian poetics, of the sort that Nussbaum is outlining, and defines it as 'monoglossic', arguing that it 'give[s] expression to . . . centripetal forces in socio-linguistic and ideological life' (M. M. Bakhtin, *The Dialogic Imagination*, p. 271). That is, it represents an approach to language that aims to create a strong notion of homogenous shared communal identity which overrides individual or cultural differences (Nussbaum writes in *The Fragility of Goodness*, p. 14, that literature aids the Aristotelian project 'whose aims are ultimately defined in terms of a "we"'.) Bakhtin goes on to argue that a monoglossic understanding of language and the novel leads to enslavement and control, and that the novel and a free society are both based on shifting viewpoints expressed by different language uses, what he names heteroglossia.

20. *Love's Knowledge*, pp. 8–9. Nussbaum takes her position principally from Wayne Booth, *The Company We Keep*, especially Chapter 6 (pp. 169–98), and *The Rhetoric of Fiction* (London: University of Chicago Press, 1961), especially Part 2, 'The Author's Voice in Fiction'.

21. Freadman and Miller, *Rethinking Theory*, p. 27.

22. Geoffrey Hartman, *Criticism in the Wilderness* (London: Yale University Press, 1980), p. 299.

23. In her article replying to criticism of her essay 'Flawed Crystals' (not included in her collection *Love's Knowledge*), she is pressed to admit that she is 'speaking now only about James'. 'Reply to Richard Wollheim, Patrick Gardiner, and Hilary Putnam', *New Literary History*, vol. 15 (1983), pp. 201–7 (p. 202).

24. Richard Wollheim 'Flawed Crystals: James's *The Golden Bowl* and the Plausibility of Literature as Moral Philosophy', pp. 189–90.

25. Hilary Putnam 'Taking Rules Seriously – A Response to Martha Nussbaum', *New Literary History*, vol. 15 (1983), pp. 193–200 (p. 199).

26. The 'probably' in this sentence is itself indeterminate. It could mean either that Adam had never seen a work of art as valuable as he appears to Maggie (i.e. that he is very valuable), or that he was placed as no work of art could be (i.e. he was beyond value). This very indeterminacy, however, strongly suggests that Nussbaum's reading cannot be easily accepted.

27. In this light, see also her list discussing 'two normative conceptions of human rationality' (*FG*, p. 20).

28. There seem to be gendered assumptions behind this list: philosophy as male, literature as female.

3

READING (:) THE ETHICS
OF DECONSTRUCTIVE CRITICISM

To stress the by no means self-evident necessity of reading implies at
least two things. First it implies that literature is not a transparent
message in which it can be taken for granted that the distinction
between the message and the means of communication is clearly
established. Second, and more problematically, it implies that the
grammatical decoding of a text leaves a residue of indetermination that
has to be, but cannot be, resolved by grammatical means, however
extensively conceived.

Paul de Man[1]

Each reading is, strictly speaking, ethical, in the sense that it *has* to
take place, by an implacable necessity, as the response to a categorical
demand, and in the sense that the reader *must* take responsibility for it
and for its consequences in the social, personal and political worlds.

J. Hillis Miller[2]

THE `MULTIFORM MOVEMENT
CALLED DECONSTRUCTION´

Martha Nussbaum's approach to the problem of ethical criticism is blind to
textuality, to 'literariness' and to the self-reflexive nature of reading and of
criticism. In stark contrast, deconstructive criticism, especially in the form
in which it flourished in the late 1970s and 1980s, concentrated on
precisely these areas. Where Nussbaum tries to offer a solution to the
problem of the ethics of criticism through what Donoghue calls 'epi-
reading', restoring 'the words to a source, a human situation involving
speech, character, personality and destiny', the so-called Yale Critics or
Deconstructors offered the strictest version of epi-reading's opposite,
'graphi-reading'. They prioritised language, text and reading over a
nostalgia for the human. Though both Nussbaum, as the best example

of a renegotiated humanism, and the Yale Critics approach the same problem – the interrelationship between ethics, criticism and texts, the problem of ethical criticism – they have very different strategies.

The work of J. Hillis Miller in the last ten years is perhaps the most concerted attempt to explore the ethical ramifications of this form of criticism, in no small part as a response to those who accuse deconstruction or deconstructive criticism of being unethical or a-ethical. In *The Ethics of Reading* and a number of other texts, Miller analyses the question of ethics and its interrelationship with reading, criticism and the critical strategy known as deconstruction. Miller's work, then, offers a clear example of the way in which graphi-reading, centrally understood as deconstructive criticism, might approach the ethics of criticism.

Before examining Miller's work, a more general question needs a response: can deconstruction, given its philosophical origins, exist as a literary critical method? What is the interaction between deconstruction and the discourse of literary criticism? If they are incompatible, then the question of the ethics of deconstructive criticism would seem to make no sense at all.

Asked 'can deconstruction serve as a method of literary criticism?', Jacques Derrida replied:

> I am not sure that deconstruction can function as a literary *method* as such. I am wary of the idea of methods of reading. The laws of reading are determined by the particular text that is being read . . . Deconstruction asks *why* we read a literary text in this particular manner rather than another . . . Deconstruction teaches us to read literature more thoroughly by attending to it *as language*.[3]

If deconstruction can be a way of doing literary criticism, it will have a different relation to literature from other critical approaches: it will be an approach that reads and responds to the text on the text's own terms, an approach, as much as possible, without *being* an approach.

However, a number of thinkers and critics have resisted the idea that deconstruction can play any part in literary analysis: they argue it is only by chance that deconstruction in the anglophone world became known through film and literature departments rather than through philosophy departments.[4] This view is expressed by Rodolphe Gasché, in 'Deconstruction as Criticism', in which he locates Derrida's work firmly in a genealogy of philosophical thought and specifically as a reaction to Husserlian phenomenology. He argues that if this is not fully understood by 'philosophically untrained readers' then the application of these philosophical debates to literary analysis will be 'naive and . . . ridiculous'.[5] He suggests that Derrida's 'developments concerning literature and literary criticism . . . [need to be] understood within the boundaries of his debate with the philosophy of phenomenology'.[6] For Gasché, Derridian concepts of writing, text and metaphor 'cannot simply, without mediation, be integrated into literary criticism'.[7] Richard Rorty is even blunter: literary deconstructors, he writes,

> think of [Derrida] as providing new, improved tools for unmasking books and authors – showing what is really going on behind false fronts. I do not think that a critic of metaphysics, in the tradition of Nietzsche and Heidegger, should be read in this way.[8]

Christopher Norris follows the same line of argument. He is contemptuous of 'the US-domesticated variant' of literary critical deconstruction and argues that Derrida's work is philosophical, not to be understood in literary critical terms.[9] If Gasché's, Rorty's and Norris's arguments are correct, Miller's work on the ethics of criticism cannot even take place or 'make sense', since it already presupposes deconstruction can be applied to literature and to criticism.

There seem to be three general responses to arguments like these which rule deconstruction, and thus all of Miller's arguments about ethics and criticism, as *prima facie ultra vires* for literary critical practice. The first is to suggest there can be no clear distinction between philosophic and literary texts, since all forms of writing are simply text. This idea underlies Geoffrey Bennington's reply to Gasché arguing that 'there is no linear scale with a literary end and a philosophical end'.[10] Rorty himself also suggests this: literary, critical and philosophic texts all analyse, or 'criticise', texts and, more vicariously perhaps, deal with 'the fundamental issues of human life'.[11] This response would argue that deconstruction can be 'applied' as a literary critical strategy, as texts in general have no inherent generic or disciplinary differences – there are no specifically literary or philosophic texts, for example. As a consequence, attempts like Norris's and Gasché's to argue that deconstruction can be applied to one form of text and not to another fail because there are no generic textual difference of this sort.

The second response might agree with Norris and Gasché in accepting a distinction between the two genres or discourses, but suggest that the distinction is so unclear as to be impossible to apply. As Stanley Cavell wrote in 1969: 'I do not deny that there are differences . . . between philosophy and literature or between philosophy and literary criticism; I am suggesting that we do not understand these differences.'[12] Although there are obvious affinities between deconstruction, philosophy and literary criticism their relationship is not clear or straightforward. Derrida, in an interview suggests that the 'hierarchies . . . [and] relations of force' in criticism and philosophy are different, but that literary criticism is 'very philosophical in its form . . . perhaps structurally philosophical'.[13] In the broadest sense, both philosophers and critics 'criticise' other texts. This response to Gasché, Rorty and Norris suggests that those critics who practice 'deconstruction' (or those philosophers who practise 'literary criticism') will risk straying over borders which exist but have not been fixed: it implies profound, if indefinable, generic and disciplinary boundaries.

The third, and perhaps most convincing, response to the arguments of Gasché, Rorty and Norris is the position taken by Miller. Miller, especially from the mid-1980s, argues for plural 'deconstructions': he describes 'the multiform movement called "deconstruction"'.[14] For Miller, deconstruction is 'nothing more or less than good reading as such' (*ER*, p. 10). This position would seem to tally more with Derrida's remarks cited earlier that deconstruction 'teaches us to read literature more thoroughly by attending to it *as language*'. This understanding of deconstruction as 'good reading' of any text, whether described as philosophical or literary (or as anything else), seems to be a common denominator between the Gasché/Norris/Rorty position (that deconstruction is subversive only within philosophy) and the Bennington/Miller position (that it can be used as a way of reading literary texts because it is a way of reading any texts). This is because to understand deconstruction as 'good reading' refers to the way in which deconstruction happens. A deconstructive reading is not the result of a set of rules or preconceptions about the world or the text applied to the text because it is not a machine for reading. This is what Derrida seems to mean when he says that deconstruction is not a method. Deconstruction is performed in deconstructive readings, and the readings create deconstruction, not the other – more usual – way around. A humanist critic, for example, will take into a text the preconception that it is about certain forms of human ethical relationships, but be blind to that preconception. She or he will, as a consequence, find those relationships in the text. In contrast, a deconstructive critic will respond to the text itself, with as much an awareness as possible of her or his own preconceptions and blindnesses, including the awareness of blindnesses to which she or he is blind. There is no risk of setting up an opposition between theory and practice because, in an act of deconstruction, the practice and the theory are the same.

However, this common denominator of 'good reading' needs to be qualified. Deconstructions exist in a number of different discourses, each responding to the texts of different discourses in different ways since, in Derrida's words, the 'laws of reading are determined by the particular text that is being read'.[15] The different discourses may well have different horizons or points of view which are open to deconstruction. An act of deconstruction of a history text, or a gendered piece of social behaviour, or a work of philosophy, or an archaeology textbook, will look radically different from the deconstruction of a novel. The acts of deconstruction character-istic of Miller and Paul de Man – who deal principally novels, poetry and the philosophy of language – seem to be one particular way amongst many, one branch of the 'multiform movement': this version of deconstruction is perhaps best named deconstructive criticism. This stresses both its affilia-tion to, and differences from, Derrida's deconstruction. Miller has claimed that 'deconstruction is really an American thing', a remark which makes clear how wide the 'family' of deconstruction and deconstructive criticism has become, and how impossible it is to delimit deconstruction and deconstructive criticism simply to Derrida's own work.[16]

The differences between deconstruction and deconstructive criticism are based on their contrasting approaches to texts. Paul de Man, discussing the differences between his work and Derrida's, stated that he

> would hold to the statement that 'the text deconstructs itself' rather than being deconstructed by a philosophical intervention from outside the text. The difference is that Derrida's text is so brilliant, so incisive, so strong that whatever happens in Derrida, it happens between him and his own text. He doesn't need Rousseau, he doesn't need anybody else; I do need them very badly because I never had an idea of my own, it was always through a text, through the critical examination of a text . . . I am a philologist and not a philosopher.[17]

It is this reliance on the reading of texts which marks out deconstructive critics: Miller and de Man are the strictest graphi-readers, relying on 'good reading'. The second half of this chapter will examine this claim in more detail because this simple claim for deconstruction as 'good reading' has two implications: first, it makes an unsettling pun on 'good' (morally correct, epistemologically accurate); second, it seems to understand both decon-struction and deconstructive criticism as the inheritors of New Criticism.

Miller sums up the argument over deconstructive criticism by asserting, rather bullishly, that the 'ultimate justification for this mode of criticism, as of any conceivable mode, is that it works'.[18] Miller understands decon-structive thought as a mode of criticism and that this criticism is a functioning mode of criticism amongst others. Deconstruction can be (an act of) criticism, as deconstructive criticism, and, as a result, the ethics of this 'mode' of criticism, derided and attacked from all sides needs to be explored. It is in relation to the ethics of criticism that Miller again draws this distinction between deconstruction and deconstructive criticism: 'my interest is not in ethics as such but in the ethics of reading and in . . . the ethical moment in reading' (ER, p. 15). An interest in ethics as such would seem to be the realm of 'deconstructive philosophy': 'deconstructive criticism' considers specifically the ethics of reading.

The issue of the ethics of deconstructive criticism has arisen specifically because of the way deconstructive criticism questions the dominant paradigm of modernist criticism. Much has been written on the relationship between deconstructive criticism and the American critical heritage.[19] However, it is important to stress the challenge that deconstructive criticism made, not just to the more conservative New Criticism, but to more radical left-wing criticism, which still shares the assumptions of modernist criticism. Deconstructive criticism, as practised by de Man and Miller, represents the strictest version of graphi-reading, as the ironic start of de Man's *Allegories of Reading* makes clear:

> [W]ith the internal law and order of literature well policed, we can now devote ourselves to the foreign affairs, the external politics of literature . . . Behind the assurance that valid interpretation is possible, behind the recent interest in writing and reading as potentially effective public speech acts, stands a highly respectable moral imperative that strives to reconcile the internal, formal, private structures of literary language with their external, referential, and public effects.[20]

Here de Man's opposition of the internal and external roles of literature is a reflection of the epi-/graphi-reader opposition. The external politics of literature, seeking the world beyond the text, represents the 'moral imperative' for literary criticism, which Nussbaum, after James, called 'the civic use of the imagination'. In contrast, de Man and others sought to show how the validity of interpretation was critically in doubt and that assumptions based on referential structures were deeply problematic. In contrast to the relatively simple application of ethics offered in epi-reading, deconstructive criticism appeared to exclude this ethical base of literary criticism.

Miller's 1986 presidential address deals specifically with this issue of ethics. Miller concentrates his discussion on the role of theory; as Barbara Johnson writes, often "theory' refers primarily to deconstruction' and this is the case with Miller, since by theory, in this address, he clearly means deconstruction, or more accurately that version of deconstruction which he practises, deconstructive criticism.[21] The address is concerned with both defending deconstructive criticism from attacks launched by both the right and the left and insisting that deconstructive criticism is the future of literary criticism. In it, he argues that both political sides 'need to point the finger of blame against theory to avoid thinking through the challenge theory poses to their own ideologies' and that this 'blind refusal to read flouts the minimal obligations of our profession' (p. 284). To those on the right, Miller suggests that the 'most traditional of humanistic responsibilities and missions . . . will be performed effectively only if the university remains open to the kind of questioning posed by deconstruction' (p. 290). To those on the left, with whom it is clear that Miller himself is in broad political sympathy, he declares:

> [Y]our commitment to history, to society, to an exploration of the material base of literature, of its economic conditions, its institutions, the realities of class and gender distinctions that underlie literature . . . will inevitably fall into the hands of those with antithetical positions to yours as long as you hold to an unexamined ideology of the material base, that is, to a notion that is metaphysical through and through, as much a part of western metaphysics as the idealism you would contest. 'Deconstruction' is the current name for the multiple and heterogeneous strategies of overturning and displacement that will liberate your own enterprise from what disables it. (pp. 290–1)[22]

Underlying this line of argument is Miller's work on the ethics of deconstructive criticism or the ethics of reading:

> [if] this phrase means anything, it must have something to do with respecting any text discussed, with accepting an obligation to read – to read carefully, patiently, scrupulously, under the elementary assumption that the text being read may say something different from what one wants or expects it to say or from what received opinion says it says. (p. 284)

Miller is not denying the importance of political engagement, but he is insisting that before this engagement can take place, there is the ethical obligation to read. It is this obligation which he explores at length in *The Ethics of Reading*, and which provides both his answer to the question of the ethics of deconstructive criticism and his refutation of claims that deconstruction and deconstructive criticism is nihilistic and amoral. Miller's recent work aims to answer the question that his presidential address seems to beg: '[I]n what sense can or should the act of reading be itself ethical or have an ethical import?' (*ER*, p. 1). He asserts that 'there is a necessary ethical moment in that act of reading as such, a moment neither cognitive, nor political, nor social, nor interpersonal, but properly and independently ethical' (ER, p. 1). This claim rests on a complex two stage argument and a number of performative readings.

MILLER AND THE ETHICS OF READING

Ethics into Narrative

Miller's first step is to argue that ethics have a particular relation to language and to narrative: 'without storytelling there is no theory of ethics' (ER, p. 2/3). Miller is not following Nussbaum's line of argument – indeed, he writes that it is 'not because stories contain the thematic dramatization of ethical situations, judgements and choices' (ER, p. 3) that ethics, narrative and language are interwoven. Instead, he argues that ethics are only, and can only, be expressed in a narrative, rather than a transcendent commandment. Where for Nussbaum, narratives enact and reflect back on ethical rules, for Miller, ethical or moral rules themselves can only exist in narrative form.[23] For Miller,

> ethics is not just a form of language but a running or sequential mode of language, in short a story. Ethics is a form of allegory, one form of those apparently referential stories we tell to ourselves and to those around us. (ER, p. 50)

Whether ethical are transcendent commandments beyond language or not, they can only present themselves as a narrative in language. To understand ethics, then, it is necessary to understand the story by which the ethical tells itself. As a consequence, the ability to understand ethics lies in the act of interpreting a narrative, the activity 'usually thought to be the province of the literary critic' (ER, p. 3).

This action of naming something unnameable in language is, as Miller points out, the same rhetorical trope as catachresis (etymologically: 'against usage'), 'an example of the forced or abusive transfer of terms from an alien realm to name something that has no proper name in itself since it is not an object which can be directly confronted by the senses' (ER, p. 21). This is a central point on which Miller will expand in his reading of de Man. Moreover, it is clear that Miller understands ethics in what sounds like Kantian terms: his version of ethics is ethics as law or commandment. Indeed, in order to illustrate and explore the first step of his argument, Miller chooses to read – to perform an act of deconstructive criticism on – a passage from Kant. This choice, as Miller makes clear, is an attempt to discuss the whole ethical approach of the Enlightenment and post-Enlightenment period. More significantly for Miller, Kant's ethical philosophy sets up a transcendental metaphysical law, on which such a deconstructive reading, undoing laws set up in language and in narrative, can gain the best foothold.

It is through a footnote that Miller starts his reading, concentrating on the phrase "[A]ll respect for a person is only respect for the law . . . (of righteousness etc.) of which the person provides an example" (*ER*, p. 18).[24] Miller suggests that, just as our respect for an individual comes only from our respect for the law, our respect for a text comes because that text is also an example of the law, above and beyond the particularity of that text. Thus 'the effect on the reader of the text would be like the effect on him of the moral law, that is, a categorial imperative, necessarily binding his will or leading him willingly to bind his own will' (*ER*, p. 18). However, the law, even Kant's pure practical reason, is embodied in a text – it cannot not be – and because of this, as Miller has argued, it 'involves narrative, as its subversive accomplice' (*ER*, p. 23). There can be 'no theory of ethics, no theory of the moral law as such and of its irresistible, stringent imperative . . . without storytelling and the temporalisation (in all senses of the word) which is an intrinsic feature of all narrative' (*ER*, p. 23).

Scattered throughout *The Groundwork* there are little stories, experiments, narratives which serve as 'illustrations' of Kant's argument: they often sound like summaries of novels. According to Miller these are, in fact, where the law in Kant's philosophy actually appears, in narrative. Miller's argument is that the limits of insight into the necessary moral truths are limited by condition, by events, by narrative in language. As a result, the 'satisfaction of reason' is constantly deferred by a perpetual inquiry into condition, into narrative. Reason is prevented from encountering the actual moral law by the very thing that embodies the actual moral law, the narratives in which it is demonstrated. The signifier of the law, the narratives, presupposes the absent signified of the law, which itself can never be reached. There can be no appeal to 'tables of the law', because they are always already in language and have a narrative format. Any attempt to articulate the law is bound to fail, precisely because it is an articulation of the law. The law does not exist except in its articulations, which by their existence presume both the presence of the law, for Kant, and which seemingly deny the law its very existence by their incomprehensibility.

The stories that embody the law, by which the law is comprehended, are based on an incomprehensibility because nothing outside the stories gives us the tools to make them comprehensible. The stories seem to give vicarious access to the moral law and at the same time deny any sort of perception or articulation of it, save as incomprehensibility. This is the 'very limit' of philosophy Kant discusses in his concluding note (*The Moral Law*, p. 123), where philosophy runs up against the condition of narrative, but is not subsumed within it. The law is not part of a text, not a highlighted episode or statement, but that which is exemplified throuhg a text. If philosophers seek the law, they can only seek it through narrative, through language – it is this disjunction that de Man exploits in *Allegories of Reading*, and which forms the second step of Miller's argument.

Narrative into Unreadability

The difference between de Man and Kant . . . is that Kant can have confidence in the ability of language and reason to formulate an understanding of a non-linguistic possibility, whereas in de Man's case it is a matter of encountering the limits of the possibility of under-standing the laws of language within language.

J. Hillis Miller (*ER*, p. 56)

If Miller was claiming only that philosophical thinking – on ethics in this case – worked through language, there would be nothing essentially new or radical about *The Ethics of Reading*. In insisting on the importance of the interrelationship between narrative and ethics and denying the possibility of a transcendent truth that would need no interpretation, Miller might seem to be following the same lines as a number of other contemporary thinkers on ethics: Nussbaum, Williams, Ricoeur, MacIntyre. Even to concentrate on the way in which language 'deforms' the thought of ethics would cover ground opened up by, for example, 'White Mythology', in which Derrida argues that it 'is not so much that metaphor is in the text of philosophy . . . rather these texts are in metaphor', and that philosophy – specifically metaphysics – is constrained by figures in language.[25] If Miller's work only discussed the significance of narrative, it would be similar to Jonathan Reé's *Philosophical Tales*, which investigates the effect of narrative on philoso-phy.[26] However, Miller argues that because the law is embodied in a narrative text, the law 'falls victim' to all the consequences of being textual. It is at this point that the importance of Paul de Man's thinking on language becomes apparent. For Miller and de Man, the ethical law in narrative is both limited to language and springs from language, as opposed to being a transcendental 'merely' embodied in language. The ethical law, in language, therefore becomes unreadable.

In *Allegories of Reading*, Paul de Man discusses ethics as a form of rhetoric in a passage central to Miller's argument:

> The concatenation of the categories of truth and falsehood with the
> values of right and wrong is disrupted, affecting the economy of the
> narration in decisive ways. We can call this shift in economy *ethical*
> since it involves displacement from *pathos* to *ethos*. Allegories are
> always ethical, the term ethical designating the structural interference
> of two distinct value systems. In this sense, ethics has nothing to do
> with the will (thwarted or free) of a subject, nor a fortiori with the
> relationship between subjects. The ethical category is imperative (i.e.,
> a category rather than a value) to the extent that it is linguistic and not
> subjective. Morality is a version of the same language aporia that gave
> rise to such concepts as 'man' or 'love' or 'self', and not the cause or
> consequence of such subjects. The passage to an ethical tonality does
> not result from a transcendental imperative but is the referential (and
> therefore unreliable) version of a linguistic confusion. Ethics (or, one
> should say, ethicity) is a discursive mode among others. (*AR*, p. 206)

De Man is arguing that ethics, a sort of language use he names 'ethicity',
occurs only in language and not in some transcendental realm. By an act of
catachresis, the 'forced or abusive transfer' of names from one discursive
mode to another singled out by Miller, the category 'ethicity' is applied to
other categories – events in the world, actions – to which it can have no
claim except by the solely linguistic act of catachresis. This act names and
creates morality, in the same way the name 'man' or 'self' creates a category
which did not exist previously. To name an action 'wrong' is precisely (and,
for de Man and Miller, only) to name it by an act of catachresis. This is not
to suggest that the name 'ethics' has no meaning, and remains a 'humpty-
dumpty' word to be used in any sense at will. Rather, just as the name 'man'
invents and becomes a practical used category, the name 'ethicity' names
and creates a category which is made important by its social use. De Man's
point is that it relies on and 'originates' from its use in language, not from
anywhere 'outside' language.

Barbara Johnson perhaps sums this point up writing on the representation of minorities (in relation to Harvard Law School and *Pilgrim's
Progress*). She states that each

> time a person chooses to speak 'as a', he or she is attempting the
> 'ethical' leap that de Man's later analysis associates with allegory: to
> combine referentiality (the question of identity) with judgement (the
> question of social change), to make the true/false distinction line up
> with the right/wrong distinction.[27]

Thus for Miller, ethical necessity is

linguistic rather than subjective or the effect of a transcendental law . . . In the case of ethics it is a necessity to make judgements, commands, promises about right and wrong which have no verifiable basis in anything outside language. It is in this sense that ethics (or ethicity) is a discursive mode among others . . . Ethics is a form of allegory. (ER, pp. 49–50)

'It is impossible to get outside the limits of language', Miller writes, 'by means of language' (ER, p. 59).

Miller and de Man argue for the 'unreadability' of texts. De Man argues that a text 'cannot be closed off by a single reading' but 'engenders . . . a supplementary figural superposition which narrates the unreadability of the prior narration' (AR, p. 205). In his earlier essay discussing Shelley's *The Triumph of Life* and its readings, Miller argues that the poem 'like all texts, is 'unreadable', if by readable one means a single, definitive interpretation . . . neither the 'obvious' nor the 'deconstructionist' reading is 'univocal'. Each contains, necessarily, its enemy within itself, is itself both host and parasite.'[28]

This 'unreadability' leads to the paradox of reading. Miller claims that the actual act of reading has two movements. One is the pragmatic impossibility of not reading, 'that insistence on necessary referential, pragmatic function of language' (ER, p. 44): this realisation, he argues 'distinguishes de Man's work from certain forms of structuralism or semiotics. It also gives the lie to those who claim 'deconstruction' asserts the 'free play' of language in the void, abstracted from all practical, social, or political effect.' (ER, p. 44). The second movement is the realisation of the unreadability of texts. Reading has to happen and/but it is bound to be a misreading, an allegory of unreadability, in accordance with the law that all reading is misreading. This structure is central to Miller's thought on deconstruction generally, appearing at the core of his 1979 essay 'The Critic as Host', where he places a text, its reading and the deconstruction of that reading in an unbroken unhierarchical chain, continually interacting with each other, each interdependent on the other. 'The understanding of a text', Miller writes, 'is prior to its affirmation as an ethical value, but both are necessary' (ER, p. 52). The referential function of language, its illusion or 'necessary lie' in de Man's terms, cannot be avoided. In this, for Miller, ethicity follows the same pattern as de Man's analysis of the word 'man', a metaphor that literalises, or lies about, particulars in order to turn them into serviceable universals, which in turn form the basis of society:

[E]thicity . . . is no more than another version of the same form of lying. It is story telling in more than one sense. An ethical judgement, command, or promise is like the concept 'man' in both senses, that it has no ground in truth and in the sense that it universalises without grounds, makes equal the always different moral situations in which men and women find themselves . . . It is by no means true, but at the same time it cannot be measured as false by reference to any possible ascertainable true ethical judgement. (*ER*, pp. 50–1)

By reading de Man, Miller has developed his reading of Kant. Miller had shown that Kant covered up the importance of narrative which, in fact, 'serves for Kant as the absolutely necessary bridge without which there would be no connection between the law as such and any particular ethical rule of behaviour' (*ER*, p. 28). After de Man, however, the position of ethical law has changed. Language and narrative are no longer a subversive 'bridge', but rather the place in which the ethical law is brought into existence. Moreover, just as for Kant, the ethical law in language is subject to the law of language: it has become unreadable, although it must be read. It is in this context that Miller views de Man's comments on the line of Hölderlin's 'what is true is what is bound to take place'.[29] Indeed, de Man's words take up a totemic significance throughout Miller's work: reading 'is an argument (which is not necessarily the same as a polemic) because it has to go against the grain of what one would want to happen in the name of what has to happen' (cited in *ER*, p. 52)

In summary, Miller argues first that the ethical law as conceived by Kant can only be approached through narratives, and these narratives are subject to the laws of reading. Following de Man, he then argues that the ethical is, in fact, created only in language by an act of catachresis. The narrative is in itself unreadable, that is, no determinate meaning can be assigned to it, but there is no choice but to read it. This is ethical because it is 'the experience of an "I must" that is always the same but always unique, idiomatic' (*ER*, p. 127). This leads Miller to conclude that he 'is unable . . . to know whether . . . I am subject to a linguistic necessity or to an ontological one . . . I am unable to avoid making the linguistic mistake of responding to a necessity of language as if it had ontological force and authority' (*ER*, p. 127). This is the conclusion to the problems raised by his reading of Kant. The law, 'embodied' in (not through) texts can only be read (that is, misread) and understood, through deconstruction/deconstructive criticism, as misread and misinterpreted: this 'law forces the reader to betray the text or deviate from it in the act of reading it, in the name of a higher demand that can yet be reached only by way of the text' (*ER*, p. 120).

An Example: Reading the Veil

In a reading of Hawthorne's 'The Minister's Black Veil', Miller illustrates how reading with this sort of ethical awareness might proceed. The text and Miller's readings of the text concentrate on the meaning of the veil. The Minister himself, Hooper, claims it to be a 'type and symbol' to which the Minister's fiancée Elizabeth – and assorted literary critics – plaintively ask 'type and symbol of what?'.

Miller charts the effect of this question in relation to others: for example, 'it puts in doubt his parishioners' sense of themselves'.[30] Moreover, it leads another critic to offer a sexual reading of the veil. This reading becomes the target of Miller's argument. He writes that sexuality 'is more an allegorical vehicle in Hawthorne's story for something else' (*HH*, p. 82). Although the mask does have sexual connotations, those connotations lead to something else – the impossibility of reading – and are not an end in themselves.

When challenged by a suggestion that this reading paralyses political or other forms of action, Miller responds by arguing that his strategy 'makes possible a more responsible exercise of administrative or educational power' (*HH*, p. 81). Accused of 'masking an authority by displacing and neutralising it', Miller argues that he has, in contrast, explained 'how Hawthorne shows the authority of Hooper's donning of the veil gives him to be without authority, either transcendent or social' (*HH*, p. 81). Moreover, he has shown how an interpretation which makes 'sexual secrets an ultimate explanatory ground' is only 'another version of the metaphysics of unveiling' (*HH*, p. 81). In a gesture reminiscent of his Modern Language Association of America (MLA) presidential address, he claims his reading strategy is 'an unveiling and putting into question of the ideology of unveiling' (*HH*, p. 104). Miller unveils the 'promise of an imminent unveiling' as 'a promise that can never be kept' (*HH*, p. 91).

Miller argues that the story reveals two presuppositions: first that the face is the sign of the person and, second, that that sign can be read. Veiled, the face becomes unreadable: the veil

> is the type and symbol of the fact that all signs are potentially unreadable, or that the reading of them is potentially unverifiable. If the reader has no access to what lies behind a sign but another sign, then all reading of signs cannot be sure whether or not it is in error. Reading would then be a perpetual wandering or displacement that can never be checked against anything except another sign. (*HH*, p. 97)

The text, then, bears within it not only an allegory of its own unreadability, but also a rejection – an ethical rejection in Miller's terms

– of readings which rely on introducing external factors into the text – the history of sexuality in New England, for example. By simply reading the text, Miller is able to show how the text itself, in the sign of the veil, cannot be read and makes other readings impossible.

PROBLEMS WITH MILLER'S ACCOUNT

The second half of this chapter aims not to critique Miller, in the sense of contrasting his position with another, but rather to draw attention to moments of blindness and of self-contradiction in his argument and its development. The argument seems to be problematic within its own terms. These very terms, in their turn, limit and constrain his approach to the issue of the ethics of criticism. This reading will approach Miller's work in two interrelated ways: first, his conception of ethics and second, his conception of reading.

THE ETHICS OF *THE ETHICS OF READING*: OR, A `MILLENNIUM OF GOOD READERS´

Ethics as such?

Miller claims that his interest is not in 'ethics as such but in the ethics of reading and in the relation of the ethical moment in reading' (ER p. 15). However his own argument – the interrelationship of ethics only in its concrete embodiment in narrative and ensuing unreadability – makes this claim impossible: the ethics of reading must be 'ethics as such'. This is clear in his discussion of Kant. He claims that his analysis of Kant avoids dealing with 'ethics' in the abstract, but rather discusses ethics in the concrete, in Kant's narratives. However, he then claims that this is the only way ethics can be discussed. This has the result of making the claim that he does not wish to discuss ethics in the abstract spurious: there is no 'abstract' in which to discuss ethics for Miller. Ethics are the ethics of reading and a distinction between 'applied' ethics and 'abstract' or 'pure' ethics can have no meaning at all. Miller sums this up at the end of *The Ethics of Reading* when he claims that he is unable to tell whether his experience of the law of reading, and the law in general, is 'a linguistic necessity or an ontological one' (ER, p. 127). Ethics in the traditional sense has been subsumed into reading – quite the opposite approach to Nussbaum, who subsumes reading into thinking about ethics. This opens, for Miller, the question of what remains of 'ethics' apart from narrative unreadability.

In *Versions of Pygmalion*, the sequel to *The Ethics of Reading*, Miller claims to understand ethics in the same general way as Henry James. In the preface to *The Golden Bowl*, James wrote that

> the whole conduct of life consists in things done, which do other things in their turn, just so our behaviour and its fruits are essentially one and continuous and persistent and unquenchable, so the act has its way of abiding and showing and testifying, and so, among our innumerable acts are no arbitrary, senseless separations.[31]

Miller's aim is to ask in what sense a reading of a text is a thing which 'does other things in its turn'.[32] Moreover, he relates this to the (very Kantian) demand that an ethical act be free from self-interest and from other influences, and at the same time be directed by an imperative, by the law, as a response to an 'I must'. As Harpham argues, the

> problems of ethics are for Miller the problems of Kant: how can we wish to obey a law that negates our wishes? How can a choice be considered free when the law compels it? How can we know a law that resists specificity?[33]

Why, then, does Miller choose Kantian ethics in order to discuss the ethics of reading? There are two answers to this, both of which illustrate problems or blindnesses in Miller's arguments.

Miller's Ethics and History

The first concerns history. Kantian ethics, as Miller makes clear, demand to be outside history: the categorical imperative is '*act only on that maxim which you can at the same time will that it should be a universal law*' and, formulated in terms of nature, it becomes '*act as if the maxim of your action were to become through your will a universal law of nature*'.[34] These formulations, by appealing to transhistorical universals immediately seem to abolish both history and any particular location in the world. This has two functions for Miller's argument. First, it pulls the philosophical writing away from any consideration of context, historical or political: Miller is not unaware of this (see *ER*, pp. 13–14), and this choice is made for clear reasons and has clear consequences. Accepting without question Kant's demand for ahistoricity as a key element in the formulation of his own laws, Miller is able to dissociate himself from arguments based on a historical perspective against his reading of Kant. These arguments would be similar to arguments about the role of history in criticism which he condemns in the first chapter of *The Ethics of Reading* and in his presidential address. Second, it shifts the focus from Kant's ideas *per se* on to Kant's language, 'the words on the page' (*ER*,

p. 6), the 'real situation of a man or a woman reading a book' (*ER*, p. 4), those things that Miller counts as central to the act of criticism. An ethical reading, as we have seen for Miller, 'cannot . . . be accounted for by . . . social and historical forces' (*ER*, p. 8), and any attempts to do so will be 'vague and speculative' (*ER*, p. 5). Ethical reading in Miller's terms comes from the language of the text itself and not from anything 'outside' or transcendental.

In choosing to read Kant's ethics in this way, Miller has already chosen a way of reading that demands an ethical reaction to the language alone, in order to prove that ethical response in general is to the language alone and not to wider historical or other factors. Kant's ethics prove Miller's ethics which in turn have proved Kant's ethics in a circular argument. This might suggest that Miller has chosen Kantian ethics for performative reasons. In response, Miller would argue that this again demonstrates the unreadability of narratives, since it is impossible to validate his – or Kant's – argument by any standards outside language: the only way to 'prove' anything is within language.

However, there is a blindness here. Miller is arguing that ethics only exist in concrete narratives, and is using Kant to prove this. Narratives create ethics, and the ethics claim to deny history. However, what are narratives but histories? Narratives depend primarily on other narratives – other histories – for their meaning. The narratives Miller uses only have power as narratives because they depend on other narratives. The example used by both Miller and Kant of the narrative of the man who promises a better meal to cannibals if they do not eat him (*ER*, p. 37) depends for its narrative sense on an understanding of exactly what (sort of western, eurocentric invention) a cannibal is, and in what situation they (are supposed to) eat people. Miller's example of the narrative of marital fidelity (*ER*, p. 37) assumes a narrative of marriage and an understanding of fidelity. Both of these narratives rely for their sense and meaning, that is, for their ability to be (mis)read, on a whole set of narratives over time which are usually known as history or culture. Thus, the claim that these narratives are free from interpretations based on historical understandings turns out to be false: these narratives are precisely those which are deeply dependent on a certain sort of – western – history in order to make any sense at all. In direct contrast to Miller's claim, and Kant's wish to escape history, the unavoidable use of narrative to embody ethics does not deny history but smuggles in historical understandings at a deeper level. This confounding of Kant's ahistorical philosophy is made clear, ironically, by Miller's analysis concentrating on language and narrative. Miller's argument, which relies on narratives claiming to be ahistorically transcendent has, in fact, relied on precisely the lack of this ahistoricism, on the grounding of narratives in historical contexts.

'It works': Ethics and Miller's Performative Argument

The second reason for choosing a Kantian approach to ethics also turns out to be performative. In the structure of deconstructive critical reading, illustrated by Miller in 'The Critic as Host', a text is given a univocal reading which in turn plays host to a deconstructive reading. Each text contains within itself the other element. Miller imports this structure into his consideration of the ethics of reading. This means that he has to analyse an ethics that looks, or can be acted on, like a text. For Miller, ethics are a set of textual rules, commandments or laws, actually written down to be followed. As a text, as only, following de Man, another mode of discourse, ethics for Miller are open to deconstructive reading. Although it may be that all approaches to ethics function in this way (textuality certainly raised problems for Nussbaum's approach), some texts dealing with ethics engage specifically with their very linguistic nature – Levinas's *Otherwise than Being; or, Beyond Essence* is one such example.

Miller, whilst claiming to come to no conclusions about the nature of ethics as such, has always already presupposed that ethics function in relation to language in this textual way. If his prime command is that reading 'is an argument . . . because it has to go against the grain of what one would want to happen in the name of what has to happen' (*ER*, p. 52, p. 116), he has contradicted himself because he has already made ethics 'happen' in one relation to language, subsumed by, rather than in contention with, language. This functions in exactly the same way in which a critical reading of a text assumes that text is referential 'beyond' that text itself and aims to deconstruct this. It is these sorts of readings, like the critic's suggestion that Hawthorne's Minister's mask covers a sexual secret, that Miller is used to deconstructing. However, the relationship between ethics and language may be different from Miller's assumption that ethics are beyond language.

Miller cannot offer a convincing account of ethics because he is doing two things at once. His work sets up a binary opposition between ethics as transcendent (beyond language) and immanent (in language). He deconstructs the presupposition that ethics must come from beyond language, by showing how the ethical is always constructed in and by language. This is the first part of his argument, which reverses the binary opposition. The second part bypasses the opposition altogether and is illustrated by his claim that it is impossible to tell whether the ethical demand is ontological (from

Being, beyond language) or linguistic (immanent, in language). Confusingly, however, he also supports the de Manian claim that ethics originate in language, that the traditionally rejected term in the opposition is in fact the dominant one. He seems to want the 'origin' of ethics to be both determinate (in language) and indeterminate (linguistic or ontological).

Pedagogic and Apolitical

In addition to these problems with Miller's text a number of writers have criticised Miller, from a variety of perspectives, for the deficiency of his understanding of ethics. Simon Critchley argues that Miller's idea of text is limited to books rather than having a wider Derridian idea of text, resulting in an understanding of ethics which is only pedagogical, and thus unable to deal with more wide-ranging debates.[35] In response, it is possible to argue that Miller concentrates on books as a way of concentrating on what he perceives to be the central issue, language, and that although he discusses reading in a limited sense he would not be unwilling to follow Paul de Man and find this limited sense expanded to a universal one. This would explain his statement 'I would even dare to promise that the millennium would come if all men and women became good readers in de Man's sense' – that is, it would come if everything were read as de Man read books (*ER*, p. 58).[36] Strangely, this in turn can be reread in the light of another of Critchley's criticisms, that Miller's work is limited to reading texts in the context of a North American university. If everyone alive could be taught to read at Yale as de Man read, in what could be understood as a western European capitalistic hegemonic way, then the millennium, the 'end of history', at least in Fukuyama's sense, might well have come. Critchley also suggests that Miller only presents ethics as a traditional region of philosophical inquiry (this chapter has suggested that Miller only really explores Kantian ethics), and thus ethics for Miller are 'thinner' than Critchley would wish. Moreover, for Critchley, the link between ethics and politics has not been made clear; for Miller, ethics is 'simply and entirely a formal, universal command to respect, an 'I must' or moment of sublimity derived from a text and then somehow translated into political action' (*ED*, p. 48). Again, this criticism circles around the weakness of the ethics that Miller espouses.

Ethical but Amoral?

Geoffrey Galt Harpham, in his review of *The Ethics of Reading*, also argues that Miller's understanding of ethics is too weak: Miller is 'purporting to define and defend the ethics of reading, but [produces] an apology for a particular critical practice'.[37] Harpham also draws on the distinction between ethics (the idea of doing right) and morality (a specific set of values or obligations) developed by Bernard Williams. In the light of this distinction, Harpham suggests that Miller

> makes no provision for the possibility that the competition among evaluative systems for the right to describe is eventually won. He tries . . . to rule out morality, with its choices and particularities. Ethics may suspend choice, may resist settled determinations . . . But non-philosophers may not have this luxury. They must be moral as well as ethical, must interpret as well as understand.[38]

This seems to miss precisely the claim of Miller's second step, that we are forced to make a choice but that choice is continually open to deconstruction and disruption: we have to (mis)read and be aware of the (mis)reading. This choice is, for Miller, not a 'luxury' but a vital need in any ethical, social or political project. Indeed, in contrast to Harpham and following Williams, it might be more accurate to describe Miller's work as 'The morals of reading', so central is this de Manian claim. It is because of Miller's understanding of ethics as a moral obligation to a certain practice that Harpham's first point – that for Miller the practice of reading is centrally important – has weight. It is as if Miller has first worked out how to read and then worked out from that how an ethics should be applied, in manner analogous to an act linguists call backformation. (Backformation is the creation of a new word following an often fallacious etymological model of an old one: examples are cheeseburger from hamburger, Irangate and Whitewatergate from Watergate.) For Miller, Norris writes, 'ethics becomes just the name for a certain, albeit highly sophisticated practice of reading, one that obeys the deconstructionist imperative to take nothing on trust and attend always to the letter of the text.'[39]

For Miller the laws of text, the rules of reading, come before the law of ethics: his first ethical imperative is to read. What Miller proclaims is not the importance of 'the ethics' of reading but rather the significance of 'the reading' of ethics. The reading process, the unveiling of unveiling, is the focus of his work on ethics – a concern for ethics as such has disappeared.

Miller and the Thickness of the World

If the reading process is understood as prior to ethical or social obligation, Norris asks what can be the status of an ethics (even an 'ethics of reading') that reduces all questions of truth, responsibility and self-knowledge to a play of rhetorical codes and figurations; that rejects any appeal to human agency or will as inherently self-deluding for the same reason; and that always arrives at a stage of ultimate undecidability where the 'structural interference' of two linguistic codes is the end point of ethical reflection?[40]

For Norris, the world has 'thickness', an extra-linguistic basis, with which we must engage. Tobin Siebers, too, argues that Miller's approach represents 'an isolated linguistic morality [which] robs ethical theory of its social content'.[41] In contrast, it is part of Miller's argument that the ethics of reading only has force by 'excluding all reference to those thematic, historical or 'moral' concerns that provide the only point of contact between ethics and lived experience'.[42] This, for Norris, makes Miller's ethics anaemic and empty. Norris cites Harpham's review: 'deconstruction is both fanatically ethical and amoral.'[43] For Norris, Miller's reading or deconstruction demands an ethical purity, which is truly 'theoretical' since it depends more on looking than on acting. Norris argues that this ethical demand to follow one practice through to its logical conclusion is not in any way compatible with the moral, historical and practical demands that are placed upon us by the world. For Norris, Miller's inability to tell the difference between an ontological ethical necessity and a linguistic necessity is simply an abrogation of responsibility.

Following Harpham, Norris argues that Miller's claims are essentially ascetic, following 'the law that identifies resistance to desire as the production of ethics, but which also defines ethics itself as the desire to resist its own more generalised or blandly accommodating precepts'.[44] Further, by suggesting that these ethics lead an active subject or agent to resist, even in an abstract way, this line of criticism implies that Miller has slipped into a traditional approach to agency subjectivity that he and de Man specifically deny.[45] Thus, Miller would seem to be caught in a logical double bind: denying agency and yet, by his reformulation of an ethics as an ascetic imperative, affirming it. However, it would be possible to outline Miller's response to this: the self, a fiction, acts as if it is not a fiction. Agency, like ethics, is a 'necessary lie'. Miller's response to accusations of asceticism and abrogation of responsibility – and indeed the trajectory of his entire argument – would simply have to be that this melancholy conclusion is what reading reveals and that the process of reading comes before any actual ethical obligation. The two different approaches to reading, neatly summarised in Donoghue's opposition between graphi-reading and epi-reading, simply reach an impasse, an aporia, an incommensurability. There seems to be no common ground between the two, save the fact that both claim to be dealing with the same set of problems.

At this point the trajectory of Miller's work is closest to thinkers and critics like Richard Rorty, Stanley Fish and the school of American Pragmatists. Rorty claims that 'the world does not provide us with any criterion of choice between alternative metaphors, that we can only compare languages or metaphors with one another, not with something beyond language called "fact".'[46] For Rorty, it is the power of metaphor and language which move one to moral action, precisely because it is impossible to find any transcendental ahistorical truths. Moreover, the understanding of these linguistic constructions, whether in the discourse of literary criticism or elsewhere, are dependent on what Stanley Fish calls 'interpretative communities'. Societies have seemingly always already decided on what the misreadings are: for example, what misreading of a particular (e.g. man) constitutes the general (e.g. men). Transcendental truth is unreachable, leaving only a succession of misreadings. That Miller's work runs parallel in some ways to Rorty's neo-pragmatist philosophy is not surprising, despite Rorty's somewhat disparaging comments on Miller in essays like 'Two Meanings of Logocentrism' and 'De Man and the Cultural Left'. Both have been influenced by Derrida and by other thinkers in the continental tradition. Their differences stem in part from the different intellectual traditions with which they engage, and from their very different aims.

This section has discussed the ethics of Miller's work in two ways.

Miller's own text, then, has offered a deconstruction of the 'ethics' in *The Ethics of Reading* on two grounds. First, from 'within' Miller's own text, the repression of history served only to highlight and so to 'return' the historically grounded nature of language. This has revealed how Miller has chosen the limits of the field of his argument to draw out his own conclusions. Second, Miller has implicitly denied his own leitmotif in *The Ethics of Reading* by always already assuming that 'ethics' exists in a certain relation to language which may not be the case – as a result he offers a weak and seemingly insubstantial understanding of 'ethics'. This 'weak' understanding of ethics is highlighted by Critchley, as pedagogic and specifically American, and by Harpham and Norris as simply unethical, turning ethical concerns into simply a way of reading. These problems with Miller's work do not deny its rigour as criticism *per se*. Rather, they suggest that the ramifications for ethics of this way of reading – deconstructive criticism – are highly problematic. Having explored reactions to Miller's conceptions of ethics, the chapter turns to his conception of reading. If, as Norris suggests, Miller's ethics are a secondary 'backformation' from his principles of reading and ethics are collapsed into a reading strategy, his reading strategy asks for close concentration.

READING READING

Miller's 'Constitution of Reading' and its Problems

Miller is blind to a number of assumptions that he makes about his critical practice. This is clearest in the 'laws' of reading that he offers in *Versions of Pygmalion*, the sequel to *The Ethics of Reading*. This passage echoes Derrida in *Of Grammatology*, in the section entitled 'The Exorbitant. Question of Method' (pp. 157–64). Derrida writes about the production of critical reading and, dealing with the question of what 'produce' might mean, he argues that in an 'attempt to explain that, I would initiate a justification of my principles of reading. A justification, as we shall see, entirely negative, outlining by exclusion a space of reading that I shall not fill here: a task of reading.'[47] Miller, in contrast, attempts to undertake this task by offering four positive rules of reading. Miller's list also has an echo of I. A. Richards's 1929 *Practical Criticism*, a founding text for the New Critics. Richards provides a number of lists and rules, perhaps most significantly a list of the 'chief difficulties of criticism' which seem to foreshadow Miller's work.[48]

Miller's first law in *Versions of Pygmalion* states that the 'relation of literature to history is a problem, not a solution' (*VP*, p. 33). The second rule goes on to argue that historical context 'does not exempt the scholar-critic from the fulfilment of the patient task of actually *reading* the text' (*VP*, p. 33). For Miller, repeating his de Manian ethical 'law of reading' from *The Ethics of Reading*, the key assumption is that reading

> should be guided by the expectation of surprise, that is, the pre-supposition that what you actually find when you read is likely to be fundamentally different from what you expected . . . Good reading is also guided by the presupposition of a possible heterogeneity in the text. (*VP*, p. 33)

For Miller, here as in the earlier work, the

> ever-present danger in reading is that it will not be reading at all, but just finding in the text of what the reader already knew he or she was going to find there and therefore has posed as a screen between himself or herself and the actual text. (p. 33)

Miller's third rule is that context and text have a relationship in language, not in materiality: 'the relations of literature to history and society is part of rhetoric, not part of physics, however 'material' history may be' (*vp*, p. 34). Miller's fourth rule argues that reading is transformative, that a work of literature 'intervenes in history when it is read' (*vp*, p. 34).

These four rules repeat the arguments Miller made in *The Ethics of Reading* which criticised attempts to explain works of literature by reference to things outside the text. Miller suggested that this was difficult because of 'ennui and fatigue' in keeping one's attention on the text, a sense of guilt in the study of something so seemingly unworldly as literature, a fear of the anarchic and subversive power of literature and the promise of 'intellectual mastery' (*ER*, p. 5) offered by Marxist, Gadamerian or psychological approaches 'measuring and ascertaining . . . the meaning of a text by something nontextual outside that text' (*ER*, p. 6). These 'vague and speculative' (*ER*, p. 5) approaches merely form a metaphorical gloss on the text, an allegory of its explanation or reading: it 'is another way of saying that the study of literature, even the study of the historical and social relations of literature, remains within the study of language' (*ER*, p. 7). Moreover, Miller argues that extra-textual 'evidence' will lead the text to be read as a symptom rather than a cause: the critic already knows what will be found in a text. This, for Miller, carries the risk of simply reprogramming the text in the light of an extra-textual approach, to deny it any 'performative power' (*ER*, p. 8) of its own. The four rules offered in *Versions of Pygmalion* simply codify in a positive way these arguments from *The Ethics of Reading*.

Indeed, these rules do more than codify. They seem to be part of a prescriptive constitution. Miller, in an evocative legislative performative act, claims 'I hold these truths to be self-evident, but even self-evident truths need occasionally to be enunciated' (*vp*, p. 35). Their status is no longer that of assumptions, of one way of reading amongst other, but rather of constitutional demand – an appropriate register, perhaps, for the one-time president of the MLA.

These rules also illustrate Miller's hostility to history and historical readings: again these rules seem to be aimed at Marxists and '"new historicists"' (*vp*, p. 34, Miller's inverted commas). Although Miller's key rule is his second, he emphasises his hostility to history by dealing with it in his very first rule and more or less repeating the same point in the third. It is also of central importance here that Miller simply does not rule 'history' out of court, in the way that he ruled ontological ethical demands out: history, Miller could argue but does not, simply occurs in language. The conclusion that history itself is only composed in and of language, an argument like Hayden White's on the rhetoric of history, would seem to be the clearest result of Miller's argument, but a conclusion that Miller does not reach. The reason for this is that Miller does not wish the purity of the 'act of reading' literature to be contaminated with 'history' at any level. In *The Ethics of Reading*, Miller elevated reading to an ontological status beyond history and situation; it became the pure relation of the individual to the text. Although the act 'spreads out to involve institutional, historical, economic, and political "contexts" . . . it begins with and returns to the man or woman face to face with the words on the page' (*ER*, p. 4). If history were understood as literature by Miller it would be impossible for him to determine whether one was reacting 'freely' to a 'literature' language act or to a 'history' text language act. By denying history the same linguistic status as literature, by swerving in his argument at this point and not following his assumptions about language to their conclusions, Miller is retaining a strong sense of the literary text as separate from the historical text, which in turn seems to imply that Miller is not really discussing the role of reading *per se* (as he claims) but the role of reading (a category of texts defined as) literature.

Finally, in relation to his key second law, there is a contradiction which is made more apparent here than in his previous work. One the one hand, the critic must read 'guided by the expectation of surprise', the de Manian rule; on the other, good reading is also 'guided by the presupposition of a possible heterogeneity in the text'. Reading, then, has two contradictory rules: to be in a state of expectation for a particular thing from a text (heterogeneity) and to be in a state of expectation for anything and specifically not any particular thing (surprise). To be in a state of 'preparing to be surprised' (expectation of something but nothing specific) cannot include a presupposition of heterogeneity: no one is surprised by something they expect or have consciously taken as a presupposition. Although this paradox may seem insignificant, it seems to show up a wider incoherence in Miller's thought. Miller's insistence on the primacy of the act of reading in relation to ethics is incoherent in its own right because it places too much emphasis on the act of reading itself. Following an examination of these 'laws', it is possible to suggest that it is not reading that is primary as Miller suggests, but rather the openness to surprise.

Reading and the World

For Miller, reading is the 'real situation of a man or woman reading a book' (*ER*, p. 4). Although reading 'leads to an act' and 'enters into the social, institutional realms' (*ER*, p.4), the ethical moment for Miller is unaffected by its institutional, political, social and historical world: it occurs in a vacuum. Yet the act of reading must occur within the world. This might be seen as one of the principle claims of Derridian deconstruction itself, demanding a self-reflexivity even about self-reflexivity. This interrogation would include questioning the claim that some things (e.g. art, race, and in this case the practice of reading) are ahistorical. Miller opposed the insistence, by critics like Jameson, that the demand to historicise is transcendental and ahistorical. Miller himself, however, has offered an ahistorical practice of reading in its stead.

Any reader is always already located in the world and the ideal ahistorical 'reading situation' that Miller posits is a myth. It is impossible to read without being located, as if one were a neutral pure (enlightenment) 'reading' being. A text cannot be in any sense 'understood' until it has been read through our own reading-perception which will itself determine our understanding of it: however hard we try to 'bracket off' our opinions, conceptions, lived experience, skills of analysis and so on, these factors still delimit our reading-perception. To state this is not simply to contradict Miller when he argues that literature is 'a source of political or cognitive acts' (ER, p. 5) or that literature 'must be in some way a cause not merely an effect' (ER, p. 5), but rather to problematise the idea of reading on which Miller puts such weight. Simply, reading must take place as 'a reading' by 'an individual' in the world. 'Reading' in the abstract cannot exist. To read is not to start from a neutral position.

Indeed, Miller's description of the 'real situation of a man or woman reading a book' can easily be read as implicitly acknowledging this, against his intentions. By attempting to escape gendered assumptions ('a man or a woman' instead of just 'a woman' or 'a man') it re-imposes a binary metaphysics of sex ('a man *or* a woman') which serves to position everyone as gendered on one side or other. This attempt to avoid positioning by Miller simply serves to re-emphasise the impossibility of circumventing a binary metaphysics of sex. Readers are positioned as men or women, located in the world. In contrast, it might be possible to argue from Miller's position that this positioning was simply a linguistic situation; or, rather, just as with ethical demands, one's actual position is indistinguishable from one's linguistic position. However, this argument can be destabilised by suggesting that – even if it were possible – to claim to be without a 'position' in the world, in a 'reading vacuum', 'contentless', is also a location, even if it represents a null location. Thus this position, if it is possible and even if it only exists in linguistic systems, is already to be located in history by denying history. Again, Miller seems blind to this implication of his own argument.

Deconstruction and Reading

For Miller, the term 'reading' carries a great deal of emphasis and is identified with 'deconstructive criticism'. However, the relationship between the two is not as unproblematic as it at first appears. Indeed, there seems to be a trajectory in Miller's work away from deconstructive criticism and towards the idea of 'reading'. In 'The Critic as Host', of 1979, Miller writes of the necessary deconstruction any text bears within it. However, by 1987, the name of this action is less clear: Miller is torn between 'reading' and 'deconstruction'. E. S. Burt sums up Miller's understanding of 'reading' as

> a term that, through overuse, easily becomes confused with interpretation. But in fact there is a crucial difference: reading involves the undoing of interpretative figures for it questions whether any synthesis, any single meaning, can close off a text and satisfactorily account for its constitution. Unlike interpretation, which implies a development over the course of a narrative toward a single figure reconciling all its diverse moments, reading states the logic of figures and the logic of narrative to be continually divergent.[49]

Miller follows this line in his presidential address, naming the way of reading he champions deconstruction. In contrast, although his book of 1987 concerns deconstruction specifically, it is entitled *The Ethics of Reading* not 'the ethics of deconstruction'. The act of reading has become linked to deconstructive criticism but is no longer simply an act of 'deconstruction'.

This slow shift away from deconstruction is even more marked in *Versions of Pygmalion* where Miller avoids any mention of deconstruction or deconstructive criticism at all. This is perhaps why Miller has to invert Derrida's refusal to name his protocols of reading. Where Derrida drew up 'laws of reading' negatively, delineating a 'space of reading' by saying what it was not, Miller is forced to lay out his new positivistic rules of reading which, although similar to deconstructive critical readings, are not, in fact, the same. Where Derrida offered rules of indeterminacy, Miller offers determinate rules.

Interviewed in 1991 Miller stated:

> I'm prepared to say that all good readers *are* deconstructionists, but remember I said there are deconstructionisms. I don't mean that everybody has to read de Man and Derrida . . . the good readers are those readers who are, for whatever reason, sensitive to the kinds of

rhetorical complexities that Derrida, for example, sees in works. This sensitivity may be found in otherwise diverse critics . . . the sort of people who notice anomalies, who are not bamboozled by their preconceptions about what they're going to find, that are prepared to notice what's really strange about works. (*HH*, p. 158)

At this point, Miller seems to have abandoned deconstructive criticism as a critical method and to have moved to a position of making 'deconstruc- tionisms' a version of 'good reading'. 'Deconstructionisms' has become so vague and amorphous for Miller that it ceases to have any clear meaning. This, in a sense, allows Miller to sidestep all the issues of the ethics of criticism that deconstructive criticism raised in the first place – it is almost as if Miller wants to return to an earlier paradigm of literary studies in which all 'good' critics are 'deconstructionists'. This in itself implies that there need not, in fact, be any discussion over the 'ethics of criticism' at all since there has been no change in literary studies. It also suggests that Miller has started to use this rhetoric of 'reading' in order to negotiate stresses from two directions: to distance his work from the changing understanding of deconstruction and deconstructive criticism as well as to counter anti-deconstructive trends in academic discourse.

'Good' Reading?

Miller claims that deconstruction 'is nothing more or less than good reading as such' (*ER*, p. 10). It is good reading which underlies the ethics of reading in general. This claim is deeply ambiguous. If Miller wants to claim that 'good' means accurate, in the sense of correct and true to the text, his own argument in *The Ethics of Reading* would seem to make this claim impossible. For Miller, the actual act of reading implies, on the one hand, the pragmatic impossibility of not reading and, on the other, a realisation of the unreadability of texts: reading has to happen and it is bound to be a misreading. Truth, like ethics, is a 'necessary lie', so to claim a reading is 'good' (accurate) is to rely again on the referential, the power of language, which has already been unsettled and is thus a nonsensical claim. If Miller wants to claim that 'good' reading is ethically good and has ethically good effects, he has already put his own text into a *mise èn abyme*. How would it be possible to show or to judge or even to do 'good' (ethical) reading? Only by an ability to already do 'good' (accurate) reading, which is impossible, but demanded for by good (ethical) reading. 'Good' in 'good' reading, in 'deconstructive' reading, refers back to 'good' reading, the only way in which the 'good' can be made manifest. In this case again the 'good' is meaningless and solipsistic: reading simply depends on reading. Reading, in turn, for Miller, depends on all the exclusive assumptions of his 'rules'.

Miller and New Criticism

Miller's thought seems to ignore the concerns in Derrida's work for history and political engagement. These have always been present: *Of Grammatology* aims to focus attention on 'the most original and powerful ethnocentrism, in the process of imposing itself upon the world' and in more recent work these concerns have come to the fore.[50] Miller's concentration on 'reading' does not engage directly with political or historical issues and this would seem to support a distinction between deconstruction and Miller's deconstructive criticism. In this light, Miller's work bears similarities to New Criticism, concentrating on the 'words on the page' and refusing to deal with wider concerns: Girard suggests that 'we look at deconstruction as the child of New Criticism'. Deconstruction, in all its myriad forms, is too wide to simply be descended from New Criticism, but certainly Miller's deconstructive criticism is very influenced by New Criticism.[51]

Miller's insistence on the 'man or woman face to face with the words on the page' is an echo of I. A. Richards's experiments with 'protocols' – poetic texts given to students with no other context at all. Indeed, there are similarities between Richards's work and Miller's. Both eschew history as a means of interpretation; both are very much on their guard against critical preconceptions; both have a pedagogical emphasis, Richards explicitly, Miller implicitly. Perhaps the key difference is that Richards's experimental work supports the contention, contra Miller, that the location and status of the reader is of unavoidable importance in reading. It is Miller's New Critical heritage which distances his work from the more politically active deconstructive criticism of, for example, Homi Bhabha and the more politically engaged deconstruction offered by Derrida and other thinkers.

Miller's work also shares with New Criticism its innate canonical conservatism. Barbara Johnson perceptively comments that

> because deconstruction has focused on the ways in which the Western, white male, philosophical-literary tradition subverts itself *from within*, it has often tended to remain within the confines of the established literary canon. If it has questioned the boundary lines of literature, it has not done so with respect to the noncanonical but with respect to the line between literature and philosophy or between literature and

criticism. It is as a rethinking of those distinctions that deconstruction most radically displaces traditional evaluative assumptions.[52]

This is pre-eminently true of Miller's work, which has remained very much within the canon and has not followed anti-canonical movements in contemporary criticism.[53] His version of deconstructive criticism, which he calls 'reading', allows him to remain within the canon and to 'uncouple' his thought from more recent developments in deconstructive thought in general.

If the term 'reading' allows Miller to ignore both the demands of 'context' – politics, history – and the demand to engage in an evolving 'multiform' (to use his phrase) deconstructive movement, it also makes his work less radical. 'Deconstruction', as Chapter 1 detailed, has been under constant attack from all directions. To use a much more 'polemically neutral' term, such as 'reading', allows Miller to align his work with the long New Critical tradition in the American academies and thus to make his work seem less threatening.

Miller's ('deconstructive') criticism ('reading') and New Criticism share a denial of history and politics, a canonical conservatism and reading strategies. There remain, however, some differences between them – these differences are precisely what makes Miller's justification of the ethics of reading so tenuous. The differences seem to be three. First, the extremely rigorous readings, in the mould of de Man, that Miller demands and enacts are more intensive than New Critical readings: this is a difference not in kind but in degree of intensity. Second, Miller tries to sweep away all presuppositions about language and meaning that have adhered to texts and to reading in general. Assumptions about the referential power of language, for example, are both made and suspended. It is at exactly this point that Miller's argument becomes blind to its own assumptions – it makes assumptions and is blind not only to those assumptions but to the ramifications of those assumptions. Third, Miller's argument allows an understanding of reading as an ongoing process that cannot be closed off, as a continual process of 'deconstruction' (whatever status that claim has) which means that his reading is always more open to rereading. It is this acknowledged facet of his work, of which his text is aware (see, for example, his remarks on Kant in ER, p. 13), which will not let his 'reading' ever develop an ethics in a recognisable sense: any conclusion will have to be read, that is (mis)read continually.

These differences distinguish Miller (and de Man) from New Criticism; however, it is quite possible to read Miller's work as both New Criticism and deconstructive criticism. In the words of Paul de Man:

I don't have a bad conscience when I'm being told that, to the extent it is didactic, my work is academic or even, as it is used as a supreme insult, it is just more New Criticism. I can live with that very easily because I think that what is, in a sense, classically didactic, can be really and effectively subversive.[54]

Miller would seem to support this statement. It is this understanding of the power of reading, misreading and rereading – simply put, of the power of textuality over referentiality – that prevents Miller from unproblematically introducing a theory of ethics.

CONCLUSION: ETHICS IN GREEN GLASSES

The world appears green. This may be because we are wearing green glasses. But the world may really be green. There is no way to tell, since there is no way to take off the glasses.

J. Hillis Miller[55]

This chapter has explored Miller's understanding of the ethics of criticism, by examining a number of works where he specifically examines his own approaches to reading. It has suggested that his approach to the ethics of criticism is flawed in a number of ways. Miller assumes ethics to be simply Kantian or neo-Kantian ethics, and eschews any relation to history or to the world, partially in order to apply his literary critical method to philosophical texts. Moreover, his ethics remain unpoliticised and pedagogic; both Harpham and Norris suggest that to ignore the 'thickness of the world' is immoral, sacrificing moral engagement to ethical purity. However, it is important to note that this disagreement cannot, in fact, be resolved and their positions are incommensurable. This is because Miller argues that there are no standards outside language by which his argument (in language) can be judged, and thus arguments that invoke the 'world' can carry no weight. There seems to be no common ground over the issue of ethics. In relation to Miller's practice of reading, it seems clear that his four assumptions are more in reaction to other models of reading (suggested by the left, for example), and that they have internal contradictions. Again, his practice of reading is blind to the location of the reader in the world, and the principle of 'good' reading is logically incoherent. Moreover, Miller's use of the term 'reading' is an escape from the philosophical demands of deconstruction and from the critical demands of deconstructive criticism, to the more widely accepted assumptions of New Criticism. These assumptions about reading, and the importance that 'reading' takes on for Miller, prevent him from successfully proposing a theory of ethics.

Contrasting Nussbaum and Miller

Miller and Nussbaum have a number of fundamental differences that are summed up in Donoghue's epi-reader/graphi-reader opposition. In relation to the action of reading, Nussbaum does not find the textuality of texts problematic: for her a text can be a direct lesson in morals or, as Henry James would say, an experiment in life. The text disappears as the characters, with whom we, the readers, unproblematically identify, live out our lives and dilemmas for us. This is epi-reading on a grand scale: literature becomes no more than a cypher, an example for philosophy, a heuristic testing ground for ideas, by assuming real presence beyond the text. Despite Nussbaum's protests to the contrary, she dissolves literature into philosophy. The trope involved, as Miller's work in *Versions of Pygmalion* reveals, is prosopopoeia: 'the ascription to entities that are not really alive first of a name, than of a face and finally . . . of a voice' (*VP*, p. 5). Nussbaum does not analyse her use of this trope, which forms the basis of her critical method. She also absolves herself of what Miller would call the task of reading. Nussbaum's analyses, as have been shown, fail to pick up on ambiguities and moments where the text is not clear. Nussbaum's work also has problems with fictionality: her texts, as dry-runs for life, have to be as 'realistic' as possible, which is why her literary canon is taken principally from the realist or realist-influenced modernist works and, when confronted with an anti- or unrealist text – Beckett, for example – reads it as if it were a realist text.

In relation to the question of ethics *per se*, Nussbaum offers a coherent and convincing neo-Aristotelian argument in the idea of perceptive equilibrium, which both accepts the idea of principles and the understanding that the world will always modify these principles in a continual process of phronesis. Nussbaum offers a convincing case for Aristotelian ethics, but not a convincing method of dealing with the problems of texts.

Miller, the graphi-reader, on the other hand, is very different, despite the admiration he shares with Nussbaum for Henry James. His work is concerned only with the textuality of texts – so much so, that the world seems to disappear in relation to the individual looking at the words on the page. Moreover, and despite his claims for the importance of literature, in contrast to Nussbaum, he reads philosophical texts not in search of some sort of clear meaning but rather as a competing battle of tropes and figures.

With literary texts, he starts by putting out of bounds the very referentiality that Nussbaum claims to be centrally important. Miller is self-reflexive about his way of reading, although it does have blindnesses and unquestioned assumptions within it; as Paul de Man argues in his essay 'The Resistance to Theory', it is impossible to avoid this. Miller is a close reader who follows textual anomalies and twists through to their often disparate conclusions. For Miller, fictionality is not the problem it is for Nussbaum, since all forms of discourse are, following de Man, 'fictional', necessary lies, allegorical rather than referential.

However, as a result of this practice of reading, he is unable to offer a coherent theory of ethics. Indeed, so much is he constrained by his practice of reading that his understanding of ethics is always already constricted to a version of transhistorical Kantian ethics, a far cry from the historically involved, 'thick' phronesis of Nussbaum's approach. Finally, Miller's ethics dissolve into his practice of reading: he cannot tell whether he is responding to an ethical demand or a linguistic demand. In direct contrast to Nussbaum, Miller offers a rigorous reading, a possibly unsurpassable approach to a text; however, his attempt to generate an ethics from this turn out to be paradoxical and problem-ridden.

Ethics beyond Graphi-reading and Epi-reading

The previous three chapters have explored three general responses to the issue of the relationship between ethics, literature and criticism. First, the 'anti-theorists' demand a return to a relatively unsophisticated humanism, reacting to the challenges of 'postmodernity' by trying to grasp certainties that are no longer certain. Second, Martha Nussbaum, as an exemplary epi-reader, found ethics unmeditated through the literary texts she read. She compensated for the lack of a person in the text (a lack signified, as Derrida argues, by the very presence of writing) by ignoring the very textuality of text and assuming a clear referentiality. Nussbaum's ethical understandings are convincing but her criticism is not since it fails to deal with the text itself – this in turn, perhaps, shows up a weakness in her thought, in its refusal to engage with the nature of language. In contrast, and aiming to deal with this specific problem, Miller, the 'deconstructive' graphi-reader, explores only the textuality of a text, denying the validity or even the possibility of reference outside the text. However, his ethical position is too weak to be sustained in the light of the blindnesses and paradoxes it contains. It is also contested from another, incommensurable, point of view as it could be read as being unethical because it simply ignores the world in favour of the text.

The problems that these critics and philosophers have are created by their understandings about the interrelationship between language in texts and ethics. For Nussbaum and epi-readers, language or text simply does not exist: ethical positions shine through like light through a perfect window. This assumption has been revealed by deconstructive thought as being problematic. Following this approach, for Miller and for other graphi-readers, only language or text exists. Miller assumes that language operates as a plane of glass that it is impossible to see through and might, in fact, be a screen with nothing behind it. Rather like Kleist's green glasses, Miller cannot tell the world from the way the world is represented or created in language.

The ethical theories of Emmanuel Levinas in relation to language offer a way out of this oppositional dilemma, a way out which is particularly relevant to literary analysis at the current moment. Levinas's work shows how the ethical signifies in language. From this understanding, which comes only after an engagement with Derrida's thought, it is possible to explore the role of the ethical in language, which in turn, and drawing further on Levinas, will make the ethical role of criticism apparent. Nussbaum ignores language and consequently opens her argument to the sort of deconstructive reading offered in Chapter 2: ethics are for her beyond language. Miller cannot offer a convincing account of ethics because he is acting on the presupposition that ethics are a linguistic category. However, an awareness of the special ethical nature of language as revealed by Levinas will go beyond this opposition. In the light of this understanding, Miller's final comment in *The Ethics of Reading* can be reread. Miller is unable to tell whether the ethical demand he is subject to in relation to reading is 'a linguistic necessity or an ontological one' (*ER*, p. 127). After reading Levinas, this presupposed distinction between the two will disappear: ethical demands are linguistic demands, ethics and language are intertwined in an inescapable way.

NOTES

1. Paul de Man, *The Resistance to Theory* (Minneapolis: University of Minnesota Press, 1986), p. 15.
2. J. Hillis Miller, *The Ethics of Reading* (New York: Columbia University Press, 1987), p. 59. Further references to *The Ethics of Reading* will be given in the text with the abbreviation *ER*.
3. Richard Kearney, *Dialogues with Contemporary Continental Thinkers* (Manchester: Manchester University Press, 1984), pp. 124–5.
4. For a version of this history see Anthony Easthope, *British Poststructuralism since 1968* (London: Routledge, 1988).
5. Rodolphe Gasché, 'Deconstruction as Criticism', *Glyph 6* (1979), pp. 177–216 (p. 183, p. 178).
6. Rodolphe Gasché, *The Tain of the Mirror* (London: Harvard University Press, 1986), p. 270.
7. Gasché, *The Tain of the Mirror*, p. 318.
8. Richard Rorty, 'Remarks on Deconstruction and Pragmatism', in *Deconstruction and Pragmatism*, ed. Chantal Mouffe (London: Routledge, 1996), p. 14.

9. Christopher Norris, *What's Wrong with Postmodernism* (London: Harvester Wheatsheaf, 1990), p. 139.

10. Geoffrey Bennington, 'Deconstruction and the Philosophers (The Very Idea)', *Oxford Literary Review*, vol. 10 (1988), pp. 73–110 (p. 112).

11. See, for example, Richard Rorty, 'Heidegger, Kundera, and Dickens', in *Philosophical Papers*, 2 vols (Cambridge: Cambridge University Press, 1991), vol. 2, pp. 66–82.

12. Stanley Cavell, *Must We Mean What We Say?* (Cambridge: Cambridge University Press, 1976), p. xviii.

13. Jacques Derrida, Geoffrey Bennington, Rachel Bowlby, '"This Strange Institution Called Literature": An Interview with Jacques Derrida', in *Acts of Literature*, ed. Geoffrey Bennington (London: Routledge, 1992), pp. 33–75 (p. 53).

14. J. Hillis Miller, 'Presidential Address 1986: The Triumph of Theory, the Resistance to Reading and the Question of the Material Base', *PMLA*, vol. 102 (1987), pp. 281–91 (p. 290).

15. Kearney, *Dialogues with Contemporary Continental Thinkers*, p. 124.

16. Imre Salusinszky, *Criticism in Society* (London, Methuen, 1987), p. 223. In *Deconstruction and Pragmatism*, Derrida echoes this and discusses 'American deconstructionism' (p. 77).

17. De Man, *The Resistance to Theory*, p. 118.

18. J. Hillis Miller, 'The Critic as Host', in *Deconstruction and Criticism*, ed. Harold Bloom (London: Routledge and Kegan Paul, 1979), pp. 217–53 (p. 252).

19. See, amongst others: Frank Lentricchia, *After the New Criticism* (London: Methuen, 1983); Paul Bové, 'Variations on Authority: Some Deconstructive Transformations of the New Criticism', in *The Yale Critics: Deconstruction in America*, eds Jonathon Arac, Wlad Godzich, Wallace Martin (Minneapolis: University of Minnesota Press, 1983), pp. 3–19; Allan Bloom, *The Closing of the American Mind* (New York: Simon and Schuster, 1987); Wayne Booth, *The Company We Keep: An Ethics of Fiction* (London: University of California Press, 1988); Paul Bové, *Mastering Discourse: The Politics of Intellectual Culture* (London: Duke University Press, 1992); René Girard, 'Theory and Its Terrors', in *The Limits of Theory*, ed. T. M. Kavanagh (Stanford: Stanford University Press, 1989), pp. 225–55; David Lehman, *Signs of the Times: Deconstruction and the Fall of Paul de Man* (London: André Deutsch, 1991).

20. Paul de Man, *Allegories of Reading* (London: Yale University Press, 1979), p. 3. Further references to this text will abbreviated to *AR*. Paul de Man's personal history has become part of the debate about the ethics of deconstructive criticism. De Man's anti-semitic writings are less unpleasant than those of, for example, T. S. Eliot, and were written in a considerably more dangerous situation. It is impossible to excuse de Man's wartime journalism and anti-semitism, but its context is important. See: Paul de Man, *Wartime Journalism, 1939–1943*, eds Werner Hamacher, Neil Hertz and Thomas Keenan (London: University of Nebraska Press, 1988); *Responses to Paul de Man's Wartime Journalism*, eds Werner Hamacher, Neil Hertz and Thomas Keenan (London: University of Nebraska Press, 1989); Christopher Norris, *Paul de Man* (London: Routledge, 1988); Jacques Derrida, 'Like the Sound of the Sea Deep within a Shell: Paul de Man's War', trans. Peggy Kamuf, *Critical Inquiry*, vol. 14 (1988), pp. 590–652; Lehman, *Signs of the Times*; Shoshona Felman and Dori Laub, *Testimony* (London: Routledge, 1992), ch. 5, 'After the Apocalypse: Paul de Man and the Fall to Silence', pp. 120–64.

21. Barbara Johnson, *The Wake of Deconstruction* (Oxford: Basil Blackwell, 1994), p. 79.

22. This summarises two main objections to left-wing criticism from a deconstructive critical perspective. The first is the response to claims for history. For example, Fredric Jameson's *The Political Unconscious* begins with the injunction '[A]lways historicize!' and goes on to describe this as 'the one absolute and we may even say 'transhistorical' imperative of all dialectical thought' (Fredric Jameson, *The Political Unconscious* (London: Methuen, 1981), p. 9). Although deconstructive criticism obviously accepts the importance of history, it is also 'suspicious of the metaphysical concept of history', of the assumption that history is transcendental, outside language and thus able to ground or justify literary critical judgement (Derrida, 'This Strange Institution Called Literature', p. 54; see also the preface to *Of Grammatology*). The second objection is, as Miller suggests, to the use of criticism as an explicitly political tool without offering an analysis of its own rhetoric.

These opinions are not an innovation in Miller's thought. In 1980, he wrote 'I do think the conservative aspect of deconstruction needs to be stressed. Its difference from Marxism, which is likely to become more sharply visible as time goes on, is that it views as naive the millennial or revolutionary hopes still in one way or another present even in sophisticated Marxism. This millenarianism believes that a change in the material base or in the class structure would transform our situation in relation to language or change the human condition generally. Deconstruction, on the other hand, sees the notion of a determining material base as one element in the traditional metaphysical system it wants to put into question' ('Theory and Practice: Response to Vincent Leitch', *Critical Inquiry*, vol. 6 (1980), pp. 609–14 (p. 612)). When Salusinszky put this same quotation directly to Miller in the interview in *Criticism in Society*, Miller responded '[D]id I say that?' (p. 221). The innovation in Miller's thought is the understanding that this questioning is now in response to some sort of ethical demand.

23. Miller, unlike Bernard Williams (in *Ethics and the Limits of Philosophy*, (London: Fontana/ Collins, 1985) pp. 6–7), makes no distinction between the ethical and the moral.
24. Miller's translations have come under attack for being inaccurate. See: the introduction to J. Hillis Miller, *Hawthorne and History: Defacing it* (Oxford: Blackwell, 1990); Valentine Cunningham, *In the Reading Gaol* (Oxford: Blackwell, 1994), p. 382. H. J. Paton translates the same phrase '[A]ll reverence for a person is properly only reverence for the law (of honesty and so on) of which that person gives us an example' (*The Moral Law: Kant's Groundwork to the Metaphysics of Morals*, trans. H. J. Paton (London: Hutchinson, 1948), p. 67).
25. Jacques Derrida, 'White Mythology: Metaphor in the text of philosophy', *New Literary History*, vol. 6 (1974), pp. 8–74 (p. 60).
26. Jonathan Reé, *Philosophical Tales: An Essay on Philosophy and Literature* (London: Methuen, 1987).
27. Johnson, *The Wake of Deconstruction*, p. 72.
28. Miller, 'The Critic as Host', p. 226.
29. The discussion occurs in de Man's foreword to Carol Jacobs, *The Dissimulating Harmony* (London: Johns Hopkins University Press, 1978), p. xi.
30. Miller, *Hawthorne and History*, pp. 75–6. Further references to this text will be abbreviated to HH.
31. Henry James, *The Golden Bowl* (Harmondsworth: Penguin, 1985) p. 36.
32. J. Hillis Miller, *Versions of Pygmalion* (London: Harvard University Press, 1990), p. 15. Further references to this book will be given in the text as VP.
33. Geoffrey Galt Harpham, 'Language, history and ethics', *Raritan* 7, (1987), pp. 128–46, (p. 138).
34. Kant, *The Moral Law*, p. 84 (italics in original).
35. Simon Critchley, *The Ethics of Deconstruction: Derrida and Levinas* (Oxford: Blackwell, 1992), p. 47.
36. Miller repeats this claim in Salusinszky, *Criticism in Society*, p. 221: this section's title is taken from there.
37. Harpham, 'Language, history and ethics', p. 137.
38. Harpham, 'Language, history and ethics', p. 145.
39. Christopher Norris, *Deconstruction and the Interests of Theory* (London: Pinter, 1988), p. 165.
40. Norris, *Deconstruction and the Interests of Theory*, p. 182.
41. Tobin Siebers, *The Ethics of Criticism* (London: Cornell University Press, 1988), p. 39.
42. Norris, *Deconstruction and the Interests of Theory*, pp. 182–3.
43. Harpham, 'Language, history and ethics', p. 144; also cited Norris, *Deconstruction and the Interests of Theory*, p. 182.
44. Norris, *Deconstruction and the Interests of Theory*, p. 182.
45. See, for example, de Man, *Allegories of Reading*, p. 173.
46. Richard Rorty, *Contingency, Irony and Solidarity* (Cambridge: Cambridge University Press, 1989), p. 20.
47. Jacques Derrida, *Of Grammatology*, trans. Gayatri Chakravorty Spivak (Baltimore: Johns Hopkins University Press, 1976), p. 158.
48. I. A. Richards, *Practical Criticism* (London: Routledge and Kegan Paul, 1973), pp. 13–17.
49. E. S. Burt, 'Developments in Character: Reading and interpretation in "The Children's Punishment" and "The Broken Comb"', *Yale French Studies*, vol. 69 (1984), pp. 192–210 (p. 192).
50. Derrida, *Of Grammatology*, p. 3. See, for more recent examples: Jacques Derrida, 'Racism's Last Word', trans. Peggy Kamuf, *Critical Inquiry* vol. 12 (1985), pp. 291–9; Jacques Derrida, 'Force of Law: The "Mystical Foundation of Authority"', in *Deconstruction and the Possibility of Justice*, eds Drucilla Cornell, Michel Rosenfeld, David Gray Carlson (London: Routledge, 1992), pp. 3–67; Jacques Derrida, *Specters of Marx*, trans. Peggy Kamuf (London: Routledge, 1994).
51. René Girard, 'Theory and Its Terrors', in *The Limits of Theory*, ed. T. M. Kavanagh (Stanford: Stanford University Press, 1989), pp. 225–55 (p. 253).
52. Barbara Johnson, 'Rigorous Unreliability', *Yale French Studies*, vol. 69 (1985), pp. 73–80 (p. 75).

53. For examples of noncanonical literary traditions of the sort that Miller avoids, see: *Left Politics and the Literary Profession*, eds Lennard J. Davis, M. Bell Mirabella (New York: Columbia University Press, 1990), especially section IV, 'Tracings: Developments and Trends in Noncanonical Literary Traditions', pp. 209–84.
54. Paul de Man, 'Interview with Paul de Man', in *The Resistance to Theory*, p. 117.
55. Miller is summarising Heinrich von Kleist writing on Kant (*vp*, p. 98).

4

'COLD SPLENDOR': LEVINAS'S SUSPICION OF ART

> That art is one of the best witnesses of the spiritual worth of civilisations, that it is the universal expression of a search for the absolute, that to be beyond Good and Evil is appropriate to art's inalienable quality of an unprescribed ethics, that after the failures of intellectuals, of dogmas and of systems, artists are the truly inspired, the real prophets, the last guardians of hope; these truisms of modernity which come to a reader of Nietzsche . . . Levinas disputes all of these claims.
>
> Françoise Armengaud[1]

INTRODUCTION:
LEVINAS ON REPRESENTATION AND AESTHETICS

At the conclusion of the previous chapter, an impasse was reached in the debate about the ethics of criticism. One the one hand were those who could be characterised as graphi-readers, exemplified by J. Hillis Miller, and on the other hand those who could be classified as epi-readers, exemplified by Martha Nussbaum. It was suggested that the philosophy of Emmanuel Levinas, especially in the way it understands language, would offer an alternative to both of these approaches. Indeed, recently, many critics have turned to Levinas's thought to provide an ethical grounding for a range of different types of criticism.[2] Others have turned to Levinas to offer an ethical justification for postmodern thought in general.[3] However, appealing to Levinas's philosophy on these issues is not straightforward. In using or applying Levinas's thought, many of these accounts oversimplify his work, especially in relation to aesthetics in particular and to representation in general. This chapter seeks to problematise such readings by exploring Levinas's deep-seated antipathy to art, from his early work to his first major book, *Totality and Infinity*.

Rather than rushing to offer a 'Levinasian' solution to the question of the ethics of criticism, then, this chapter is an enforced hiatus, which aims to examine the reasons for Levinas's antipathy to art and to argue that this antipathy is such that it simply prevents any direct attempt to apply his work to the aesthetic, or to the interpretations of works of art. Few critics seeking to utilise Levinas have taken this antipathy into account. Levinas's 'aesthetic essays are . . . really still essays in ethics':[4] in his understanding of ethics, art is treated with such great suspicion as to make using his thought in relation to any artistic discourse highly problematic. If Levinas is as opposed to the aesthetic in general as these writings suggest, a Levinasian ethics of criticism will be either impossible or, at best, weak to the point of incoherency.

In brief, and to highlight the key strands of argument in this chapter, Levinas' suspicion of art comes from two complementary and profoundly interlinked directions. First, Levinas wishes to reject ontological claims for art as something which can give us knowledge of the absolute (for example, Hegel's claim that 'art has the vocation of revealing the truth') or which claim for art a transcendent role beyond ethics and truth (Nietzsche's claims for art, for example).[5] Perhaps more significantly, he also rejects Heideggerian claims for art which argue that art as poetry is 'founding' or an 'origin'. In this he reflects both a Platonic and, perhaps, a Jewish tradition. As if in response to Wellek's and Warren's question about the ontological status of art in their *Theory of Literature*, Levinas assigns art a secondary status, at the same level as straightforward materiality. As Françoise Armengaud points out in this chapter's epigraph, Levinas sets himself against the modern truisms of art's status.

Second, Levinas's work is troubled by the problem of representation. In Levinas' work, up to and including *Totality and Infinity*, ethics stem from the face-to-face relationship, guaranteed by an assumption of presence. To suggest that presence is only re-presented in material forms, to confuse the issue of presence with the issue of how presence is represented, is to challenge the actual face-to-face relationship with the Other, one of Levinas's most central ideas. It is because of this that Levinas is suspicious of the idea of representation, in art or otherwise, and either ignores representation or attempts to circumvent it. In *Totality and Infinity*, he places great stress on the way in which the face surpasses the constraints of form and matter, yet, paradoxically, exists within those constraints. A consideration of the aesthetic particularly highlights this difficulty in Levinas' thought.

Levinas in his early work insists that all art is mimetic. He writes that even when realism is repudiated in art, it is 'in the name of a higher realism. Surrealism is a superlative'.[6] Readers of Auerbach's *Mimesis* will realise that, combined with Levinas' two suspicions or problems, this means that art comes under a double exclusion. First, ontologically, an art work has, for Levinas, only an illusory being. Second, as representation or mimesis, the artwork is excluded because of Levinas's distrust of the act of representation itself. Indeed, the art works which Levinas does discuss at length, and sometimes favourably, attempt to be non- or anti-realist: Sonso's sculptures, Leiris's poetry, Jean Atlan's paintings, Blanchot's novels and other writings.[7]

In addition to problematising reductive readings of Levinas's work in relation to art by exploring both how and why Levinas reaches his position on the aesthetic, this chapter also aims to uncover some of the tensions which are created by this double exclusion of the aesthetic. These tensions are interrogated by Derrida and, as a result of this interrogation, Levinas renegotiates his philosophical approach in *Otherwise than Being; or, Beyond Essence* in a way that will allow for a development of the ethics of criticism in the next chapter.

`IF POETRY CAN CONTAIN LESSONS . . .´: LEVINAS´S EARLY WORK ON AESTHETICS

Levinas's early work which touches on aesthetics sets the tone and introduces the themes which will reappear, in greater depth, in *Totality and Infinity*. In addition to his short early essay on Leiris, Levinas wrote on Proust and, in passing, on Shakespeare.[8] However, his key early work in this field is 'Reality and its Shadow', first published in *Les Temps Modernes* in 1948. It was written at a significant time in Levinas's philosophical development, a year after the publication of both the first version of *Time and the Other* and *Existence and Existents* and it extends the themes – being, time, ethics – of these works into a consideration of the aesthetic.[9] Adriaan Peperzak suggests that it is one of 'five dense thematic studies, in which an original philosophy became visible' and, as such, it can be taken as the central statement of Levinas's early thought on aesthetics.[10]

As Seán Hand argues in his introduction, this essay is in no small part a reaction to the work of Sartre, and indeed, the 'Sartrean objections' offered by the editorial board of *Les Temps Modernes* confirm this. To Levinas's thought on art, 'plus pessimiste',[11] they oppose Sartre's thought on the use of literature, 'plus optimiste'. The essay is also part of Levinas's lifelong engagement with the work and thought of his pre-war friend, Maurice Blanchot. However in the light of Levinas's other early work, it is perhaps more useful to see this essay in relation to Heidegger's 'On the Origin of the Work of Art'.[12] This would seem to be a crucial comparison in terms of specific subject-matter and as an expression of Levinas's thought which echoes but veers away from Heidegger's work. It is, perhaps, only in relation to Heidegger's understanding of art that 'Reality and Its Shadow' makes sense: it is Levinas's reaction to Heidegger that shapes this response.

Levinas's relationship with Heidegger's thought is vexed. Levinas's respect for Heidegger's pre-war thought is undiminished: he considers *Sein und Zeit* as 'one of the finest books in the history of philosophy', it 'completely altered the course and character of European philosophy'.[13] Even in relation to Heidegger's Nazism, Levinas still maintains that 'here was someone . . . all modern thought would soon have to answer'.[14] Indeed, this was a task that Levinas took upon himself, in an attempt to move beyond Heidegger. In a widely quoted passage from *Existence and Existents*, Levinas writes that if

> at the beginning our reflections are in large measure inspired by the philosophy of Martin Heidegger, where we find the concept of ontology and of the relationship which man sustains with Being, they are also governed by a profound need to leave the climate of that philosophy, and by the conviction that we cannot leave it for a philosophy that would be pre-Heideggarian. (*EE*, p. 19)

Heidegger, perhaps more than any other philosopher, forms both the horizon of Levinas's thought and his most severe opponent. This orientation and this struggle are clear in 'Reality and Its Shadow'. Further, by reading Levinas's early aesthetics in the light of Heidegger's, Levinas's objections to the art work are thrown sharply into focus.

Heidegger's 'On the Origin of the Work of Art': Art as 'the becoming and happening of truth'

The original painter or the original writer proceeds on the lines of the oculist. The course of treatment they give us by their painting or by their prose is not always pleasant. When it is at an end the practitioner says to us: 'Now look!'. And, lo and behold, the world around us (which was not created once and for all, but is created afresh as often as an original artist is born) appears to us entirely different from the old world but perfectly clear.

Marcel Proust[15]

'On the Origin of the Work of Art' was written at the very moment of Heidegger's *Kehre*, and shows the traces of his turn from considerations of Being to a more complex interaction with issues of language. The essay both reflects back to *Being and Time* and indicates the path of his later thought. The essay begins with a discussion of 'the thing', reminiscent of the analysis of equipment ('*Zeug*') in *Being and Time* (*BT*, H. 67–72, pp. 96–102; H. 106–7, pp. 141–2). For Heidegger, an art work partakes of 'things', but 'is something else over and above the thingly element' and this 'something else . . . constitutes its artistic nature' (*OW*, p.p 19–20). This leads him to an analysis of Van Gogh's painting of peasant shoes. The shoes in themselves do not reveal the 'equipmental being of the equipment in truth', but the painting of them reveals something:

> [from] the dark opening of the worn insides of the shoes the toilsome tread of the worker stares forth. In the stiffly rugged heaviness of the shoes there is the accumulated tenacity of her slow trudge through the far-spreading and ever uniform furrows of the field swept by a raw wind . . . perhaps it is only in the picture that we notice all this about the shoes. The peasant woman, on the other hand, simply wears them. (*OW*, pp. 33–4)

It is this discovery that opens up the key area of Heidegger's discussion. The truth of the being of the equipment is revealed by the painting: this 'painting spoke', it 'is the disclosure of what the equipment, the pair of peasant shoes, *is* in truth' (*OW*, p. 35). Heidegger is not proclaiming that a depiction of reality is simply transposed into art but that the work of art 'opens up in its own way the Being of beings' (*OW*, p. 37). For Heidegger, this opening up or unconcealing is the action of art.

This 'opening' or 'unconcealing' is explored by considering a paradigmatic example, a Greek temple: the temple as art work 'opens a world' (*OW*, p. 42). The world, understood in the terms of a concept evolved from *Being and Time*, is perceived through the art work in its world-ness: the '*world worlds*' (*OW*, p. 45).

> By the opening up of a world, all things gain their lingering and their hastening, their remoteness and nearness, their scope and limits . . . The work as work sets up a world. The work holds open the Open of the world. (*OW*, p. 45)

This 'worlding' is made clear in a less abstract way by considering how an art work makes its materiality appear: in an art work the 'rock comes to bear and rest and so first becomes rock; metals come to glitter and shimmer, colours to glow, tones to sing, the word to speak' (*OW*, p. 46). It is because of this that an art work, for Heidegger, leads to the unconcealing of truth.

For Heidegger, in *Being and Time* and here, truth is not correlative but '*alethia*, the unconcealedness of beings' (*OW*, p. 51). Truth occurs in art as unconcealedness: it reveals that which is 'familiar, reliable, ordinary' to be 'extra-ordinary, uncanny' (*ow*, p. 54). In Van Gogh's painting, for example, 'the revelation of the equipmental being of the shoes . . . attains to unconcealedness' (*ow*, p. 56). This unconcealedness is the nature of the art work and of aesthesis itself:

> [the] more simply and authentically the shoes are engrossed in their nature . . . the more directly and engagingly do all beings attain to a greater degree of being along with them. That is how self-concealing being is illuminated. Light of this kind joins its shining to and into the work. This shining, joined in the work, is the beautiful. (*ow*, p. 56)

For Heidegger, beauty 'is one way in which truth occurs as unconcealedness' (*ow*, p. 56): beauty is truth, brought out by the act of artistic creation. Moreover, the more an art work stands out, the 'more solitary the work . . . and the more clearly it seems to cut all ties to human beings' (*ow*, p. 66) the greater the power of that art work. This separation from humanity allows that art work to 'transport us into this openness and thus at the same time transport us out of the realm of the ordinary' (*ow*, p. 66). This is how an art work transforms 'our accustomed ties to the world' (*ow*, p. 66).

Art is able to break 'open an open place, in whose openness everything is other than usual' (*ow*, p. 72) because of its nature as what Heidegger names 'poetry'. It is 'poetry' because language is the paradigm of how all art works work, since 'language alone brings what is, as something that is, into the Open for the first time' (*ow*, p. 73). Thus, for Heidegger, the 'nature of art is poetry. The nature of poetry, in turn, is the founding of truth . . . art lets truth originate' (*ow*, p. 75, p. 78).

In summary, Heidegger's argument may be seen as a development from a German Romantic position, perhaps unsurprisingly, given Heidegger's predilection for Hölderlin. It even shares features with an English Romantic position. Poets are the 'unacknowledged legislators of the world': it bears a family resemblance not just to Shelley but also to Eliot's conception of literature in 'Tradition and the Individual Talent' – the artist, the legislator, can change the world by his or her reworking in and of the tradition. Art gives each of us, according to Heidegger, an unmediated view of the world worlding and the earth earthing: it is a 'founding presence'. Art uncovers, it opens up, the world, not just as representation but as world. In reading 'Reality and Its Shadow', it will be clear how Heidegger's argument orients Levinas's, but also how Levinas opposes Heidegger's position.

'Reality and its Shadow':
The Irresponsibility of Art and the Question of 'Non-truth'

'Reality and its Shadow' is usually read as an essay on aesthetics, but its key question is not an aesthetic one: Levinas, in relation to Heidegger, wishes to investigate 'non-truth of being' (RIS, p. 132). It is through a consideration of aesthetics that he approaches this question, and his answer has significant results for his understanding of aesthetics.

The essay starts with the apoditic argument that art, as it is generally and dogmatically affirmed, reveals the essences of things. It is generally held that 'a poem or a painting speaks . . . an artwork is more real than reality . . . [and] sets itself up as knowledge of the absolute' (RIS, p. 130). This description of the role of the art work refers to Heidegger's analysis – it uses the same vocabulary and even the same catachrestical phrase, 'a painting speaks'. Yet what puts both this general unreflective assumption and Heidegger's argument into question for Levinas is the existence of criticism. Criticism would appear to be pointless – it apparently adds nothing to the art work – yet it exists. This step, to analyse art by the way in which it stimulates criticism, to take criticism seriously as a 'distinct function' (RIS, p. 130) and analyse it phenomenologically, is highly unusual. For Levinas, 'criticism exists as the public's mode of comportment' (RIS, p. 130). The critic is 'the one who still has something to say when everything has been said, that can say about the work something else than the work' (RIS, p. 130). The fact that there are things to say about an art work, the very fact that there is criticism, means that for Levinas the art work is 'neither language nor knowledge', and that art is 'outside 'being-in-the-world'' (a reference to section 44 of *Being and Time*, 'Dasein, Disclosedness and Truth', H. 212–30, pp. 256–73). This is because the very existence of criticism seems to show that there is a need to bridge the gap between the world in which we live and the world of the art work. The art work is outside 'our world', outside our language or knowledge. Criticism intervenes between human life and 'the inhumanity and inversion of art' (RIS, p. 131).

An art work, complete in itself, 'does not give itself out as the beginning of a dialogue' (RIS, p. 131), and it is this which 'situates it outside the world like the forever bygone past of ruins' (RIS, p. 131). (This use of ruins must surely reflect Heidegger's use of a ruined Greek temple as an example.) This disengagement from the world means that, in turn, to consider art valuable for its own sake is immoral since it would put art above reality. Moreover, its distinction from reality means that art is not, as Heidegger argues, revealing, unconcealing, alethia, but quite the opposite. Art is non-truth, obscure, made up from the very act of obscuring being-in-the-world. Art, for Levinas, then,

> does not know a particular type of reality; it contrasts with knowledge. It is the very event of obscuring, a descent of the night, an invasion of shadow . . . art does not belong to the order of revelation, nor does it belong to the order of creation. (*RIS*, p. 132)

Levinas has offered an opposite interpretation of art to Heidegger: it neither opens up the world nor unconceals truth. However, this argument is set within the terms laid out by Heidegger, in discussing the interrelationship of art, truth and being.

The art work, rather than revealing the truth of being through the representation of object, like the painting of the peasant's shoes, instead 'consists of substituting for the object its image' (*RIS*, p. 132). This image, like 'magic' (*RIS*, p. 132), takes our initiative from us. Art does this through what Levinas calls rhythm, by which art works 'impose themselves on us without us assuming them' (*RIS*, p. 132), like dreams, in which we are participants without having chosen to be.[16] We become involved – fallen into – images and thus the world, our world, is deconceptualised. Reality is disincarnated by the simple action of supplying an image for an object: the actual world is left behind. For Heidegger, art 'worlds' the world, it brings us into closer ontological contact with a more real reality. For Levinas, art bewitches us into involvement, but specifically not with the world as reality, but with something else, with non-being.

To uncover this 'something else', Levinas analyses the relationship between the image and its object. Traditionally, the phenomenology of the image has presumed that the image is transparent, that it simply represents the 'real' object, and that the link between an image and an object is the resemblance of the image to the object. Levinas makes the point that resemblance is not the comparison between object and image, but the grounds of the image existing at all. It is, after all, resemblance which 'engenders the image' (*RIS*, p. 135). A thing is itself, but also its double, its shadow. A thing 'is what it is and it is a stranger to itself, and there is a relationship between these two moments . . . the thing is itself and is its image. And this relationship between the thing and its image is resemblance' (*RIS*, p. 135)

In allowing both the thing and its appearance as resemblance to figure in the argument, Levinas is following *Being and Time* strictly. Heidegger discusses inadequacies in Kant's understanding of the phenomenon:

'Phenomenon', the showing-itself-in-itself, signifies a distinctive way
in which something can be encountered. 'Appearance' . . . means a
reference-relationship which is an entity in itself, and which is such
that what does the referring . . . can fulfil its possible function only if it
shows itself in itself and is thus a 'phenomenon'. Both appearance and
semblance are founded upon the phenomenon, though in different
ways. (*BT*, H. 31, p. 54)

That is, a thing and its appearance both 'appear' and are both phenomena,
different but, as Heidegger suggests, linked. As Levinas argues, a 'being is
that which is, that which reveals itself in its truth and, at the same time, it
resembles itself, is its own image' (*RIS*, p. 135). In a very Platonic
formulation, this applies to everything; the 'whole of reality bears on its
face its own allegory' (*RIS*, p. 136).

With something 'non-artistic', the relationship between the image and
the object is clear, and would seem to follow Heidegger's discussion of the
hammer as 'equipment'. As we use the hammer, we encounter its being
more primordially as 'ready-to-hand', as 'manipulability' ('*Handlichkeit*'); at
the same time, its outward features, its appearance as hammer 'withdraws' –
the 'peculiarity of what is proximally ready-to-hand is that, in its readiness
to hand, it must . . . withdraw in order to be ready-to-hand quite
authentically' (*BT*, H. 69, p. 99). Its being, as 'readiness to hand', comes
to the fore as its being as appearance withdraws. Glasses, for Heidegger, are
most authentically glasses when we forget that we are wearing them and, as
a consequence, are unable to find them (*BT*, H. 107, p. 141 – this is,
incidentally, about as close as *Being and Time* gets to a joke). The hammer is
most authentically a hammer when it is being used for hammering, and we
are no longer thinking about it as an object: its 'object-ness' has withdrawn.

The art image has a different relationship with the object however. Here,
'Levinas upholds a Platonic view, since he interprets the work of art as the
substitution of an image for being itself'. When we look at the image we are
aware of the absence of the object: the object has abandoned the image. A
picture's presence insists on the object's absence 'as though the represented
object died, were degraded, were disincarnated in its own reflection' (*RIS*, p.
136). Unlike the hammer, which is the phenomenon of both image and
object, an art work is just the phenomenon of image. The picture itself
cannot take us to the real world but only to 'the hither side' (*RIS*, p. 136).

In approaching the world through its image, paradigmatically through
art, Levinas has uncovered 'unrevelation' or 'non-truth', 'not an obscure
residue of being, but its sensible character itself, by which there is
resemblance and images in the world' (*RIS*, p. 136). Non-truth is

tangible, part of being: without non-truth things would have no images. Non-truth is, in fact, equiprimordial with truth in the Heideggerian sense, with alethia. The image uncovers the non-truth of being at the same time as it uncovers the truth of being. Again, Heidegger's work has formed the horizon for this conclusion, following the phenomenological process of unconcealing, but Levinas has shown how Heidegger's own approach contains a blindspot within itself in relation to the question of 'non-truth'.

The art work then, as an objectless image, pertains not to truth and objects, but to a strange non-truth. This is not without importance. Indeed, Levinas writes that the 'image *qua* idol leads to the ontological significance of its unreality' (*RIS*, p. 137). Art is a 'caricature, allegory or picturesque element which reality bears on its face' (*RIS*, p. 137). Just as, for Heidegger, all art was poetry, for Levinas all art is essentially sculpture, because of the relationship between art and time. It is the relationship between art and time which, in addition to the non-truth of art, leads Levinas to his aversion to the aesthetic.

Levinas's understanding of the relationship between art and time in this essay cannot be understood without reference to his near-contemporaneous work *Existence and Existents*. There, Levinas postulates that 'underneath' all being is the *There is*, the 'presence that arises behind nothingness' (*EE*, p. 65), which is felt in liminal states, such as insomnia, for example. Temporality is created by an entity taking up being, from out of this anonymous state. This occurs not in Heideggerian Being-towards-Death, but in the Instant. An Instant is not a continuation, it 'inherits' nothing, but is instead a beginning. Time is not the reality of our being, but the existent – the *There is* transformed to an 'I' – is the reality which inaugurates time: the 'present . . . is the coming out of a self, this appropriation of existence by an existent' (*EE*, p. 83). The existent, evanescent, like a wave breaks again and again in each instant: in each instant, being is begun anew, the existent takes possession and position again. For Levinas, 'the generating essence of consciousness . . . [is] commencing, instituting a here and now, a wakening' (Lingis, 'Translator's Introduction', *EE*, p. 9).

This understanding of temporality is also part of Levinas's concern with hope, liberation, freedom and the advent of justice, all of which feature heavily in *Existence and Existents* (this is perhaps more than just a reflection of the fact that Levinas wrote the text whilst imprisoned by the Nazis). Hope is also the structure of temporality: hope is 'not satisfied of a time composed of separate instants given to an ego that traverses them' (*EE*, p. 91). Temporality without being able to carry on the self-reflexive relationship with oneself which is freedom is empty, evil, meaningless, hopeless. The emerging of the existent into the instant, into time, must also be able to accept freedom, which is responsibility for an historical 'self', an 'I'. The existent must have a future, which contains the possibility of continual emergence. If we are trapped in history or the present then we can never be free.

For Levinas, in 'Reality and its Shadow', the sculpture embodies this trapped – and therefore hopeless – relationship to time:

> [a] statue realises the paradox of an instant that endures without a future. Its duration is not really an instant . . . It will never have completed its task as present . . . In this situation the present can assume nothing, can take on nothing and thus is an impersonal and anonymous instant. (*RIS*, p. 138)

Unlike a human being, art is frozen into lifelessness. It cannot take up a position in time, cannot give itself existence: it has 'a lifeless life . . . a caricature of life' (*RIS*, p. 138). It cannot take up responsibility, it cannot hope. An art work only exists in a continuous present, impotent. The art work is 'an event of darkening of being' (*RIS*, p. 139). It is not 'that an artwork reproduces time that has stopped' but rather that 'art is the falling movement on the hither side of time into fate' (*RIS*, p. 139). Fate is the 'present, impotent to force the future' (*RIS*, p. 138) which 'has no place in life' (*RIS*, p. 139): fixed, without freedom, fate is the refusal to take up existence in the evanescence of an instant and thus the refusal of hope and of responsibility. Even art forms that use narrative and so make use of the effect of time are of this sort. Characters in novels, like statues, are prisoners in a fixed situation. By being placed into a narrative, their being has 'a non-dialectical fixity': the novel 'stops dialectics and time' (*RIS*, p. 139).

It is because of this relationship to time that, for Levinas, the present in which art exists is sterile, an interval – a meanwhile – which parodies our interval of life: the 'eternal duration of the interval in which a statue is immobilised . . . is the meanwhile, never finished, still enduring – something inhuman and monstrous' (*RIS*, p. 141). The time of art is not our time and, as a consequence, the shadow non-being of art is not like our being. A work of art is literally 'time-less', trapped outside time. As such, as 'time-less', it can play no part in our world, which involves the constant taking up of a position in time. For Levinas, there is nothing art, in its hither, time-less world of resemblances, can teach about the real world: the 'proscription of images is truly the supreme command of monotheism, a doctrine that overcomes fate, that creation and revelation in reverse' (*RIS*, p. 141). Fate is 'creation and revelation in reverse' because fate – like history, always written after the event – makes a false world of resemblances from a real world of beings. A statue is a paean to fate, to a possibility of being that is not being, but resemblance.

At the conclusion of the essay, Levinas rounds off his attack on the aesthetic. Art does not deal with real life but its resemblance: it is essentially disengaged, separate, evasion, a disavowal of responsibility. For Levinas, in art, the

> world to be built is replaced by the essential contemplation of the shadow. This is not the disinterestedness of contemplation but of irresponsibility. The poet exiles himself from the city. There is something wicked and egoist and cowardly in artistic enjoyment. There are times when one can be ashamed of it, as of feasting during a plague. (*RIS*, p. 142)

This statement obviously has echoes in Adorno's famous dictum about the impossibility of art after Auschwitz.

The only salvation for art is for the critic or the philosopher to cross that distance between the resemblance and the real: 'the immobile statue has to be put in movement and made to speak' (*RIS*, p. 142). It is necessary to reintroduce the hither world of art 'into the intelligible world in which it stands, and which is the true homeland of the mind' (*RIS*, p. 142). The role of the critic, Levinas argues here, is to imbue that text with an intelligible meaning in concepts from the world, to speak in 'the word of a living being speaking to a living being', in 'the language which makes us leave our dreams'. Levinas offers the grounding of a 'philosophic' criticism which is the equivalent of epi-reading, restoring the art work to a world of persons: Levinas would move swiftly from 'from print and language to speech and voice and the present person'. To refuse to do this, to be lost in contemplation in the 'rhythm' of the work, is irresponsible and immoral. Committed art, Levinas argues, cannot exist, but committed criticism, that can make art committed by leaving the world of art to appeal to the real world, can and must exist. Levinas has presented a justification for criticism, but not a methodology.

However, Levinas's position on criticism here is deeply problematic. The essay begs the question of why anybody should be concerned with art at all. The first ethical duty of the critic would appear to be to exile art altogether, thus depriving him or herself of a profession. Moreover, the boundaries between 'criticism' and 'the aesthetic' are not as clearly drawn as Levinas's essay suggests. Geoffrey Hartman argues that criticism is a genre of literature.[20] If this is the case, criticism, for Levinas, would fall into the monstrous category of the aesthetic. Conversely, George Steiner suggests that all 'serious art, music and literature is a critical act', drawing art, in

Levinas's sense, out of the sphere of the inhuman into critical communication.[21] To ask for criticism to save art may be like trying to jump higher
than one's shadow: asking art to save itself from art. Levinas's conclusion
leads on to the question of representation in language which will dog
Totality and Infinity.

Levinas's response to Heidegger's thought, especially 'On the Origin of
the Work of Art', seems clear. For both, art opens: but for Heidegger, it
opens up the Being of beings; for Levinas, art opens to the inhuman. For
both, art 'worlds': for Heidegger, the world was 'worlded'; but for Levinas, a
strange and monstrous 'hither world' is opened. Art reveals or discloses for
both, but for Levinas it does not disclose truth, but 'non-truth'. Indeed,
where for Heidegger, the more solitary the art work, the more it reveals, for
Levinas, the more solitary and further from the public sphere, the more
alien and other-worldly the artwork becomes. Heidegger claims poetry as
the basis of art and of everything; Levinas claims sculpture as the basis of art
but that it is secondary and parasitic. For Heidegger, art is founding,
beyond judgement of good or evil; Levinas judges art and concludes that it
is 'wicked and cowardly'. For Levinas, ethics are prior to aesthetics. Levinas
continually shares the same orientation as Heidegger, but comes to very
different, often opposite, conclusions.

As has been suggested, two sets of Levinas's ideas come together here.
First is the general distrust of art. Levinas follows both a Platonic line,
opposing art for its resemblance to things, for its nature as shadow.
Moreover, as his passing reference to the first commandment might
suggest, he may also be influenced by his Jewish heritage. Secondly, it is
clear that in 'Reality and Its Shadow' his focus is on the problem of
representation more than on the problem of art. The essay circles around
the suggestion that a thing re-presents itself at the same time as being itself
in itself. On the one hand, this shows up a blindness in *Being and Time*,
which is Levinas's aim. On the other hand, it destabilises any attempt to
offer a philosophy based on or guaranteed by presence, because presence
and representation have become problematic categories.

Levinas highlights this in discussing 'two contemporary possibilities of
being' (*RIS*, p. 136). He writes that alongside 'the simultaneity of the idea
and the soul – that is, of being and its disclosure . . . there is the
simultaneity of being and reflection' (*RIS*, p. 136). The two possibilities
assume either a world of presence and revelation of that presence – idea and
soul – or a world of being only representing itself in images, its essence
beyond any grasp. In summary, he writes that the 'absolute at the same time
reveals itself to reason and lends itself to a sort of erosion' (*RIS*, p. 136):
revelation of the absolute and its erosion go hand in hand. This is perhaps

the first inkling of the structure of the Saying and the Said which will play such a key role in his later work. However, this essay neither explores nor resolves this issue. In fact, it attempts to avoid the dilemma altogether by returning to the issue of art, despite commenting that 'the whole discussion of art is subordinate' (*RIS*, p. 132). Levinas writes, for example, that '[H]ere we leave the limited problem of art' (*RIS*, p. 140), and yet he then returns to it for another three pages. This tension, and his evasion of the problem with representation, troubles his thought on aesthetics and his philosophy as a whole, as the discussion of aesthetics in *Totality and Infinity* will make clear.

`BEYOND . . . THE CANONS OF THE BEAUTIFUL`: THE AESTHETIC IN *TOTALITY AND INFINITY*

The truth of being is not the image of being.

Emmanuel Levinas[22]

Levinas makes his position on art clear from the declamatory preface of *Totality and Infinity*: when (messianic) peace superimposes itself on the ontology of war, morality 'will have gone beyond . . . the canons of the beautiful' (*TI*, p. 22). Art and the beautiful are not, for Levinas, capable of reaching beyond the world. They are firmly located in the understanding of the world constituted by war, 'fixed in the concept of totality, which dominates western philosophy' (*TI*, p. 21). The thinking behind this as yet unjustified assertion is slowly revealed in *Totality and Infinity*.

Art is constantly marginalised in *Totality and Infinity* and discussions of the aesthetic generally occur only in passing. Despite this, the aesthetic is a site of disquiet. The aesthetic in Levinas's work comes under a double exclusion: once because of Levinas's opinion of the ontological status of art and once because of the problems for Levinas's thought of the idea of representation, although these are interlinked. These two exclusions, the ontological argument and the representation argument, continue to be central to Levinas's position on aesthetics in this work, as they were in the earlier essay.

Totality and Infinity offers a series of interlinked arguments against the achievement of transcendence through the aesthetic, against a philosophical approach to aesthetics exemplified most clearly perhaps by Hegel in the *Lectures on Aesthetics*. Each argument is related to the argument of 'Reality and its Shadow' but is subtler and more complex, since the aesthetic here is related to the wider and more profound trajectory of *Totality and Infinity*. The issue of aesthetic transcendence, even spurious transcendence, could not be ignored in such a major work on ethics, metaphysics and transcendence. Just as in 'Reality and its Shadow', Levinas tries to limit the importance of art in his consideration of ethics: art for Levinas is secondary, derivative and, most dangerously, misleading. He writes in section I.B.6, 'The Metaphysical and the Human', that he wishes to establish the 'primacy of the ethical': setting out the

> primacy of an irreducible structure upon which all other structures rest (and in particular all those which *seem* to put us primordially in contact with an impersonal sublimity, *aesthetic* or ontological), is one of the objectives of this work. (*TI*, p. 79, italics added)

Here, Levinas denies the possibility of any transcendence through the art work, contra Hegel, Nietzsche and Heidegger, and insists on the primacy of the ethical over the aesthetic. Art may seem to put us in contact with an absolute, but, for Levinas here, it does not. Poets are not the legislators of the world.

Representation throughout *Totality and Infinity* is the site of a tension 'between the figural transfers operating within the sequential narrative of Levinas's description and the anteriority of the founding experience that is described'.[23] Levinas is arguing that the transcendental 'founding experience' is beyond form and the representation of form. Within form, this founding experience cuts through form and representation. It represents itself without representation. The several tensions between the represented and the beyond-representation represented, these 'two contemporary possibilities of being', and Levinas's representation of this paradox, have profound implications for his thought as a whole, especially in relation to his claims for language, which seem to ignore language's role as representational – the crux of Derrida's later reading. Levinas is keen to repress this paradox of 'representation without representation' in *Totality and Infinity*. However, it is precisely the return of this problem, in a number of different ways, that this chapter details. This tension undermines Levinas's position, at least on aesthetics.

Derrida, seemingly in an allusion to the start of Maurice Blanchot's *Thomas the Obscure*, describes *Totality and Infinity* as the action of waves on a beach, returning and returning to the same themes.[24] The discussion of aesthetics follows this pattern: in each section in which the issue is discussed, the discussion becomes more profound, touching the area, then coming back to it in more detail, revealing the thought behind previous conclusions. This discussion forms one thread amongst the many that, like a tapestry, make up *Totality and Infinity*. Concentrating on the relationship between art and the face, this chapter traces this idea through

I.B.5, 'Discourse and Ethics', to a fuller development of the argument in III.B.2., 'Ethics and the Face'. Then, turning to the relationship between materiality, art and transcendence, it analyses section II.B.4, 'Sensibility'. Finally, it unites the two threads in section III, 'Exteriority and the Face', the central and most important moment of Levinas's argument. This section covers both the ontological status of art and deals with the problem of representation by examining sensibility. The aesthetic and art do re-emerge later in the text, in IV.B, 'The Phenomenology of Eros', and in IV.G, 'The Infinity of Time', but only as adjuncts to the general discussion and only repeating points made in the crucial section III. These arguments are not separate from each other but twist together in the weft of the book: each supports and develops from the other.

Art and the Face: Problems with Representation and Artwork

The Beautiful is not the ultimate. The Beautiful can be discussed as a Face. But in it there is also the possibility of enchantment, and, from that moment, a lack of concern or ethical cruelty.

Emmanuel Levinas[25]

In section I.B.5., 'Discourse and Ethics', Levinas discusses the role of language. He finds it necessary to draw a distinction between 'the nakedness of the face' (*TI*, p. 75) and the 'disclosure of the thing illuminated by its form' (*TI*, p. 75). Following Heidegger, a thing in use withdraws, or 'disappear(s)' (*TI*, p. 74) in its function: it is, for Levinas, metaphorically naked. In a passage that echoes 'Reality and Its Shadow', he draws attention to the way in which things are made individual when they are not absorbed in their use: a thing stands 'out in itself' (*TI*, p. 74) because its form doubles its being. A thing is no longer metaphorically naked. A thing's beauty or aesthetic quality 'introduces a new finality' (*TI*, p. 74) to a thing because it draws that thing into a new classification. A beautiful object is classified by – or clothed in – its form, extrinsic to its use. This classification, this disclosure 'by science and by art' (*TI*, p. 74), can only function in the light of a totality which defines and perceives things as forms. Objects 'have no light of their own; they receive borrowed light' (*TI*, p. 74). Beauty and the category of the aesthetic has imposed itself and obscured the nudity of a thing by doubling the thing's being in form, bringing form to light and drawing the object through its form into a totality. In contrast, the work of language involves entering into a relationship with 'a nudity disengaged from every form' (*TI*, p. 74), the face. Thus the beautiful is not a relation like language. Beauty, as in 'Reality and its Shadow', relies on the doubling of being in form, and not going through form to the nudity of the face. The work of language, and the relation to the face, go through form to 'the primordial discourse whose first word is obligation' (*TI*, p. 201).

This distinction between form and what lies beyond but through form is repeated from a different perspective in III.B.2., 'Ethics and the Face'. The face, which is a central concept for Levinas, 'breaks through the form that . . . delimits it' (*TI*, p. 198).

> To manifest oneself as face is to impose oneself above and beyond the manifested phenomenal form, to present oneself in a mode irreducible to manifestation, the very straightforwardness of the face to face, without the intermediary of any image, in one's nudity. (*TI*, p. 200)

The 'manifestation' of the face is not a manifestation: it is 'naked' or 'true representation' (*TI*, p. 200). In this relation, forms manifest themselves 'unbeknown to the radiating being' (*TI*, p. 200) as 'splendor' (*TI*, p. 200) or 'cold splendor' (*TI*, p. 200): this 'is perhaps the definition of beauty' (*TI*, p. 200) for Levinas. This manifestation of objects is secondary, separate, misleading in relation to the 'true representation'. Here Levinas's problem with representation has become acute. In order to stress that the face is *not* a representation, he is forced to use phrases like 'true representation', 'nudity', 'present oneself in a mode irreducible to manifestation', 'very straightforwardness', 'appealing to me in destitution' (all *TI*, p. 200). Levinas is trying to suggest that the face, although made manifest like objects, is beyond manifestation: it represents itself without representing itself, it has access to infinity.[26] This is why he is so antipathetic to art as representation. If an art work could represent itself without representation, it, too, would portray (or, rather, be) the transcendence, the infinity which 'presents itself as a face' (*TI*, p. 199). It would not masquerade as infinite, like a person, but actually be 'equivalent' to a person (although, like infinity, beyond values: 'the face does not have the status of a value' *TI*, p. 202). This, in a manner of speaking, would be blasphemous for Levinas, and this is the blasphemy that art threatens. Thus he has to distinguish between a representation and a 'true representation'. This distinction comes under great pressure, which is reflected in his multiple choice of synonyms.

Art and the Thing: Problems with the Ontological Status of the Art Object

The 'light' metaphor which Levinas uses to discuss the appearance of the form of things (*TI*, p. 74) recurs in the second section, 'Interiority and Economy'. Things 'have a form, are seen in the light – silhouettes or profiles', whereas 'the face signifies *itself* (*TI*, p. 140). As a profile or silhouette 'a thing owes its nature to a perspective, remains relative to a point of view; a thing's situation constitutes its being. Strictly speaking it has no identity . . . Things have no face' (*TI*, p. 140).

Levinas has been detailing how interiority – crudely, the idea of an inside self – is built up by the phenomena of separation and thence by enjoyment, or 'living from . . .': life 'is love of life, a relation with contents that are not my being but more dear than my being' (*TI*, p. 112). Life is involved with things. Things, for Levinas, are important and make up the world and are to be enjoyed. Things, even aesthetic things do not, however, provide access to the transcendental. Levinas writes that the

> aesthetic orientation man gives to the whole of his world represents a return to enjoyment . . . The world of things calls for art, in which intellectual accession to being moves into enjoyment, in which the Infinity of the idea is idolized in the finite, but sufficient, image. All art is plastic . . . They are playthings: the fine cigarette, the fine car. They are adorned by the decorative arts; they are immersed in the beautiful, where every going beyond enjoyment reverts to enjoyment. (*TI*, p. 140)

An art work is to be enjoyed; it is not different in kind from other objects Levinas says we enjoy, such as 'good soup, air, light, spectacles' (*TI*, p. 110). Confirming and helping to construct interiority, art is not transcendent, nor does it bear any sign of the ethical. It is something with which we fill our lives, and is dear to us, but does not represent the breaking of the totality that the face does. This is repeated in the fourth section, 'The Ambiguity of Love', IV.A, where Levinas writes that 'a thing, an abstraction, a book can . . . be objects of love' (*TI*, p. 254). However, he makes the claim that this sort of love is a love based around need, in this case a need for aesthetic enjoyment, which is a love divested of transcendence. This makes clear the other exclusion by which the aesthetic is bound in *Totality and Infinity*: here, just as in 'Reality and its Shadow', Levinas refuses the possibility of transcendence through art. Art is simply a thing – a 'plaything' – and nothing more. It cannot reveal the absolute or the transcendent.

Representation, Aesthetics and Sensibility

These two strands of argument, about the impotency of the aesthetic and the problem of representation, come together at the beginning of part III, 'Exteriority and the Face', in the section entitled 'Sensibility and the Face'.

Levinas asks a key question: how can 'the epiphany as a face' be different from 'that which characterises all our sensible experience'? (*TI*, p. 187). Levinas's attempt to answer this question will involve the core of his account of the aesthetic. Levinas attempts to 'show that . . . the peculiar awareness of the face differ[s] . . . from representational knowledge' by discussing the role of vision and light and the way in which the face is manifest.[27]

The 'object disclosed . . . is the visible or touched object' (*TI*, p. 188): vision and touch are used to understand all sense experience 'even when it involves other senses' (*TI*, p. 188). Objects are only encountered in the light, but light itself is not an object: the 'eye does not see the light, but the object in the light' (*TI*, p. 189). Vision is 'a relation with a "something" established within a relation with what is not a "something"' (*TI*, p. 189); light opens up a 'void' (*TI*, p. 190) in which objects are made manifest. However, the light only

> ascribes signification by the *relation* it makes possible. It opens nothing that, beyond the same, would be absolutely other . . . Light conditions the relations between data; it makes possible the significa- tion of objects that border one another. It does not enable one to approach them face to face. (*TI*, p. 191)

Light is the object in which relations between objects take place: the 'sensible light qua visual datum does not differ from other data . . . A light is needed to see the light' (*TI*, p. 192). Levinas argues that the sensible can only occur in the light, and that this is not an end in itself. Something else, beyond form and light, allows light to appear. Light, the horizon of form and thus of representation, only appears in the horizon of the other. Alterity, in or as the face, appears in this primordial horizon and not, first, in the realm of form. It 'represents' itself not through light, nor through representation, but beyond or before light and sensibility: it is that by which light appears.

Alterity does not manifest itself in form, which is the property of things. Things can be remade, reworked – Levinas uses the examples of boxes made into tables and of coins reminted. The 'depth of the thing can have no other meaning than that of its matter, and the revelation of matter is essentially superficial' (*TI*, p. 192). For Levinas, form betrays itself in 'its own manifestation, congealing into a plastic form' (*TI*, p. 66): form 'alienates the exteriority of the other' (*TI*, p. 66) because, in contrast to form, the 'face is a living presence; it is expression' (*TI*, p. 66).

Yet there does seem to be a difference for Levinas in the different 'surfaces' of matter: an obverse and a reverse. This again repeats the argument of 'Reality and Its Shadow', that an object is itself and its double by virtue of having an individual form. The obverse is the essence of the thing, supported by the reverse, its form. 'Proust', writes Levinas, 'admired the reverse of the sleeves of a lady's gown, like those dark corners of cathedrals, nonetheless worked with the same art as the façade' (*TI*, p. 192). This is the role of art: it 'endows things with something like façade, by which objects are . . . as objects on exhibition' (*TI*, p. 192). An art work has only façade, and 'is constituted in the beautiful, whose essence is indifference, cold splendor and silence . . . It captivates by its grace as by magic, but does not reveal itself' (*TI*, p. 193).

Again, this repeats the structure of the earlier essay: the beauty of an object's form does not relate back to anything but its form, it has no ontological status save as form. Moreover, this form has the ability to bewitch with beauty, with 'magic'. Just as in 'Reality and its Shadow' the art work is not of this world, it is alien, alone in cold splendor: it cannot speak. Possessing only form, façade, art cannot aspire to transcendence and overcome the egoistic, ontologically centred thought of western culture and history.

The ontological status of the art work is contrasted with the face by suggesting that the face 'cuts across' sensibility. This argument gives the art work a secondary, derivative and essentially superficial position. It also plays a part in Levinas's attempt to bypass the question of how the face is actually presented or represented.

Transcendence cuts across sensibility, including vision. In contrast, the art work appears only in relation to, or in, sensibility. Transcendence can be revealed neither in form, nor 'in terms of contemplation nor in terms of practice' (*TI*, p. 193) – only the face, the relation with the other can lead to transcendence. Levinas does not, in fact, argue for this – rather, he just asserts it. This perhaps is a weakness in this section. Levinas relies on the claims made for the transcendence of the face to simply sweep away the problem of how the face represents itself without representing itself. Here, the face both is and is not material form.

The face is fully present for Levinas, a presence that art cannot achieve: this distinction is important in relation to language and the literary art work. The face is 'this exceptional presentation of self by self, incommensurable with the presentation of realities simply given, always suspect of some swindle' (*TI*, p. 202). Art works here, as in 'Reality and its Shadow', are swindling, intoxicating, 'where events other than that of the presentation of the original being come to overwhelm or sublimate the pure sincerity of this presentation' (*TI*, p. 202). As Levinas has argued, an art work has nothing to do with original being. He seems here to be following a

Nietzschean understanding of the aesthetic as Dionysiac. Poetic activity, 'where influences arise unbeknownst to us out of this nonetheless conscious activity' (*TI*, p. 203), threatens to envelop the ethical relation and 'beguile it as a rhythm' (*TI*, p. 203): this concept of 'rhythm' has already appeared in 'Reality and its Shadow'. However, the ethical relation in language 'dispels the charm of rhythm and prevents the initiative from becoming a role' (*TI*, p. 203). Language is 'rupture and commencement, breaking of rhythm which enraptures and transports the interlocutors – prose' (*TI*, p. 203).[28] Art is again feasting during a plague, blinding, illusory, and is now understood to be opposed to the expression of the other, to language.

In addition to the larger question of the success of the argument about representation, which will be taken up in the next chapter, the question arises of the meaning of 'cutting across' (*TI*, p. 193) sensibility. Levinas argues specifically that the project of *Totality and Infinity* is to show how the 'beyond' is 'reflected within the totality and history, *within* experience' (*TI*, p. 23, original italics). Yet, the implication of 'cutting across' is that the 'beyond' appears not through or within experience but by a violation of it. As Robert Bernasconi argues, Levinas seems to want to maintain both an 'empirical' and a 'transcendental' understanding of the face. Bernasconi concludes that 'Levinas is using the language of transcendental philosophy and the language of empiricism . . . in an effort to find a way between these twin options given to us by the philosophical – and nonphilosophical – languages we have inherited'.[29]

This would mean that a clear answer to the questions raised by issues of representation in general would be impossible, as Levinas's language would finally appear to be indeterminate, both transcendental and empirical. In relation to aesthetics in particular, this indeterminacy would not be enough in itself to displace Levinas's rigid disapproval of aesthetics.

Levinas's position on art in *Totality and Infinity* is neatly summarised by the Levinasian thinking of the French theologian Jean-Luc Marion, who understands the transcendent as the divine. In *God Without Being* Marion contrasts the idol and the icon: in Levinas's terms, the idol is the material art work, the 'plaything' (*TI*, p. 140), whereas the icon is the face of the other, the divine Other. The idol is created by, in and for the gaze, as spectacle: 'it supposes an aesthesis that precisely imposes its measure on the idol.'[30] That is, the idol is measured only in terms of the aesthesis, the experience of an art work. It is the aesthetic object, façade, frozen, with no access to transcendence. The icon, on the other hand, 'summons the gaze to surpass itself by never freezing on a visible . . . the icon opens in a face that gazes at our gazes in order to summon them to its depth . . . only the icon shows us a face'.[31] The icon is plainly what Levinas recognises as the face, calling us to responsibility, the 'visibility of the invisible as such' which 'unbalances human sight':[32] the idol is that which fits the terms Levinas has already used to discuss the art work in which 'the Infinity of the idea is idolized in the finite' (*TI*, p. 140). All art is idolatrous for Levinas, unable to achieve the transcendence that is sometimes ascribed to art. Art is constituted by idols, ethics by icons.

A discussion of the aesthetic occurs in one other place in *Totality and Infinity*, during Levinas's highly problematic discussion of the feminine in section IV.B, 'The Phenomenology of Eros'. The alienness of art is used as a contrast for the depth of the feminine face and the primordial feminine beauty. Feminine beauty is converted into 'weightless grace' (*TI*, p. 263) by being represented. For Levinas, the

> beautiful of art *inverts* the beauty of the feminine face. It substitutes an image for the troubling depth of the future . . . announced and concealed by the feminine beauty. It presents a beautiful form reduced to itself in flight, deprived of its depth. (*TI*, p. 263)

Again, the creation of an image has destroyed the essence of the face it represented. Levinas continues, echoing 'Reality and its Shadow', by suggesting every work of art 'is painting and statuary, immobilized in the instant' (*TI*, p. 263). Art substitutes the magical enchantment of rhythm for the feminine, and beauty 'becomes a form covering over indifferent matter, and not harbouring mystery' (*TI*, p. 263). Here the themes of the meaninglessness of matter and the entrapment of art appear again. Art covers up the feminine, and reduces it from a 'mystery' to the dead art work, just as the aesthetic does for everything. Levinas's sexism has frequently been challenged, reappraised and negotiated. Here this disputed passage is cited for its relevance to Levinas's discussion of the aesthetic.[33]

The Role of Literature in Totality and Infinity

It might be suggested that the art work, or the literary art work at least, is rehabilitated for Levinas through a consideration of either the use of references to art works and literature or, more significantly, by an appreciation of the significance of language itself in *Totality and Infinity*. Perhaps surprisingly, the work also makes a large number of literary allusions, both implicit and explicit, although other art forms do get mentioned.[34] It is with an adaptation from Rimbaud's 'Une Saison en Enfer' – ' "The true life is absent". But we are in the world' (*TI*, p. 33) – that Levinas chooses to start the text proper (*TI*, p. 33).[35] However, the three most significant literary figures in *Totality and Infinity* are Shakespeare, Proust and Dostoyevsky.

Shakespeare's 'sorcerers' are described as using 'antilanguage' (*TI*, p. 92) to illustrate a point about language, and in a similar context later (*TI*, p. 263); *Hamlet* is alluded to in a discussion of discourse (*TI*, p. 64); *Macbeth* is used in a discussion of death and suicide (*TI*, p. 231). Dostoyevsky's presence is felt throughout Levinas's work although never mentioned by name.[36] For example, an allusion to the famous discussion of the wall in *Notes from Underground* occurs very obviously twice, in the context of will and reason (*TI*, p. 217) and will and death (*TI*, p. 236). Levinas writes that the opposition to the identification of will and reason

> does not consist in shutting one's eyes to being and thus striking one's head madly against the wall so as to surmount in oneself the consciousness of one's deficiencies of being, one's destitution, and one's exile, and so as to transform a humiliation into a desperate pride. (*TI*, p. 217)

This, of course, describes precisely the action of the narrator of *Notes from Underground*.

According to Lescourret's biography, Blanchot introduced Levinas to the work of Proust in the 1930s and Proust figures significantly in *Totality and Infinity*. References to him occur at the conclusion of the longest section which discusses art (*TI*, p. 192), and Proust is alluded to in a section on the infinity of time: '[M]emories, seeking after lost time, procure dreams, but do not restore the lost occasions' (*TI*, p. 281). This itself is foreshadowed by a discussion of history earlier in the text which also seems to concern Proust: 'there is no purely interior history' (*TI*, p. 227) writes Levinas. In all his discussions of time, and most of his discussions of history, *À la Recherche du Temps Perdu* seems to be just behind the text: the influence of Bergson on Levinas, on Proust and on the understanding and interpretation of Proust forms common ground.[37]

Levinas does not use references to literature as an integral part of his philosophical argument, nor as ornament; they certainly serve, however, as examples and clarifications of his thought, but not as heuristic examples. As with his citations from the Talmud (e.g. *TI*, p. 201), his literary references are not used to add to his philosophical argument, nor to provide spurious anthropological evidence for 'eternal human truths', nor to argue his view from theological presuppositions – with or without these citations the philosophical argument stands or falls on its own grounds. Indeed, having outlined his position on art works in general, it would seem to be more coherent if these 'playthings' (*TI*, p. 140) were totally excluded. At best, they would seem to hinder or delay the text. At worst, their 'rhythm' (*TI*, p. 203) would mislead or entrap readers and, as such, their very presence seems to threaten his argument. It has been suggested that Levinas calls literary works as 'witnesses' to his thought.[38] However, given his antipathy to art and his understanding of it as unable to portray transcendence, they would seem to be very unreliable witnesses. Despite this, Levinas obviously admires these texts. Indeed, he wrote that 'it sometimes seems to me that the whole of philosophy is only a meditation of Shakespeare', and his admiration for 'the great writers of Western Europe' is on record.[39] It is possible that these texts and their use stand exactly on the fault line in Levinas's thought about language, representation and art. One the one hand, Levinas appeals to these works; on the other, he removes their status as anything more than beguiling 'rhythm', and thus removes the very reason he makes appeals to them in the first place. Their use symbolises exactly the difficulties in his discourse that Derrida will highlight. His use of literature in *Totality and Infinity* is another example of the tension between his views on art and his thought in general, a tension made most acute by a consideration of the importance of language.

Language in Totality and Infinity

> To see the face is to speak of the world. Transcendence is not an optics, but the first ethical gesture.
>
> Emmanuel Levinas (*TI*, p. 174)

If *Totality and Infinity* is seen as a tapestry of ideas woven together, ideas about language are a central recurring pattern throughout: indeed, it would be impossible to draw out this thread without repeating most of the argument of the book. His consideration of language can, however, be juxtaposed with his consideration of the aesthetic.

For Levinas, it is the face to face relation, the essential moment of ethics that 'first institutes language' (*TI*, p. 42) and, as a result, 'the relation between the same and the other . . . is language . . . primordially enacted as conversation' (*TI*, p. 39). Thus, the

> relationship of language implies transcendence, radical separation, the strangeness of the interlocutors, the revelation of the other to me . . . Discourse is thus the experience of something absolutely foreign, a pure 'knowledge' or 'experience', a traumatism of astonishment. (*TI*, p. 73)

Levinas repeats this key formula frequently in different ways: language is 'an original relation with exterior being' (*TI*, p. 66); language is 'produced only in the face to face' (*TI*, p. 295); in language 'exteriority is exercised, deployed, brought about' (*TI*, p. 296); 'language . . . announces the ethical inviolability of the Other' (*TI*, p. 195); the 'essence of language is the relation to the Other' (*TI*, p. 207); 'the essence of discourse is ethical' (*TI*, p. 216); the 'work of language . . . consists in entering into relationship with a nudity disengaged from every form . . . Such a nudity is the face.' (*TI*, p. 74). Language reveals the other, the ''vision' of the face is inseparable from this offering language is' (*TI*, p. 174).

It is from this understanding of language as the relation to the other expressed, not represented, that the ethical importance of language emerges. Language is where and how we are put into question by the other, and drawn to our responsibilities: the 'calling into question of the I, coextensive with the manifestation of the Other in the face, we call language' (*TI*, p. 171). Language teaches or reveals. This is a key point for Levinas: he rejects maieutics and the whole Socratean tradition of philosophy which reveals the world from the One, as if 'I' remembered it. In its place, he suggests that language 'teaches and introduces the new into a thought' and that the 'absolutely new is the Other' (*TI*, p. 219). It is in language that 'absolute difference' is presented (*TI*, p. 194, p. 195) without reintegrating that difference, which is 'inconceivable in terms of formal logic' (*TI*, p. 195), back into a totality. Language fractures the totality. Language, the site of the ethical relation, is how the other puts us into question.

Language is where transcendence takes place. Language is more than labour, things or material, which are 'already situated in the world established by language – by transcendence' (*TI*, p. 70). Language, by its revelation of the other, establishes the world, offers the world to us, above and beyond labour, things and material. Language does partake of these things, but they 'hide the profound essence of language' (*TI*, p. 101). Indeed, true language has no materiality or action: Levinas writes that 'language is possible only when speaking precisely renounces this function of being action and returns to its essence of being expression' (*TI*, p. 202). Thus, for example, demagogy is rhetoric and action, and although it is 'absent from no discourse' (*TI*, p. 70), in fact demagogy 'resists discourse' (*TI*, p. 70). As action, it is not true language for Levinas. Only when language is not action or material is it truly language.

It is this which produces a difficulty over language in *Totality and Infinity*. How is it possible to differentiate between Levinas's true language, and a language-event or language-work, in which, writes Levinas, 'I am

only deduced and am already ill-understood, betrayed rather than expressed' (*TI*, p. 176)? Can there be language that is all work or material and
thus, paradoxically, not language? Indeed, as Levinas suggests, considering
injustice and demagogy, not 'every discourse is a relation with exteriority'
(*TI*, p. 70). This is another version of the problem of representation Levinas
had with the face: how can the appearance of language lead beyond its
appearance to the other?

Levinas's solution to this problem, which follows the same structure as
his understanding of art as derivative and of the face as primary, relies on
an argument based on presence: language is only language if the
interlocutor is actually present. Levinas stresses that the materiality of
language, language-works, are different from the 'languageness of language'. Language-works can 'recount their author . . . but only if they
have been clothed with the signification of language, which is instituted
above and beyond works' (*TI*, p. 175–6). Here language is to be understood as separate from language-works. Language is guaranteed by
presence. Language-works only have access to the 'language-ness' of
language if they are supported by the face. Without the face, they can
make no claims to transcendence. Language is only a result of presence,
and so becomes effectively synonymous with presence. Levinas is explicit
about this. Language, as opposed to a language-work, can occur only in
speech in which the speaker 'never separates himself from the sign he
delivers, but takes it up again always while he exposes. For this assistance
always given to the word which posits the things is the essence of
language' (*TI*, p. 97). This 'assistance' is the face, the transcendental
signifier: 'the signifier must present himself before every sign – present a
face' (*TI*, p. 182). Language is only language as opposed to a language-
work if the interlocutor is actually physically present and speaking. The
presence of an actual face thus becomes the guarantee of ethics.

This, in turn, means that writing, which presupposes the absence of the
writer and is only material language, a language-work, is unsupported by
the face. Levinas writes that signs 'are a mute system, a language impeded.
Language does not group symbols into systems, but deciphers the symbols'
(*TI*, p. 182). To be expressed by symbols, 'by one's works, is precisely to
decline expression' (*TI*, p. 176). Although Levinas does trust that 'the
interpretation of the symbol can assuredly lead to an intention divined' (*TI*,
p. 177), this interpretation is a 'burglary' (*TI*, p. 177) and occurs 'without
conjuring the absence' (*TI*, p. 177) of the author. The importance of
language lies not in its materiality 'its density as a linguistic product' (*TI*, p.
177) but its 'language-ness', its primordial expressiveness, 'what it really
means'. If the author or speaker is not actually present, language seems not

to work as a guarantor for true expression: true expression is declined, and only a residue, interpreted or burgled, can be reached.

In this light, the art work written in language has no access to the face, to transcendence, and is secondary and derivative. The rhetorical art work 'resists discourse' (*TI*, p. 70) – true language – and it is the duty of philosophical discourse to overcome this. Moreover, art works in language, which are examples of anti-language or language with no 'language-ness' because they lack a present speaker, can be 'beguiling'. Levinas' consideration of language does not offer a defence of the literary art work from claims that it was, at best, a plaything or, at worst, wicked. Instead, it has made clear that the literary art work in language, lacking the presence of a face, is just as secondary and derivative as any other art works. However, this conclusion has drawn attention again to the tension between representation and transcendence in Levinas's thought. In addition, it has revealed that Levinas's use of the term language is highly specialised and, in fact, refers only to the experience of presence of the other, face-to-face. Language, in *Totality and Infinity*, seems to mean something other than language: it means presence, and not representation.

CONCLUSION: LEVINAS'S ANTI-AESTHETICS AND THE ETHICS OF CRITICISM

Levinas said that his 'task does not consist in constructing ethics; I only try to find its meaning' (*EI*, p. 90). If his position on aesthetics, in his earlier writings and in *Totality and Infinity*, is to be accepted, he finds no ethical 'meaning' in art works, only a dangerous and wicked distraction or swindle. His suggestion that criticism should bring the 'hither world' of art into the 'public world' assumes too great a distinction between art and criticism, and moreover, such an action would be 'wicked and egoist and cowardly' (*RIS*, p. 142), dealing with insubstantial forms and shadows. Whether a painting, sculpture or written language in its material 'density as a linguistic product' (*TI*, p. 177), an art work is only matter and 'the revelation of matter is essentially superficial' (*TI*, p. 192). Literary critics who have used Levinas's work to provide a basis for criticism have not appreciated the full weight of his arguments against aesthetics, and how this argument in turn reflects his central ethical concerns. For Levinas in these works, it is impossible to speak ethically about art, save to say that art is unethical.

In this light, a Levinasian criticism would be an anti-criticism, warding off readers from literary works. 'Ethical criticism' would be meaningless: if ethical meaning can have nothing to do with art, there simply cannot be Levinasian ethics of criticism and to look for an ethics of criticism in

Levinas's work would appear to be a dead end. Unlike Miller or Nussbaum, who at least found an ethical importance in literature, Levinas in these works only finds delusion and unethical magical beguiling. This position on aesthetics not only does not offer a way out of the opposition between readers like Miller and readers like Nussbaum, it suggests that the whole debate is meaningless and possibly immoral, like 'feasting during a plague' (*RIS*, p. 143).

Despite this, however, Levinas does make a great deal of use of literary works: he has written some 'literary criticism', defined loosely. There is, as this chapter has outlined, a profound tension in his work, between his claims against the aesthetic access to transcendence and his use of the aesthetic. There is an even more profound tension in his understanding of representation, which is brought out clearly by a consideration of the aesthetic. It seems crucial, but ultimately impossible, for Levinas to establish the difference between 'true representation' (*TI*, p. 200) and the representation of forms, between what Bernasconi describes as 'empirical' and 'transcendental' understandings of the face. His arguments which attempt to do this are, as this chapter demonstrates, unsatisfactory and rely on assertions of transcendence.

It is by exploiting this problem with representation that Derrida effects his deconstructive reading of *Totality and Infinity*, which begins the next chapter. Moreover, it is in Levinas's response to Derrida's reading, his second major work, *Otherwise than Being; or, Beyond Essence*, that these tensions over representation and over the ontological status of the art work, specifically the literary art work, break through the text and clearly show up an aporia or blindness. It is through an exploitation of this blindness that an ethics of criticism will be developed.

NOTES

1. Françoise Armengaud, 'Éthique et esthétique: De l'ombre à l'obliteration', in *L'Herne Emmanuel Levinas*, eds Catherine Chalier and Miguel Abensour (Paris: Éditions de l'Herne, 1991), pp. 499–508 (p. 499) (author's translation).
2. Some examples amongst many: Homi Bhabha reads *Beloved* through what he describes as Levinas's 'ethical-aesthetic positioning' (Homi Bhabha, *The Location of Culture* (London: Routledge, 1994), p. 16); Isobel Armstrong discusses Levinas in relation to close reading (Isobel Armstrong, 'Textual Harassment: the Ideology of Close Reading, or How Close is Close?', *Textual Practice* vol. 9(3) (1995), pp. 401–20); Levinas's work is a central concern in Adam Newton's *Narrative Ethics* (London: Harvard University Press, 1995); Gerald Burns cites Levinas in uncovering the ethical in *Finnegan's Wake* (Gerald L. Burns, 'The Otherness of Words: Joyce, Bakhtin, Heidegger', in *Postmodernism: Philosophy and the Arts*, ed. Hugh J. Silverman (London: Routledge, 1990), pp. 120–36); Michael Beehler uses Levinas to explore Eliot's criticism, ' "Riddle the Inevitable": Levinas, Eliot and the Critical Moment of Ethics', in *America's Modernisms: Revaluing the Canon*, eds Kathryne Lindberg and Joseph G. Kronick (London: Louisiana State University Press, 1996), pp. 118–34.

3. See, for some examples, the end of the introduction to *Postmodernism; A Reader*, where Thomas Docherty turns to Levinas, finding in his work 'the basis of an ethical demand in the postmodern" (*Postmodernism: A Reader*, ed. Thomas Docherty (London; Harvester, 1993), p. 26). Docherty modifies this claim, and explores a renewed approach in *Alterities: Criticism, History, Representation* (Oxford: Clarendon Press, 1996). Lyotard's work on ethics has been profoundly influenced by Levinas (see Jean-François Lyotard and Jean-Loup Thébaud, *Just Gaming*, trans. Wlad Godzich (Minneapolis: University of Minnesota Press, 1985). See also Zygmunt Bauman, *Postmodern Ethics* (Oxford: Blackwell, 1993).

4. Robert Gibbs, 'The Other Comes to Teach Me: a Review of recent Levinas Publications', *Man and World*, vol. 24 (1991), pp. 219–33 (p. 222).

5. G. W. F. Hegel, *Introductory Lectures on Aesthetics*, ed. Michael Inwood, trans. Bernard Bosanquet (Harmondsworth: Penguin, 1993), p. 60.

6. 'Reality and its Shadow', trans. Alphonso Lingis, in *The Levinas Reader*, ed. Seán Hand (Oxford: Blackwell, 1992), pp. 129–43 (p. 130). Further references to this essay will be abbreviated to *RIS*.

7. See: Emmanuel Levinas, 'La Transcendance des Mots: A propos de *Biffures*, de Michel Leiris', *Les Temps Modernes*, vol. 44 (1949), pp. 1090–5; Emmanuel Levinas, *Sur Maurice Blanchot* (Montpellier: Fata Morgana, 1975); Emmanuel Levinas, 'About Blanchot; an Interview', *Substance*, vol. 14 (1976), pp. 54–7; Emmanuel Levinas 'Jean Atlan et la Tension de l' Art', in *L'Herne Emmanuel Levinas*, pp. 509–10; Emmanuel Levinas, *De l'Obliteration: Entretien avec Françoise Armengaud à propos de l' oeuvre de Sonso* (Paris: Éditions de la Différence, 1990); 'The Transcendence of Words', trans. Seán Hand, in *The Levinas Reader*, ed. Seán Hand (Oxford: Blackwell, 1992), pp. 144–9; also translated as 'Transcending Words: Concerning Word-Erasing', trans. Didier Maleuvre, in *Yale French Studies*, vol. 81 (1992), pp. 145–50.

8. 'The Other in Proust', trans. Seán Hand, in *The Levinas Reader*, pp. 160–5; first published in *Deucalion*, vol. 2 (1947), pp. 117–23. This section's title comes from this essay, p. 165. Shakespeare is discussed by Levinas in *Time and the Other*, trans. Richard A. Cohen (Pittsburg: Duquesne University Press, 1987), pp. 72–3.

9. *Time and the Other* originally appeared in 1947 ('Translator's Note', Levinas, *Time and the Other*, p. vii); *De l' Existence a l' Existant* was first published in 1947.

10. Adriaan Peperzak, 'The One for the Other: the Philosophy of Emmanuel Levinas', in *Man and World*,vol. 24 (1991), pp. 427–59 (p. 430). The essay is not named except in a footnote (p. 457); the other four are 'La transcendence des mots' (1949), 'Liberté et commandement' (1953), 'Le moi et la totalité' (1954) and 'La philosophie et l'idée de l'Infini' (1957). On this essay, in addition to Armengaud, 'Éthique et esthétique', and Hand's introduction in *The Levinas Reader*, pp. 129–30, see: Fabio Ciaramelli, 'L'appel infini à l'interprétation: Remarques sur Levinas et l'art', *Revue Philosophique de Louvain*, vol. 92 (1994), pp. 32–52; Andrew Gibson, *Towards a Postmodern Theory of Narrative* (Edinburgh: Edinburgh University Press, 1996) pp. 184–9; Edith Wyschogrod, *Emmanuel Levinas: The Problem of Ethical Metaphysics* (The Hague: Martinus Nijhoff, 1974), pp. 71–5; Edith Wyschogrod, 'The Art in Ethics: Aesthetics, Objectivity, and Alterity in the Philosophy of Emmanuel Levinas', in *Ethics as First Philosophy*, ed. Adriaan Peperzak (London: Routledge, 1995), pp.137–48.

11. Editors' preface, 'La Réalité et Son Ombre', *Les Temps Modernes*, vol. 38 (1948), p. 770.

12. It has been suggested that Levinas is responding to Heidegger's essay 'Poetically man dwells'. However, since this essay was not given as a lecture until 1951 and did not appear in print until 1954, it seems more likely that, in 1948, Levinas was responding to 'On the Origin of the Work of Art', which was given as three lectures in 1935. (Martin Heidegger, 'On the Origin of the Work of Art', in *Poetry, Language, Thought*, trans. Albert Hofstadter (London: Harper Row, 1971), pp. 17–87). References will be abbreviated to *ow* in the text.

13. Emmanuel Levinas, *Ethics and Infinity: Conversations with Philippe Nemo*, trans. Richard A. Cohen (Pittsburg: Duquesne University Press, 1985), p. 37 (abbreviated to *EI*); Richard Kearney, *Dialogues with Contemporary Continental Thinkers* (Manchester: Manchester University Press, 1984), p. 51. Levinas's engagement with Heidegger is so central that most writing on Levinas deals with it to some extent. See specifically: Robert Bernasconi, 'Fundamental Ontology, Meontology and the Ethics of Ethics', *Irish Philosophical Journal*, vol. 4 (1987), pp. 76–93; Luc Bouchraet, 'Ontology and Ethics: Reflections on Levinas' critique of Heidegger', *International Philosophical Quarterly*, vol. 3 (1970), pp. 402–19; C. D. Keys, 'An Evaluation of Levinas' critique of Heidegger', *Research in Phenomenology*, vol. 11 (1972), pp. 121–42; Adriaan Peperzak, 'Phenomenology – Ontology – Metaphysics: Levinas' perspective on Husserl and Heidegger', *Man and World*, vol. 16 (1983), 113–27; Brian Schroeder, *Altared Ground: Levinas, History and*

Violence (London: Routledge, 1996); Robert John Sheffer Manning, *Interpreting Otherwise than Heidegger* (Pittsburg: Duquesne University Press, 1993).

14. Emmanuel Levinas, 'As If Consenting to Horror', trans. Paula Wissing, *Critical Inquiry*, vol. 15 (1989), pp. 485–8 (p. 485).
15. Marcel Proust, *Remembrance of Things Past*, 3 vols, trans. C. K. Scott Moncrieff and Terence Kilmartin (Harmondsworth: Penguin, 1983), vol. 2, *The Guermantes Way*, p. 338.
16. This conception of 'rhythm' and its effects is discussed by Blanchot in *The Writing of the Disaster*, trans. Ann Smock (London: University of Nebraska Press, 1986), pp. 112–13.
17. Wyschogrod, *Emmanuel Levinas: The Problem of Ethical Metaphysics*, pp. 73–4.
18. Levinas, 'The Transcendence of Words', in *The Levinas Reader*, p. 148; Wyschogrod, *Emmanuel Levinas: the Problem of Ethical Metaphysics*, p. 74.
19. Denis Donoghue, *Ferocious Alphabets* (London: Faber & Faber, 1981), p. 146.
20. Geoffrey Hartman, *Criticism in the Wilderness* (London: Yale University Press, 1980).
21. George Steiner, *Real Presences* (London: Faber & Faber, 1989), p. 11.
22. Emmanuel Levinas, *Totality and Infinity: An Essay on Exteriority*, 3rd printing, trans. Alphonso Lingis (London: Kluwer Academic Publishers, 1991) p. 291. References to this text will be abbreviated to *TI*.
23. Jill Robbins, '*Visage, Figure*: Reading Levinas's *Totality and Infinity*', *Yale French Studies*, vol. 79 (1991), pp. 135–49 (p. 139).
24. Jacques Derrida, 'Violence and Metaphysics', in *Writing and Difference*, trans. Alan Bass (London: Routledge and Kegan Paul, 1978), pp. 79–153, p. 312fn.
25. Emmanuel Levinas, 'Entretien', in *Répondre d' Autrui Emmanuel Levinas*, ed. Jean-Christophe Aeschlimann (Boudry-Neuchâtel: Éditions de la Baconnière, 1989), p. 15 (author's translation).
26. Deleuze and Guattari offer a very different understanding of the face in Giles Deleuze and Felix Guattari, *A Thousand Plateaus*, trans. Brian Massumi (London: The Athlone Press, 1988). Although Levinas is not mentioned, the section of the book entitled 'Year Zero: Faciality' (pp. 167–91) is implicitly aimed at his concept of face. Deleuze and Guattari suggest that the face is 'a horror story' (p. 168). Pointing out the way in which the face – or faciality – takes over and is seen in everything – heads, hands, stomachs, plug sockets – they argue that the face is not a thing in itself, but the result of an 'abstract machine of faciality' (p. 168). This thought-machine textualises or ciphers any array of what they describe as a white screen with black holes into a face: it is 'precisely because the face depends on an abstract machine that it is not content to cover the head, but touches all other parts of the body, and even, if necessary, other objects without resemblance' (p. 170). Their concept of face, unlike Levinas' concept, is 'not a universal' (p. 176) but a particular face, the white man's face. For Deleuze and Guattari, certain assemblages of power require the production of a face. As a result, the face is inhuman (p. 181) and it has nothing to do with people. A face is created by the western thought/power machine: the 'face is a politics', and not a call to peace, beyond the war of politics, as Levinas claims. Where for Levinas, the face cannot be represented or is a 'true representation', for Deleuze and Guattari, it is only representation, forced violently on to an object. For a discussion of this, see Robert Eaglestone, 'The Face of Emmanuel Levinas and Philip II of Macedon', in *Diatribe* vol. 4 (1994–5), pp. 9–20.
27. Adriaan Peperzak, *To the Other* (West Lafayette, Indiana: Purdue University Press, 1993), pp. 161–2.
28. This comparison of poetry to prose has a parallel in the work of Bakhtin. Poetry, especially epic poetry, for Bakhtin is monoglossic, follows only one voice, and thus imposes itself: aiming at a totalising control, it refuses to let the voice of the other even appear. In contrast, the novel – prose – is heteroglossic, the result of the interaction of different voices. The novel is dialogic, disruptive, it occurs in the interaction which is language. See M. M. Bakhtin, *The Dialogic Imagination*, ed. Michael Holoquist, trans. Michael Holoquist and Caryl Emerson (Austin: University of Texas Press, 1981). Levinas and Bakhtin share an influence in Buber. For Bakhtin's view of Buber, see Joseph Frank, 'The Voices of Mikhail Bakhtin', *New York Review of Books*, 23 October 1986, pp. 56–9. On Levinas and rhythm, see Gary Peters 'The Rhythm of Alterity: Levinas and Aesthetics' in *Radical Philosophy*, vol. 82 (1997), pp. 9–16.
29. Robert Bernasconi, 'Rereading *Totality and Infinity*', in *The Question of the Other*, eds A. B. Dallery and C. E. Scott (Albany: State University of New York Press, 1989), pp. 23–34 (p. 34).
30. Jean-Luc Marion, *God Without Being*, trans. Thomas A. Carlson (Chicago: University of Chicago Press, 1991), p. 20.
31. Marion, *God Without Being*, pp. 18–19.
32. Marion, *God Without Being*, p. 22, p. 24.

33. For specific discussions of Levinas and gender, see: Luce Irigaray, 'The Fecundity of the Caress: a Reading of Levinas' *Totality and Infinity* section IV.B. 'The phenomenology of Eros', in *Face to Face with Levinas*, ed. Richard Cohen (New York: University of New York Press, 1986), pp. 231–56; Catherine Chalier, 'Ethics and the Feminine', in *Rereading Levinas*, eds Robert Bernasconi and Simon Critchley (London: Athlone, 1991), pp. 119–29; Luce Irigaray, 'Questions to Emmanuel Levinas: On the Divinity of Love', in *Rereading Levinas*, pp. 109–18; Tina Chanter, 'Antigone's Dilemma', in *Rereading Levinas*, pp. 130–46; Robert Manning, 'Thinking the Other without Violence?: An analysis of the Relation between the philosophy of Emmanuel Levinas and Feminism', *Journal of Speculative Philosophy*, vol. 10 (1991), pp. 132–43; Tina Chanter, *Ethics of Eros: Irigaray's Rewriting of the Philosophers* (Routledge: London, 1995).

34. Painting is mentioned as a metaphor (*TI*, p. 128) and in a reference to the uniqueness of the Mona Lisa (*TI*, p. 117). The Eiffel Tower is also mentioned (*TI*, p. 117). Levinas remarks that architecture is 'perhaps the first of the fine arts' (*TI*, p. 193–3). Mythic or legendary characters from the classics are mentioned: in an image which is to grow in importance in Levinas's work, Ulysses becomes a figure for the journey of western thought, from the same to the same (*TI*, p. 102, p. 271); the shades Ulysses meets in Hades are also shown to be equivalent to Heideggerian Being (*TI*, p. 112); Gyges, able to make himself invisible, a figure taken from Plato and Herodotus, becomes a recurring image for interiority and a refusal of the responsibilities already inherent in being (*TI*, pp. 61, 90, 91, 170, 221 and 173); Pygmalion (*TI*, p. 267, 271), Proteus (*TI*, p. 268) and Faust (*TI*, p. 272) also appear.

35. Other writers cited include Baudelaire (*TI*, p. 156), Molière (*TI*, p. 229), Mallarmé (*TI*, p. 256), Pushkin (*TI*, p. 133, p. 220), Goethe (*TI*, p. 92), and Poe (*TI*, p. 335). Maurice Blanchot is mentioned by name twice (*TI*, p. 284, *TI*, p. 298) and is often in the background (for example, the discussion of suicide, *TI*, pp. 230–2).

36. On the influence of Dostoyevsky, see: Kearney, *Dialogues with Contemporary Continental Thinkers*, p. 67; Levinas, *Ethics and Infinity*, p. 98, p. 101.

37. See Kearney, *Dialogues with Contemporary Continental Thinkers*, p. 49.

38. Gillian Rose, 'O! untimely death/ Death!', *Mourning Becomes the Law: Philosophy and Representation* (Cambridge: Cambridge University Press, 1996), pp. 125–46 (p. 135).

39. Levinas, *Time and the Other*, p. 72; *EI*, p. 22.

5

'WHAT IS HECUBA TO ME?': LANGUAGE BEYOND BEING AND THE TASK OF CRITICISM

HAMLET:
Is it not monstrous that this player here,
But in a fiction, in a dream of passion,
Could force his soul so to his own conceit
That from her working all his visage wann'd,
Tears in his eyes, distraction in his aspect,
A broken voice, and his whole function suiting
With forms to his conceit? And all for nothing
For Hecuba!
What's Hecuba to him, or he to her,
That he should weep for her?

Hamlet (II, ii)[1]

To run into an aporia, to reach the *limit* of philosophy, is not necessarily to be paralysed. We are only paralysed if we think that to reach the limit of philosophy is to be silenced.

Drucilla Cornell[2]

INTRODUCTION

At the end of the last chapter, Levinas's thought appeared so hostile to the aesthetic that it would seem to be impossible to base any ethical criticism on his work, let alone develop an understanding which would resolve the disagreements over ethics in critical thought made so clear by contrasting epi-reading with graphi-reading. There were underlying tensions in his position, principally over difficulties with representation, and it is on these tensions, their implications and consequences that this chapter concentrates. Beginning with an examination of Derrida's interrogation of *Totality and Infinity*, the chapter will deal principally with Levinas's second major work, and his response to Derrida, *Otherwise than Being; or, Beyond Essence*.

This chapter aims to show both how and why Levinas's thought in *Otherwise than Being; or, Beyond Essence* may be a foundation for an understanding of the ethics of criticism. The path of this argument, unfortunately but unavoidably, is not straightforward: *Otherwise than Being* is a strange and complex book which partakes of both philosophy and literature and yet escapes these categories. Its peculiarities will emerge throughout the chapter. After reading the relevant sections of Derrida's essay 'Violence and Metaphysics', the chapter will analyse Levinas's renewed understanding of language and the task of philosophy in *Otherwise than Being*. In contrast, it will then explore Levinas's position on aesthetics as developed in this work. It will then show how these two aspects of Levinas's thought are incommensurable: his position on language and his position on aesthetics cannot go together. It is by working through this incommensurability in his thought and by simultaneously developing Levinas's own argument about the task of philosophy and, crucially, its relationship to language that an ethics of criticism will be made clear.

`QUESTIONS OF LANGUAGE AND THE QUESTION OF LANGUAGE´: DERRIDA ON LEVINAS AND `TRUE REPRESENTATION´

Totality and Infinity was my first book. I find it very difficult to tell you, in a few words, in what way it is different from what I've said afterwards. There is the ontological terminology. I spoke of being. I have since tried to get away from that language

Emmanuel Levinas[3]

The questions whose principles we now will attempt to indicate are all, in several senses, questions of language: questions of language and the question of language.

Jacques Derrida (*VM*, p. 109)

Central to *Otherwise than Being* is the attempt to resolve the problems of representation and ontological terminology which emerged in *Totality and Infinity*. This new focus for Levinas can be seen as a result of his own self-critique following Derrida's essay, 'Violence and Metaphysics'. The relationship between Levinas and Derrida, the 'chiasmus' between their thought, has been of great interest to many commentators and thinkers.[4] Derrida has developed a number of Levinasian concepts and themes in his own work: the 'trace' for example, is originally a Levinasian idea.[5] Contemporary interest in Levinas has been greatly influenced by Derrida's essay, itself the start of a 'dialogue' between the two philosophers.[6] Most significantly, however, *Otherwise than Being* can be read as a rewriting of *Totality and Infinity* after 'Violence and Metaphysics', although the precise status of the relationship between the two works is contested. Joseph Libertson argues that the essay shows 'Derrida's astonishing incomprehension of Levinas' and is 'a virulent attempt to reduce the pertinence and originality of all the Levinasian concepts, from a philosophical viewpoint that is surprisingly traditional'.[7] Alternatively, and perhaps more acutely, Robert Bernasconi suggests that the essay is not a critique in the traditional sense, but rather one of the earliest of Derrida's deconstructive readings: it is 'a key document both in Derrida's development of deconstruction and in the reception of Levinas' own ethical thinking'.[8] This chapter offers a brief account of the relevant points of Derrida's essay, in order to highlight the problems of representation in *Totality and Infinity*, covered in Chapter 4.

At the heart of Derrida's essay is the question of how the rupture of a totality of a system of thought, based on the transcendence of the face beyond language, can possibly be represented, or have any meaning, in language, when that Greek language (of) philosophy is based on the repression of just such ruptures. Although the essay is wide-ranging in addressing Levinas's work, it is focused on the problems of representation.

As a preface to 'Violence and Metaphysics', Derrida cites Matthew Arnold: 'Hebraism and Hellenism – between these two points of influence moves our world' (*VM*, p. 79).[9] The aim of this quotation is to illustrate the thesis that 'the founding concepts of philosophy are primarily Greek' (*VM*, p. 81). Derrida argues that in this genealogy of philosophy, pre-eminently exemplified by Husserl and Heidegger, the concept of metaphysics has been consistently diminished and ethics has become a branch of philosophy, like natural philosophy or logic. Derrida points out that Levinas, in contrast to this tradition, does not assume ethics to be a subsection of philosophy, or one particular branch among many. Indeed, the thought of Levinas 'can make us tremble' (*VM*, p.82) as it tries to liberate itself from Greek philosophy and attempts to re-establish ethics and metaphysics in the transcendence of 'a non-violent relationship to the infinite as infinitely other' (*VM*, p. 83). Derrida focuses on the problems of representation that accompany this attempt.

After briefly outlining Levinas's philosophy from *Existence and Existents* to Levinas's 'great work' (*VM*, p. 92), *Totality and Infinity*, and locating Levinas in relation to a number of other thinkers (Heidegger, Husserl, Descartes, Kierkegaard, Hegel, Merleau-Ponty, Blanchot and particularly

Plato), Derrida's essay uncovers, in a typical early deconstructive move, the idea of presence in the face and a distrust of language, both speech and writing. The rest of the essay then poses a number of questions to Levinas's thought, often from Husserlian and Heideggerian perspectives. These questions all centre on the issue of representation, and five are central to a discussion of Levinas and the ethics of criticism.

The Language of 'True Representation'

First, Derrida questions the ability of Levinas to break with philosophy because he uses language. He argues that 'the attempt to achieve an opening toward the beyond of philosophical discourse, by means of philosophical discourse, which can never be shaken off completely, cannot possibly succeed *within language*' (*VM*, p. 110). Only a language that was not a philosophical language could possibly go beyond the limits which are both from language and put upon language, but all language, at least in the west, partakes of Greek philosophical concepts: 'the only conceptual language available is that of the Greek *logos*.'[10] Only a 'kind of unheard of graphics, within which philosophical conceptuality would be no more than a function' (*VM*, p. 111) could escape this. In *Totality and Infinity* Levinas assumes that his account, his representation, of the 'true representation' of the face is able to do this. He does this partially by continually insisting that the face is not a representation: he represents in written language the face which is representing itself without representation. However this 'unheard of graphics' fails because it is in (philosophical) language. 'True representation' is still representation. As the previous chapter suggested, this is a problem in *Totality and Infinity*.

The Violence of Language

Second, Derrida argues that language as a system is always already violent: it cannot get us to announce the 'unthinkable-impossible-unutterable beyond (tradition's) Being and Logos' (*VM*, p. 114). The other's otherness is always the victim of the violence of language. It is because Levinas cannot get outside language that his work embodies precisely what it wishes to eschew, the violence of thought: it is polemical, though it has no wish to be so. As it denies polemic, it is forced, as language, to deny it polemically. Language, as system, cannot escape violence, which is 'the necessary condition of the institution of any system'.[11]

Ethics (Re)presented by Phenomenology

Third, Derrida points to a problem that results from the way Levinas's phenomenological method 'uncovers' and represents ethics. Levinas describes himself as a phenomenologist, and certainly *Totality and Infinity* is a phenomenological work. However, this would imply that it was not ethics but rather Levinas's method of 'uncovering' ethics that was fundamental. Derrida argues that this means that 'ethics finds within phenomenology its own meaning, its freedom and its radicality' (*VM*, p. 121). For Levinas, Derrida suggests, it is the way in which ethics is represented by phenomenological thought which reduces ethics to representation: the 'meaning of the non-theoretical as such (for example, ethics or the metaphysical in Levinas' sense)' is only made clear by 'theoretical knowledge' (*VM*, p. 122). Ethics are not 'first philosophy' – instead the representation of the ethical by phenomenological thought becomes first philosophy; the non-theoretical, the 'true representation' of the face, is only understood through the theoretical, in this case through the methodology of phenomenology.

The Representation of the Other

Fourth, Derrida questions the way in which the other comes to appear. Derrida asks how the other can appear as other without appearing as 'other' in me, without appearing as the same. What authorises Levinas 'to say "infinitely other" if the infinitely other does not appear as such in the zone he calls the same?' (*VM*, p.125). How can the other be perceived if not by the same and, if it is perceived, how can it be other? The other cannot be other if it is perceived through the same and if it is not perceived through the same it cannot appear at all. The only way to cope with these questions is to leave the discourse of philosophy itself, to open to what Derrida names

> the call (to) (of) an eschatology . . . the opening of a question . . . put to philosophy as logos, finitude, history, violence: an interpolation of the Greek by the non-Greek at the heart of a silence, an ultralogical affect of speech, a question which can be stated only by being forgotten in the language of the Greeks; and a question which can be stated, as forgotten, only in the language of the Greeks. (*VM*, p. 133)

Derrida suggests that this question of the representation of the other is a question that is only possible in philosophy, yet philosophy – as Greek – cannot answer it.

The Impossibility of 'True Representation'

Fifth, Derrida suggests that Levinas misreads Heideggerian Being. For Levinas, it is the priority of Being in Heidegger's work which, for Heidegger, makes ethics secondary to ontology. But Being for Heidegger, as Derrida makes clear, is 'neither ontology, nor first philosophy, nor a philosophy of power . . . one may say of it what Alain said of philosophy: it "is no more politics (or ethics) . . . than it is agriculture"' (*vm*, p. 137). Moreover, not only is Being innocent of Levinas' accusations, but Levinas's philosophy cannot function without Being in the Heideggerian sense: Levinas 'must ceaselessly suppose and practise the thought of precomprehension of Being in his discourse, even when he directs it against "ontology"' (*vm*, p. 141). This means that Levinas has been unable to leave the climate of Heidegger's thought, and is instead paradoxically using Heidegger to deny Heidegger. By

> making the origin of language, meaning, and difference the relation to the infinitely Other, Levinas is resigned to betraying his own intentions in philosophical discourse. The latter is understood, and instructs, only by first permitting the same and Being to circulate within it. (*vm*, p. 151)

Derrida claims that Levinas, in his (failed) attempt to move beyond Heidegger, relies on an appeal to empiricism beyond representation.

As Chapter 4 illustrated, it is the appeal to 'true representation', to 'nudity', to the 'very straightforwardness' of the face, present 'in a mode irreducible to manifestation . . . without the intermediary of any image' (all *TI*, p. 200) that underlies Levinas's thought. According to Derrida, this understanding of the face is a simple appeal to empiricism. Levinas attempts to 'bypass' philosophy and language by an appeal to empirical experience which claims to be beyond philosophical discourse. It is not: pure 'empiricism' cannot – could not – exist. Rather, the 'dream' of empiricism is interwoven with the history and definition of philosophy. Empiricism is a philosophical 'gesture' (*vm*, p. 151). As Derrida makes clear, however, empiricism, beyond representation, language and thought, is only a 'dream' which 'must vanish at daybreak, as soon as language awakens' (*vm*, p. 151). Thus, Levinas's attempt to get beyond representation by an appeal to empiricism is another in a line of philosophical gestures which claim not to be philosophical. Empiricism offers a representation of the 'real' and not the real itself. Representation, in language, by philosophy, is the intermediary between the observer and the empirical; more radically it is possible to suggest that this intermediary actually creates the 'empirical'.

The other, the face, must be represented, as the phrase 'true representation' (*TI*, p. 200), oxymoronic at least for Levinas, suggests. Indeed, Levinas himself makes this clear in a later essay, where he writes that pure 'receptivity, in the sense of a pure sensible without any meaning, would only be a myth or an abstraction'.[12]

To summarise: Derrida's questions concern the ultimate imposition of language over the transcendent. The success of Greek thought, of philosophy is

> the impossibility of any thought ever to treat its sages as 'sages of the outside,' according to the expression of Saint John Chrysostom . . . in welcoming alterity into the heart of the logos, the Greek thought of Being forever has protected itself against every absolutely *surprising* convocation. (*VM*, p. 153)

It is impossible, then, for Derrida, philosophically to escape philosophy. Moreover, since all language relies on Greek thought – not least the thought of presence – it is impossible in language to escape language which reduces the other's otherness. There may be an escape into silence and (religious) mysticism, but this seems a very different path from both Levinas's avowal of ethics and his attempt to find 'the meaning of ethics' (*EI*, p. 90). Derrida writes that there

> is no ethics without the presence of *the other* but also, and consequently, without absence, dissimulation, detour, difference, writing. The arche-writing is the origin of morality as of immorality. The nonethical opening of ethics. A violent opening. (*OG*, p. 140)

For Derrida, ethics cannot exist save in language or 'arche-writing', which will underlie any 'pure' ethical moment: the ethical, at least in his writing around the time of *Of Grammatology*, is a result of language. Language, or textuality, is first philosophy.[13]

In response to these problems of representation which Derrida highlights, Levinas offers an understanding of ethics in terms of language in *Otherwise than Being*. He proffers a writing which, in Derridian terms, underlies even arche-writing. Levinas abandons his previous position which demanded 'true representation' and instead offers a way of understanding ethics philosophically through representation, through the phenomenon of language. As Edith Wyschogrod argues, once it is clear that 'no visible form can go proxy for the ethical, Levinas . . . deflects his attention from the Face as bearing the warranty for language to language itself'.[14] This means, in effect, that Levinas has to rewrite his earlier work in new, strange and different terms. The thought of *Totality and Infinity* is superseded, as a consequence its basic inspiration is reworked in a response to Derrida's deconstructive interruption of its text and argument. This reworking, the book *Otherwise than Being*, will prove to be a text which takes interruptions of text and argument – interruptions of philosophy – and the response to interruption as both its leitmotif and central thought.

OTHER WORDS:
THE STRANGENESS OF *OTHERWISE THAN BEING*

Otherwise than Being . . . no attempt has yet been made to appreciate this book's strangeness, the disturbance it provokes within philosophical discourse.

Simon Critchley (*ED*, p. 8)

[A] non-site cannot be defined or situated by means of philosophical language.

Jacques Derrida[15]

Both Levinas's response to Derrida's deconstruction of his work and the development of his own thought, made clear in essays like 'Meaning and Sense' and 'Phenomenon and Enigma', lead Levinas to the purposeful inconclusiveness of *Otherwise than Being: or, Beyond Essence*. Its 'disturbance' and 'strangeness' stem from the fact that it is not at all clear what sort of a text *Otherwise than Being* actually is.

Otherwise than Being is not a straightforward work of philosophy. It argues itself beyond the limit of philosophy. It is a work that, using in part the language of philosophy, seeks to undo philosophy, to speak 'in other words'.[16] It explores, to use Drucilla Cornell's phrase, 'the philosophy of the limit'. In this *Otherwise than Being* resembles an act of deconstruction. Deconstruction is 'neither an analysis nor a critique . . . not even an act or an operation . . . It is an event that does not await the deliberation, consciousness or organisation of a subject'.[17] Derrida states that he is

> not sure that the 'site' of my work, reading philosophical texts and posing philosophical questions, is itself properly philosophical . . . I have attempted . . . to find a non-site, or a non-philosophical site, from which to question philosophy.[18]

Otherwise than Being also 'signifies a null-site (non-lieu)' (*OBBE*, p. 8) because of its attempt to escape the language of philosophy: as such, it can be read as sharing a 'direction' with deconstructive thinking. Yet, in its methods and approach, and in its aims, it is not a work of deconstruction.

For Blanchot, it represents a new philosophical endeavour. He draws attention to the dedication at the start of the text to the victims of the Holocaust and 'millions on millions of all confessions and all nations, victims of the same hatred of the other man, the same antisemitism'. In the light of this he continues, asking in the shadow of Adorno, 'how can one philosophize?'

> how can one write within the memory of Auschwitz of those who have said, oftentimes in notes buried near the crematoria: know what has happened, don't forget, and at the same time you won't be able to . . . It is this thought that traverses, that bears, the whole of Levinas' philosophy.[19]

In *Otherwise than Being*, Levinas uses the language of philosophy to show the limits of philosophy and to go beyond or 'outside' them, to speak in 'other words', to try to reshape philosophy after the Holocaust. It is because of this effort that his work remains hard to categorise. It is both outside and inside philosophy that Levinas uncovers first philosophy, ethics: ethics are not philosophy but the grounding of philosophy. In this, perhaps, Levinas's work is, as Blanchot describes in a significant phrase to which the argument will return, 'a gift of literature'.

INTERRUPTION AND AMPHIBOLOGY: LEVINAS'S CONCEPTION OF LANGUAGE

Not to philosophize would not be 'to philosophize still'·

Emmanuel Levinas

Although *Otherwise than Being* is recognisably by the same author as *Totality and Infinity* – it has the same insistence on the priority of the ethical, of obligation – it represents a profound shift in Levinas's thought.

A clear example highlights the similarities of the two works, and illustrates the core of Levinas's philosophy. In a key moment of the later work, Levinas discusses obligation: he asks why 'does the other concern me? What is Hecuba to me? Am I my brother's keeper?' (*OBBE*, p. 117). His answer to this question is to suggest that these

> questions have meaning only if one has already supposed the ego is concerned only with itself, is only a concern for itself. In this hypothesis, it indeed remains incomprehensible that the absolute outside-of-me, the other, would concern me. But in the 'pre-history' of the ego posited for itself speaks a responsibility, the self is through and through a hostage, older than the ego, prior to principles. (*OBBE*, p. 117)

By hostage, Levinas means that each of us is always already responsible for the others who people the world. Their very otherness imposes this duty upon us, before we are able to deny it. He quotes Dostoyevsky, '[E]ach of us is guilty before everyone for everyone, and I more than the others' (*OBBE*, p. 146).[22] We are fundamentally responsible for others before we can theorise this relationship, and before we can place the other in relation to our own being. The otherwise than being, the totally other, comes before our being. Our unconditional responsibility is not something we take on or a rule by which we agree to be bound: instead, it exists before us and we are 'thrown' into it, without any choice. John Caputo, very influenced by Levinas, sums this up by suggesting that obligation simply 'happens'.[23] For Levinas, obligation 'calls for a unique response not inscribed in universal thought, the unforeseeable response of the chosen one' (*OBBE*, p. 145). This argument about unconditional responsibility echoes much of *Totality and Infinity*.

What makes *Otherwise than Being* radically different from its predecessor is Levinas's 'linguistic or deconstructive turn' (*ED*, p. 8). In order to develop the idea of the ethical importance of interruption, he specifically explores the way in which language interrupts itself. His intention 'is to pass beyond the discourse of western philosophy; he summons us to a dislocation of the Greek *logos*': however, doing this is complex because 'the only means at his disposal are those of philosophical discourse itself'.[24] The only way Levinas can find to bring about this interruption in philosophy is through philosophy itself. *Otherwise than Being* is about the interruption of philosophic language, and, as this chapter will argue, all other sorts of discourse, by what is beyond being, what is otherwise. As this account will illustrate, it is this 'interruption' that allows the reformulation of ethics in the light of the problems of representation in *Totality and Infinity*.

The idea of the interruption appears at the end of the first section of the work, where Levinas contemplates the role of beginnings of philosophical works: he briefly considers the reservations that Hegel, Heidegger and Husserl had about starting philosophy. Both in contrast to these philosophers and as a leitmotif for the whole work, Levinas asks whether we should 'not think with as much precaution of the possibility of a conclusion or a closure of the philosophical discourse? Is not interruption its only possible end?' (*OBBE*, p. 20). Here, as in many other passages, Levinas uses the interrogative form for suggesting what other writers might simply state in conclusions. This stylistic choice, in itself, both echoes and affirms Levinas's philosophical trajectory – not least in this, *Otherwise Than Being* is 'performative' (*ED*, p.8). Unlike a statement, a question is to be interrupted: a question starts a dialogue. An idea phrased as a question resists closure and begs not only an answer but another question, an interruption. This style of writing also echoes Levinas' larger understanding of the history of philosophy as 'a drama between philosophers' (*OBBE*, p. 20), made up of interruptions. This stylistic trope is one example of Levinas' response to Derrida's point that an opening to the exterior of philosophical discourse cannot succeed within philosophical discourse.

Another significant gesture towards this opening or interruption is the way in which Levinas rejects traditional philosophical definitions by the performative technique of offering similar ideas over and over again with different names. A term is introduced and, suddenly, it is supplanted by another term, which recalls or circles around the same idea but in different words. For example, dazzlingly, 'substitution' becomes 'one-for-the-other' becomes 'hostage' becomes 'sacrifice' becomes 'exposure' becomes 'passivity beyond passivity' becomes 'proximity' becomes 'trauma' becomes 'here I am' (a short list), but not in any ordered developmental sequence. This prevents any one term becoming the cornerstone of the work and makes a single, simple and limiting definition (de-finition) impossible. Levinas offers multiple terms, which, because they refuse to become set definitions, cannot have a role as pieces in a more traditional philosophical argument and yet act as if they do. His terms gesture both towards and away from traditional philosophical debate. This has the same effect as writing in questions, and suggesting multiple answers in different forms. Levinas, ceaselessly, is trying to move towards an opening of philosophy. He is attempting, philosophically, to draw or write the 'unheard of *graphics*, within which philosophical conceptuality would be no more than a *function*' (*VM*, pp. 110–11) for which Derrida's deconstruction of *Totality and Infinity* called.

The understanding of interruption, both emphasised and more significantly articulated performatively by Levinas's style, is made possible by a new understanding of the significance of language. Derrida argued that *Totality and Infinity* was 'thinking by metaphor without thinking the metaphor as such' (*VM*, p. 139); in response, *Otherwise than Being* concentrates on the 'metaphor', which is, as Derrida has made clear, language itself. *Otherwise than Being* deals with the representation of ethics in and through language. It concentrates on laying out the ontological structures of language in an attempt to discuss the beyond of language. Levinas is trying to develop an 'ethical language' (*OBBE*, p. 120; p. 193 fn. 35), through phenomenology, in order to 'witness' the 'otherwise than being'.[25]

Levinas argues that the 'ethics of ethics' (*VM*, p. 111) is beyond Being and traditional understandings of Being and that this becomes apparent in language because of language's nature as an amphibology. An amphibology is a 'sentence which may be construed in two distinct senses' (*OED*) – not ambiguous or equivocal, but with two different and simultaneous meanings. Amphibology, the name for a figure of speech, is used as a metaphor to describe the condition of all language. This is very common in *Otherwise than Being*: Levinas advances by using linguistic terms as metaphors for language. (Alphonso Lingis writes in the translator's introduction that 'Levinas several times proceeds by way of language' (*OBBE*, p. xxix).) This is one of the reasons that the book's style is so complex and so excruciatingly self-reflexive: its choice of metaphors and the subject those metaphors describe, language, are the same.

Language is an amphibology because it is made up of the 'transcendent' saying (*le dire*) and the 'immanent' said (*le dit*). It is the interweaving of the two which allows the ethical to signify 'within ontological language' (*ED*, p. 7). In *Totality and Infinity* the 'beyond' was manifest 'within the totality and history, within experience' (*TI*, p. 23) in the face; in *Otherwise than Being* the infinite, the 'otherwise than being', appears within language. This is Levinas's linguistic turn. Whereas before he understood the ethical to be made manifest through the face-to-face relationship, now the ethical appears through language. The approach to the other, substitution and responsibility for the other – all terms which are effectively synonymous with ethics for Levinas in his performative attempt to escape ontological language – are made apparent, enacted, in language. Language is 'no longer simply the expression of my unique response to the other, but is the very condition or possibility of all ethics in general, prior to any unique case of ethical responsibility . . . a "metaethics", an "ethics of ethics"'.[26] For Levinas, the amphibology which both takes place in and makes up language is more primordial than both Being and time. Levinas is attempting to pass beyond the power of the verb 'to be' which dominates thought: 'what is signified by the verb to be would be ineluctable in everything said, thought and felt. Our languages woven about the verb to be . . . reflect this undethronable royalty' (*OBBE*, p. 4). Time itself, 'recuperated in retention, memory, 'tales', and books' (*OBBE*, p. 34) is the result of the verb 'to be'. Yet Being denies transcendence, and the work aims to show how transcendence – ethics – exceeds language. This reaction to Heidegger is another way of stating Levinas's conception that 'ethics is first philosophy'.

Although these ideas are briefly foreshadowed at the end of the preface to *Totality and Infinity* (*TI*, p. 30), and Levinas has stated that 'I have always distinguished . . . between the saying and the said' (*EI*, p. 88), it is only in

Otherwise than Being that these ideas are made explicit and take on such significance. It is through this linguistic turn, and the demands it makes on philosophy, that Levinas's thought responds to Derrida's deconstruction of *Totality and Infinity*. Furthermore, and despite the appearance of a position inimical to art, this turn to language will be shown to be have a central part to play in uncovering the ethics of literary criticism.

The Saying

[T]he *saying* is the fact that before the face I do not simply remain there contemplating it, I respond to it . . . It is difficult to be silent in someone's presence; this difficulty has its ultimate foundation in this signification proper to saying, whatever is the said. It is necessary to speak of something, of the rain and fine weather, no matter what, but to speak, to respond.

Emmanuel Levinas (*EI* p. 88).

The saying is the focus of *Otherwise than Being* – Peperzak argues that the whole text can be understood as 'a series of 'intentional analyses' of saying, through which the implications and conditions of saying are worked out'.[27] Offering a definition of the saying is extremely problematic for three reasons. First, the saying 'is' beyond Being, beyond 'is', in the way that it is not a statement of any sort, nor can it be 'thematised', or defined and delimited. Second, the saying is integrally interwoven with a number of other concepts as the 'place' in which they are enacted. In his attempt to escape the language of ontology by continually interrupting and disrupting it, Levinas frequently, and characteristically for this text, redescribes this term in many different ways. The very fact that Levinas redescribes (the concept of) saying in so many different ways and in so many different contexts, each with a slightly different, but complementary, emphasis, illustrates its importance for *Otherwise than Being*. Third, the saying is, in a profound sense, only a metaphor. As has already been suggested, *Otherwise than Being*, in its discussions of language, self-reflectively chooses its metaphorical tropes from language. The saying is itself a metaphor – although a key metaphor which helps to anchor the whole text – for what will prove to be unsayable.

Defining the saying, then, is not easy and would perhaps be counter-productive. It is not a being or thing, not a term and, paradoxically, only a metaphor for a non-term. It is 'a performative doing that cannot be reduced to a constative description' (*ED*, p. 7). Here are four sorts of (non)definitions:

1. The closest a traditional philosophical definition might be able to come would be to suggest that the saying is the quasi-transcendental (but non-divine), untotalisable (non)place from which ethics comes.

2. Less rigorously, but more accessibly, it might be understood as what leads one to discuss the weather with a stranger. This may be fleeting and elusive, but it is precisely this that Levinas wants to draw out.

3. A more Levinasian definition would be to refuse any single definition by offering an array of understandings of the saying. It the *condition* of ethics, its mode, that which has found us always already in a society. It is what has made our world our context before we have even entered the world. It is how 'ethics' signifies. It is the '(non)place' where what might be called 'the ethical event' occurs, the 'founding' event which Levinas hopes to uncover, and which in *Totality and Infinity* was thought to take place in the face-to-face relation. The saying occurs in language, yet it is not *a* language. It is the idea, but not actually the practice of language: it does not communicate anything except the desire to communicate. It is antecedent 'to the signs it conjugates . . . it is the proximity of one to the other, the commitment of an approach, the one for the other, the very signifyingness of significa- tion' (*OBBE*, p. 5). The saying does not convey any information: it is 'not a modality of cognition' (*OBBE*, p. 48, p. 92) but rather it is the 'publicness' or openness to the other upon which language is grounded. The 'exchange of information, the interpretation and decoding of signs' (*OBBE*, p. 92) presupposes the saying. It is 'the extreme tension of language, the for-the-other of proximity, which closes in on me from all sides and concerns me even in my identity' (*OBBE*, p. 143).

4. The concept of the saying is Levinas's response to Derrida's sugges- tion that the other cannot be represented. It is Levinas's attempt to name the 'ultralogical affect of speech' (*VM*, p. 133) which questions Greek thought. It relocates the 'true representation', the 'nudity', the 'very straightforwardness' of the face (all *TI*, p. 200) of *Totality and Infinity*, so criticised by Derrida, into the realm of representation. The saying 'shines out' from the representation which is language. The ethical no longer 'bypasses' language, as representation, but passes in and as language; as such, it attempts to answer many of Derrida's questions.

The saying is interwoven in the thought of *Otherwise than Being*. It is the site, which exists only in language, for the convergence of fundamental and interwoven Levinasian ideas: these 'different concepts that come up in the attempt to state transcendence echo one another . . . and cannot be really isolated from one another without projecting their shadows and reflections on one another' (*OBBE*, p. 19). In addition to this interweaving, Levinas typically redescribes and reinterprets these ideas in many different phrases in order to escape the language of ontology: they have no one name. The three key ideas — which are not in language, but appear in language — in which the saying plays a key part can be described, in the extended 'refusing to be defined' definitions of *Otherwise than Being*, as:

1. the break-up of identity and the approach to the other.
2. substitution, passivity beyond passivity, the state of being a hostage, exposure, proximity.
3. the relation to the other and the responsibility imposed by the other.

The saying breaks up identity and opens to the other because it is in the saying that the finite and limiting strictures of being, of essence, of identity standing alone, are overcome. The saying overcomes the closure of identity because it comes before identity. This 'breakup of essence' (*OBBE*, p. 14) allows an approach to the other because the unifying, exclusive 'one' is fractured. 'Dasein' can no longer stand alone, overlooking the world: rather, it is aware of always already being obligated. The saying leads to the 'breaking up of inwardness and the abandon of all shelter' (*OBBE*, p. 48). In terms of a conversation about the weather, Levinas is arguing that, for a philosophy which does not take account of the saying, it seems as if the solitary individual chooses freely and without obligation whether or not to have a conversation. Actually, however, the saying has already placed the individual, without engaging that individual's choice or will, in the position where he or she is bound up with the other and cannot but respond to the other. To choose *not* to discuss the weather would lead, perhaps, to a pregnant silence, and a pregnant silence is also a means of communication. Because the saying comes before our self-identity, choosing not to communicate is a mode of communication and thus a response, a performative saying. Identity is thus laid over the saying, and our illusion of a free autonomous self is broken up by the saying.

Moreover, this break-up leads directly to the idea of substitution. The idea of substitution, the subject's inescapable subjectivity, forms the kernel of *Otherwise than Being* (*OBBE*, pp. 193–4, fn. 1) and it emerges in the saying: substitution

> at the limit of being, ends up in saying, in the giving of signs, giving a sign of this giving of signs, expressing oneself . . . this saying remains, in its activity, a passivity, more passive than all passivity, for it is a

> sacrifice without reserve, without holding back, and in this non-voluntary – the sacrifice of a hostage designated who has not chosen himself to be a hostage. (*OBBE*, p. 15)

The saying is where the responsibility of each of us, 'the unqualifiable *one*, the pure *someone*, unique and chosen' (*OBBE*, p. 50), takes place. The saying is the moment of committing oneself to the other, a moment which has already been (and is not, in fact, a moment) but a continual process of substitution. Substitution is to be always already in the position of being obligated to choose to respond (even by not replying) to an enquiry about the weather. To refuse to reply does not to eschew your position as a 'hostage'. The saying is this 'passivity to which the ego is reduced in proximity' (*OBBE*, p. 92): asked a question, sheltering in a doorway in the rain with a stranger, you are passive – a 'hostage' – before you are able to choose whether to respond or not, and any response, positive or negative, will be a response. The saying thus makes 'oneself a sign' (*OBBE*, p. 143), and each of us is taken up into the saying.

Levinas often describes this in terms of the biblical response 'here I am' (*OBBE*, pp. 143, 145, 146, 149, 150, 185).[28] This response is 'identified with nothing' (*OBBE*, p. 143) with no information or material specifics, no opinion about the weather, for example, but only shows 'the very voice that states and delivers itself, the voice that signifies' (*OBBE*, p. 143). The saying is the impossibility of denying the other; the site of our responsibility for the other: indeed, Levinas writes that the 'responsibility for another is precisely a saying prior to anything said' (*OBBE*, p. 43). It is an 'exposedness to the other where no slipping away is possible' (*OBBE*, p. 50). We cannot slip away from or avoid being in a conversation about the weather, even if our contribution to the conversation is not particularly constructive.

The saying, which underlies language and philosophy, cannot be named clearly in language or by philosophy. It cannot communicate itself or be defined (de-fined). It is in order to make this clear, and attempting to do this without betraying it, that Levinas writes about the saying in so many different ways. Derrida suggested that Levinas's phenomenological method, in fact, was first philosophy and that it came before ethics because it uncovered ethics. Here Levinas goes beyond phenomenology and 'takes refuge in the superlative and in hyperbolic speaking, the emphasis of which attempts to express the all-surpassing character (excellence) of transcendence'.[29] It is his attempt to say the unsayable saying. The saying is unsayable because it is always interwoven with the said.

The Said

> The exceptional words . . . one, God – become terms . . . and are put
> at the disposition of philologists, instead of confounding philosophical
> language. Their very explosions are recounted.
>
> Emmanuel Levinas (*OBBE*, p. 169)

The said contrasts with the saying. Like the saying it is outlined in a series
of terms. The said is the saying incarnated into a concrete world of
meanings and history. As such it has an inescapable hold over the
saying, immobilising it (*OBBE*, p. 5). The said has this hold because it
designates, and, in designation, denies the transcendence of the saying: 'the
process captured by designation, even if it is a movement, shows itself but is
immobilised and fixed *in the said*' (*OBBE*, p. 23). This designation works at
the level of ontology: indeed, the said is the 'birthplace of ontology' (*OBBE*,
p. 42). The said, which is the material of language, is made clear both as 'a
system of nouns identifying entities . . . designating identities . . . But also
. . . as the verb in a predicative proposition in which the substances break
down into modes of being, modes of temporalisations' (*OBBE*, p. 40). The
said then has two aspects, as 'noun' and as 'verb' – again, Levinas is using
linguistic terms as metaphors for language. Both 'aspects' deny interruption
and offer a closure of the saying, one synchronically, the other diachroni-
cally.[30]

The 'noun'-function of the said offers a synchronic closure, designating
meaning within a totalising linguistic system. The said is a statement, made
and given meaning by its location within a system. It does communicate
'facts' or things and is that material part of language that can be written or
spoken. The act of 'naming' identifies, controls, delimits, and imposes
meaning with in a fixed totalising system. As Levinas argues, entities are
not 'first given and thematized, and then receive a meaning' (*OBBE*, p. 36),
but rather 'they are given by the meaning they have . . . the word at once
proclaims and establishes an identification of this with that in the already
said' (*OBBE*, pp. 36–7). The said creates the identity of an entity by
'thematising' it. For example, every one is named, delimited and identified
as a person, one of a genus of 'people', and thus reduced into just one of a
thing in a category. (The saying disrupts this genus: 'the other is a
neighbour . . . before being an individuation of the genus man' (*OBBE*,
p. 59)). The said is the horizon of meaning.

The 'verb'-function of the said is diachronic: the said thematises and
determines identity over time. As such it 'destroys' temporality, turns
diachrony into synchrony and so creates essence. Levinas writes that there

is 'no essence or entity behind the said . . . The said, as a verb, is the essence of essence. Essence is the very fact that there is a theme' (*OBBE*, p. 39). The 'verb'-function of the said 'designates instead of resounding' (*OBBE*, p. 42) and, by this act of designation or thematisation, identifies, names or creates fixed entities 'in themes of statements or narratives' (*OBBE*, p. 38). These narratives 'imprison' 'the lived, a 'state of consciousness', a being . . . into *essence*, into a verb . . . the same finds the same modified. Such is consciousness' (*OBBE*, pp. 36–7). The said imposes on the subject a totalising teleological narrative of identity and consciousness.

The said is where the idea of being, in Heideggerian terms, or essence lies. Just as Heidegger accuses western philosophy of having forgotten the question of the meaning of being, Levinas, in turn, accuses western philosophy of having forgotten the question of the meaning of the otherwise-than-being, the question of ethics. The said is the *logos*, and it is Levinas's distinction between the saying and the said that brings his thought closest to Derrida's. The said is Levinas's admission that, as Derrida argues, language is always already violent and that this violence is necessary for the beginning of any system. It reflects what Derrida might describe as the logocentric discourse of the west. The saying, unthematisable, becomes trapped in the said, in the *logos*:

> [the] *logos* said has the last word dominating all meaning, the word of the end, the very possibility of the ultimate and the result. Nothing can interrupt it. Every contestation and interruption of this power of discourse is at once related and invested by discourse . . . The exceptional words . . . one, God – become terms . . . and are put at the disposition of philologists, instead of confounding philosophical language. Their very explosions are recounted. (*OBBE*, p. 169)

The said stands against the ethical importance of interruption. Any saying collapses into the said, into the totality of the *logos*. The said imposes a finite meaning. The said is the content of the conversation about the weather.

`THE WISDOM OF LOVE AT THE SERVICE OF LOVE´: THE TASK OF PHILOSOPHY

The said, the appearing, arises in the saying. Essence then has its hour and its time. Clarity occurs, and thought aims at themes. But all that is in function of a prior signification proper to saying, which is neither ontological nor ontic. Our task is to establish its articulation antecedent to ontology.

Emmanuel Levinas (*OBBE*, p. 46)

The saying and the said exist in continual tension. The saying is 'incarnated' in language and made manifest, yet at a cost. This manifestation of the saying, the condition of ethics, demands

> a subordination of the saying to the said, to the linguistic system and to ontology . . . In language qua said everything is conveyed before us, be it at the price of a betrayal . . . Language permits us to utter, be it by betrayal, this *outside of being*, this *ex-ception* to being, as though being's other were an event of being. (*OBBE*, p. 6)

The saying appears only as a betrayal of itself, 'a saying teleologically turned to the kerygma of the said' (*OBBE*, p. 37). The saying is transformed into *doxa*, to such an extent that it is 'forgotten' (*OBBE*, p. 37) in the said. It is impossible to say the saying because at the moment of saying it becomes the said, betrayed by the concrete language which is the language of ontology. The saying, which is unthematisable, impossible to delimit, becomes limited, thematised, said.

Yet conversely, the saying can never be totally engulfed in the said. The saying appears through its manifestation as a disruption of the said. The saying both stimulates the said – is made manifest in the said – and ruptures it: 'an affirmation and a retraction of the said' (*OBBE*, p. 44). In the said 'the spirit hears the echo of the *otherwise*' (*OBBE*, p. 44). The significance of 'the saying that is absorbed in the said is not exhausted' (*OBBE*, p. 47). Rather, it 'imprints its trace on the thematization itself' (*OBBE*, pp. 46–7). This is the amphibology of language, which is made up of the saying and the said: an amphibology is a trope 'which may be construed in two distinct senses' with two different and simultaneous meanings. Language itself is an amphibology because it has one 'meaning' in the saying – a 'meaning' beyond meaning – and, at the same time, a different meaning in the said. Language is logocentric, closed, finite, bound up with the thinking of essence and being. Language is also un- or pre-logos, open, beyond being. This is the amphibology that Levinas wants to explore and which provides the theme for *Otherwise than Being*, in which the 'saying and the said are such that each accompanies, supports yet subverts the other'.[31]

Something of this structure might be roughly exemplified in George Weiss's and Bob Thiele's song, sung memorably by Louis Armstrong (and idiosyncratically by Nick Cave and Shane MacGowan), 'What a Wonderful World': 'I see friends shaking hands/Saying "How do you do?"/They're really saying/"I love you".' The formal 'how do you do?' is said. The phrase allows people to locate and delimit the others they meet in terms of social relations. This totalising system fixes people's identity, and is a metonym for an economics of wider interpersonal relationships and delimited civic and legal duties and obligations. The person formally greeted is 'thematised', designated as a 'person', one of a genus of 'people'. However, what they are also doing, what they are 'really' doing at the same time, is expressing the saying, the I-love-you. This is an expression of the illimitable responsibility for the actual, concrete other – the neighbour is another of Levinas's terms for this other – to which Levinasian ethics calls each of us: 'the other is a neighbour . . . before being an individuation of the genus man' (*OBBE*, p. 59). The saying, the I-love-you, expresses a relationship of responsibility, Levinasian proximity, beyond the economics of social exchange. Crucially, to the people you meet as you walk down the street, the saying could not be expressed in any other way than in the formal 'how do you do?', which covers up the saying and threatens to lose it, but it is exactly, expressly, the saying that Levinas's philosophy wants to uncover. The saying and the said exist in counterpoint to each other.

Levinas argues that it is the task of philosophy to uncover the saying. This is expressed in a number of ways: extracting 'the otherwise than being from the said' (*OBBE*, p. 7), unsaying the said, putting the same into question by the other, following the trace of the other not back to the same but to the other and the obligation to the other. Philosophy must be a radical work,

> a movement of the same unto the other which never returns to the same. To the myth of Ulysses returning to Ithaca, we wish to oppose the story of Abraham who leaves his fatherland forever, and forbids his servant to even bring back his son to the point of departure.[32]

In the name of the saying, of ethics, philosophy must 'explode' the 'exceptional words' (*OBBE*, p. 169). Yet, as Levinas makes clear, as soon as the otherwise than being is described (de-scribed) 'it is betrayed in the said that dominates the saying which states it' (*OBBE*, p. 7); indeed, everything 'shows itself at the price of this betrayal, even the unsayable' (*OBBE*, p. 7). However 'philosophy is called upon to reduce that betrayal' (*OBBE*, p. 156). The 'reduction' is the way in which Levinas aims to uncover the saying in the said.

The 'reduction' is not a tool like Heidegger's phenomenology, it is not a 'methodological conception' (*BT*, H. 27, p. 50). Nor is it the same as the Husserlian method of reduction. Nor is it an attempt to improve upon and supersede these approaches, which remain, for Levinas, within ontology, within the said and judgements of true and false. It is not a method which aims to outline the 'Being' of the saying, since the saying has no Being – Being is a quality of the said. Nor does Levinas's 'reduction' seek to explain or justify transcendence.

Instead, and again in the repeated (non)definitions of *Otherwise than Being*, it aims 'to show the signification proper to the saying on the hither side of the thematization of the said' (*OBBE*, p. 43). The reduction is 'reduction of the said to the saying beyond the *logos*, beyond being and non-being, beyond essence, beyond true and non-true' (*OBBE*, p. 45). It is the never-ending attempt to show 'how my ethical exposure to the Other underlies any ontological exposition' (*ED*, p. 164). The reduction is closer to the idea of 'prophecy' or 'witness' (*OBBE*, pp. 149–53). It draws attention to the saying in every said, to the outside, the transcendent alive but buried, encrypted in every utterance. It shows up the way in which the saying disrupts every said. Levinas sees this process at work in all significant philosophy.[33]

However, as soon as saying 'becomes dictation, it expires, or abdicates, in fable and in writing' (*OBBE*, p. 43) It becomes said: 'to expose an otherwise than being will still give an ontological said' (*OBBE*, p. 44). Philosophy, then, in the act of reduction converts the signification of the saying, which is beyond essence, 'into essence . . . by an abuse of language' (*OBBE*, p. 126), and thus destroys the pretensions of philosophy to escape the said. This is both unavoidable and necessary. The saying must

> enter into a proposition and a book . . . It must spread out and assemble itself into essence, posit itself, be hypostatized, become an eon in consciousness and knowledge, let itself be seen, undergo the ascendancy of being. Ethics itself, in its saying which is a responsibility, requires this hold. (*OBBE*, p. 43–4)

It is necessary for the saying to become 'incarnated' in the said for there to be ethics. There cannot be a 'pure' saying and without the interweaving of the said and the saying there could be no ethics. 'I-love-you', the unexpressed expression of saying, can only be said to the other at the risk of losing it in 'how do you do?', the said.

This interdependency of the saying and the said, the amphibology of language, is the central paradox of *Otherwise than Being* and the 'astonishing adventure' (*OBBE*, p. 44) of philosophy. Once written and so thematised in a work of philosophy, the saying calls again for philosophy so 'the light that occurs' illuminating what is beyond essence does 'not congeal into an essence' (*OBBE*, p. 44). Once the said has been 'reduced to the signification of saying, giving it over to the philosophical said' (*OBBE*, p. 183), that 'philosophical said' in turn must be reduced again. This means that the reduction, the task of philosophy 'is then an incessant unsaying of the said, a reduction to the saying always betrayed by the said' (*OBBE*, p. 181). The foundation of philosophy becomes 'an endless critique, or scepticism . . .

destroying the conjunction into which its saying and its said continually enter' (*OBBE*, p. 44).

This formulation of the task of philosophy raises two issues. First, Levinas suggests that this seeming 'foundation' for philosophy is distrusted by intellectuals because it sounds utopian: 'they would call it humanist and even hagiographical' (*OBBE*, p. 166). However, Levinas suggests that this understanding of 'foundation' is itself a result of following the *logos*, of 'speaking Greek'. The relation with the other, the saying which underlies and calls for philosophy is not a 'foundation' in the philosophical sense. Rather, it is 'foundation without foundation', indescribably outside discourse. Moreover, for Levinas, humanism 'has to be denounced because it is not sufficiently human' (*OBBE*, p. 128). Humanism, which understands each person as worth an equal amount, limits responsibility because it values a 'person' as a person, not as a neighbour.

Second, Levinas understands scepticism, a theme to which he keeps returning in *Otherwise than Being*, as part of philosophical thought. It is from the tension of the saying and the said that scepticism arises and, for Levinas, philosophy 'is not separable from scepticism, which follows it like a shadow' (*OBBE*, p. 168). Scepticism is sensitive to the difference between the saying and the said: indeed, Levinas writes that, because of its nature as amphibology, language 'is already scepticism' (*OBBE*, p. 170), it is already the 'unheard of *graphics*' (*VM*, p. 111) that Derrida demands. As such, scepticism works constantly to question and interrupt philosophic thought. As the shadow of philosophy, it can never be escaped or ignored, yet it is without definable substance. It is not a method of thought but rather in a constant relation to thought, interrupting and disturbing it. The difficulty is recognising this, and maintaining this interruption caused in language, since language is constructed to prevent any such interruption.[34] For Levinas in *Otherwise than Being* philosophy is precisely that site of constant, ceaseless interruption, between the said and the saying.

Levinas's recurring metaphor for this paradox is a piece of thread with knots along its length (*OBBE*, p. 25, p. 105, pp. 165–71). The thread – the said – is interrupted with knots. These knots represent the interruption of the saying: a knot is made of the thread, dependent on the thread and yet not the thread. In the same way the saying can only be expressed through that which betrays it, the said. A knot is the interruption, the saying, that disrupts the said but is dependent on it. The task of philosophy is to draw awareness to the knots, the ethical saying entwined with the said.

Levinas's metaphor should be compared to Heidegger's use of the thread metaphor in *Being and Time*, *Leitfaden* (*BT*, H. 38, p. 62; H. 436, p. 487). Literally *Leitfaden* means guide-thread, translated by 'thread' or 'clue'. ('A ball of thread employed to guide anyone in "threading" his way into or out of a labyrinth or maze': *OED*.) Heidegger's thread makes it possible for his work to follow 'universal phenomenological ontology' which 'takes its departure from the hermeneutic of Dasein which . . . has made it fast for all philosophical inquiry at the point where it arises and to which it returns' (*BT*, H. 38, p. 62). In contrast, Levinas's thread is made up of interruptions of this ontological thought. For Levinas, the task of philosophy is not to simply follow the thread, but rather to foreground those moments where the knots interrupt the thread, where the beyond being interrupts being, where the saying interrupts the said.

The thread metaphor is used by Derrida in his second essay specifically on Levinas.[35] Derrida suggests that the unthematisable proximity (the condition for language) is not of the thread, nor of the interruption of the thread by the knots but rather an 'interruption of interruptions', that cannot be part of the thread, but always puts the thread under erasure. Thus, this thread is both a *séri* (a series) *rature* (of knots) and a '*séri*' under '*erature*' 'where the continuity and repetition of the series is continually placed under erasure . . . by the energy of ethical interruption'.[36] In this light, Critchley comments that Levinas's text maintains a tension between

> the thread (the ontological said), the knot (the ethical saying or interruption), and the hiatus (the interruption of interruption) where what is unbound, nonthematizable and wholly other to ontology can only be articulated through a certain repetition of ontological or logocentric language, a repetition that interrupts that language. Levinasian textuality (and perhaps textuality in general, *the* text) obeys a sériatural rhythm of binding and unbinding which preserves the absolute priority of the ethical obligation.[37]

These commentaries on Levinas's text and its textuality draw attention to Levinas's conception of philosophy, which, as much an amphibology as the language in which it exists, oscillates between the said and the saying.

The task of philosophy, then, is the continual and eternal reduction of the said to the saying through an awareness of this textual nature. Underlying and energising philosophy is 'the ethical interruption of essence' (*OBBE*, p. 44), the perpetual attempt to uncover the saying in the said by interruption. The saying constantly disrupts the said, and those disruptions are to be made and remade by philosophic discourse. What is perpetually uncovered (and betrayed) is not, however, a platitude, not 'a poverty of the saying received in exchange for the infinite richness of the said' (*OBBE*, p. 184), but rather the 'caress of love . . . always different . . . [which] overflows with exorbitance the songs, poems and admissions in which it is said' (*OBBE*, p. 184).[38] Thus philosophy, as interruption, is 'the wisdom of love at the service of love' (*OBBE*, p. 162). It is precisely this exorbitance, this overflowing of the saying over the said in 'songs, poems and admissions' which will become the focus for an approach to the ethics of criticism, a way of 'unforgetting' the saying in the aesthetic.

`WHAT MISLEADING ANTHROPOMORPHISM OR ANIMISM!´: LEVINAS´S APPROACH TO ART IN *OTHERWISE THAN BEING*

Levinas's understanding of language however, is in very sharp contrast to his writing on aesthetics in *Otherwise than Being*. This, like the view on the subject expressed in *Totality and Infinity*, makes an application of this understanding of language to art works, including those art works in language, highly problematic. That this seems paradoxical is clear; more, this difficulty suggests an contradiction in Levinas's thought over the issue of art. *Totality and Infinity* was open to criticism on the ground that it had difficulties over the issue of representation in general and the issue of aesthetic representation in particular. Notwithstanding his reworking of the problem of representation by showing how the ethical signifies in language, Levinas seems to offer an almost contradictory understanding of the art work, and particularly the literary art work, in *Otherwise than Being*. On the one hand, he can write that the saying, as exorbitance, can overflow the said in poetry and song. On the other he presents a very different view of art, in which the saying has no part.

Art occupies less space than in *Otherwise than Being* than it did in *Totality and Infinity*. It is possible to suggest that Levinas takes his understanding of the aesthetic from 'Reality and Its Shadow' and *Totality and Infinity* and tries to integrate it into the 'schema' of the saying and the said. Art comprises only essence, it does not go over into the otherwise than being: it exists only as said. The reasons for this follow from Levinas's understanding of the said, in both synchronic 'noun'-function and diachronic 'verb'-function.

The 'Noun'-function of the Said and Art

The 'noun'-function of the said offers a synchronic closure by 'naming', identifying and imposing meaning within a limited system. Levinas argues that an entity manifests itself and makes itself understood in a proposition, a '"way" of essence' (*OBBE*, p. 38): essence or being, originating in the said, closes off the beyond essence, or the otherwise than being.

Things, incarnated in their essence, designate themselves: 'the red reddens, or A is A' (*OBBE*, p. 39). Red is made red by its 'red-ing' as material, in 'the realm' of materiality, of essence. Designating itself, 'the essence of red, or the reddening as an essence, becomes audible for the first time' (*OBBE*, p. 39). The fact that it is said, within Being, has made it appear. By appearing, as/in essence it has become said: the said is, in fact, 'the essence of essence' (*OBBE*, p. 39). Being is brought into being by the said.

Art works are the pre-eminent example of how essence resounds in the said. An art work is only essence resounding in itself. Levinas writes that the 'palette of colours, the gamut of sounds, the system of vocables and the meandering of forms are realised as a pure how . . . there is resonance of essence' (*OBBE*, p. 40). An art work is said, 'pure theme . . . absolute exposition' (*OBBE*, p. 40). It displays the 'shamelessness capable of holding all looks for which it is exclusively destined' (*OBBE*, p. 40). In an art work, the 'said is reduced to the Beautiful, which supports Western ontology' (*OBBE*, p. 40). An art work makes clear the essence from which it is made. Modern art especially, Levinas writes, understands this and aims specifically to show the essence of which it is composed, to foreground the materiality from which it is constructed.

As an example, he cites Xenakis's *Nomos Alpha for Unaccompanied Cello*: he asks if a soul is 'complaining or exulting in the depth of sounds . . . ? What misleading anthropomorphism or animism! The cello *is* a cello . . . the essence of the cello, a modality of *essence*, is temporalised in the work' (*OBBE*, p. 41). The music brings out the essence, the 'Being' of the cello, of its strings and frame. Joyce's use of language in *Finnegans Wake* serves to highlight its nature as language: words show themselves off. Picasso's semi-abstract use of tone and shape in *Les Demoiselles d'Avignon* foregrounds the features of tone and shape: the colours are shown as colours. These do not go beyond essence, but rather, they bring out or make clear essence.

In this understanding of the 'noun'-function of the said, Levinas is echoing Heidegger's understanding of an art work's origin.[40] Art for both Heidegger and Levinas make essences appear: 'essence essences' in art. This is a subtle but significant alteration of Levinas's earlier position. Levinas had argued that art, as 'monstrous', 'alien' or 'cold splendor', did not and could not reveal being. This Platonic position put him in direct opposition to Heidegger's, which understood art as revealing Being. In *Otherwise than Being*, however, he accepts Heidegger's position: art does reveal Being. But, in *Otherwise than Being*, Being is said, ontological, not transcendence, not the otherwise than being. For Heidegger 'art breaks open an open place, in whose openness everything is other than usual' (*OW*, p. 72): for Levinas that openness is the continual resounding of the said, of the Logos. For Heidegger, as for Proust, art makes the world anew; for Levinas, art is a process of 'essential renewal' (*OBBE*, p. 40), but one in which essences are made to resound in new and innovative ways, but are never able to break to beyond being. Art makes the said resound but has no access to anything beyond that. In a very Heideggerian formulation, the cello's cello-ness, for example, is made manifest, but the beyond being is not. Art no longer reveals a 'hither' shadow-world ('Reality and its Shadow') or an empty world (*Totality and Infinity*), but the Being or essence of the world. A poem is made possible by the 'the evocation of being' but this evocation 'would be to make a said resound' (*OBBE*, p.135). A revelation of the essence only reveals the said: it does not pass beyond Being to uncover the saying, Levinas argues.

The 'Verb'-function of the Said and Art

If Levinas's position on art as revealing Being and essence has been subtly changed by his developing sense of the limits of Being, his understanding of the relationship between art and temporality has not. The said 'imprisons' 'the lived . . . into *essence*, into a verb' (*OBBE*, pp. 36–7) and imposes a totalising teleological narrative of identity and consciousness. As art is made up of the said, it has, in relation to temporality, only these qualities. The 'unnarratable other loses his face as a neighbour in narration' (*OBBE*, p. 166). An art work does not have the same 'time' as humanity, but rather has an inhuman trapped time. Levinas writes that, in the evocation of Being that is a poem, signification

> intelligibility and mind would reside in the manifestation and in contemporaneousness, in synopsis, presence, in essence which is a phenomenon, that is, a signification whose very movement involves thematization, visibility and the said. Any radical non-assemblable diachrony would be excluded from meaning. (*OBBE*, p. 135)

A poem, thematised, said, lacks the 'non-assemblable diachrony' which is the fracturing of temporality by the saying: poetry is 'productive of song, or resonance and sonority, which are the verbalness of verbs or essence' (*OBBE*, p. 40). Words word, or words only make their essence as words clear in poetry, and do not open beyond. Just as in 'Reality and its Shadow', the art work is locked up in the temporalisation of essence. Art still has no access to the saying.

These two functions of the said in relation to art have an effect on exegesis or criticism. The art work, the said resounding, 're-saiding', calls for exegesis. Exegesis – another said – recognises the language of essences at work in the art work and rearticulates that language in 'the forms of prefaces, manifestos, titles or aesthetic canons – a non-eliminable meta-language' (*OBBE*, p. 41). For Levinas, the exegetical act is 'not something laid on to the resonance of the essence of the art work: the resonance of essence vibrates within the said of the exegesis' (*OBBE*, p. 41). That is, the language of essences, the said, logocentric discourse, which is the language of art, is also the language of criticism. Criticism's function is to look at how art thematises, how it brings essences to light, and in doing this criticism speaks not an ethical saying but a logocentric said.

This understanding of the aesthetic as pre-eminently said, both as 'noun' and as 'verb', echoes Levinas's earlier position. Levinas's refusal to accept claims made for the transcendental in art is clear, as is his more general distrust of art. Art is not human: it cannot 'say' anything, it just reiterates the essence, the said. Art misleads by presenting not the saying but the said. It does not have the same 'time' as a person. Just as 'Reality and Its Shadow' tried to illustrate the non-truth of Being by using art as the pre-eminent example, *Otherwise than Being* tries to illustrate the non-saying of art as an example of the 'pure said', with no reference to the saying.

One key example of this understanding of art as said resounding, with no access to transcendence or to the saying, is seen clearly in a fierce attack on Heidegger. In fact, it is Levinas's position on art which makes this particular attack possible. Levinas suggests that Heidegger is 'only' a poet. Levinas describes his language as 'magical', and his work as the 'impressionism of . . . [the] play of lights and shadows, and the mystery of light that comes from behind the curtains' (*OBBE*, p. 182). These descriptions echo Levinas's disgust with 'magical' and 'bewitching' art, both here and in earlier work. Moreover, Heidegger's language of essence is compared to 'theatre machinery behind the promise of transcendence' (*OBBE*, p. 182). Heidegger's analyses of things which transport us – Levinas, like Maria, lists a few of his favourite things, such as springtimes and landscapes – are degraded, because Heidegger understands them only in relation to Dasein and essence: they become 'reflections of our own looks . . . mirages of our needs, echoes of our prayers' (*OBBE*, p. 182). Levinas asks if Heidegger's *poetry* succeeds in 'reducing the rhetoric' (*OBBE*, p. 182). Here, Levinas is suggesting that poetry might be able to perform the act of reduction, uncovering the saying in the said in Heidegger's language. The answer, as might be expected, is in the negative (although it is unclear whether this negative refers to specifically Heidegger's poetry or to poetry in general). Essence, which resounds in Heidegger's poetry, is 'the very impossibility of anything else, of any revolution that would not be a revolving upon oneself'

(*OBBE*, p. 182). Essence, Heidegger's poetic language, always returns to essence. Levinas writes that even in 'the marvels of which essence itself is capable, even the surprising possibilities of renewal by technology and magic . . . There is not a break in the business carried on by essence' (*OBBE*, p. 183). Even marvellous essence resounding cannot break through to the beyond essence. Essence cannot say. Only the 'meaning of the other' (*OBBE*, p. 183) cannot be recouped by essence. Levinas writes that a 'voice comes from the other shore. A voice interrupts the saying of the already said' (*OBBE*, p. 183). There are many criticisms of Heidegger's philosophy in Levinas's work; in this passage, Levinas attacks Heidegger by focusing on the nature of Heidegger's language as poetry, as the said echoing itself. This attack only has value because of Levinas's understanding of the aesthetic as said.

In a sense, and if this was incontestably Levinas's position on the aesthetic, this would make him the strictest of graphi-readers, in contrast to his earlier position as an epi-reader. Graphi-reading has no nostalgia for the human within a literary text: a text is the play of language, foregrounding its nature as language. If this is Levinas's last word on the aesthetic, then his thought here, as in *Totality and Infinity*, would resist any attempt to relate criticism to ethics. Critical exegesis would have to limit itself to a comparison of shapes and forms or to philological elucidation. Criticism could not appeal to the beyond or to ethics. Using *Otherwise than Being* to explore ethical criticism – if this was unquestionably Levinas's position as his explicit statements on art seem to imply – would be a blind alley: the 'ethics' of criticism would be a meaningless phrase.

However, there is a self-contradiction in Levinas's work.

SPEAKING, ONLY PHILOSOPHY? THE SAYING IN ART AND A CONTRADICTION IN LEVINAS'S APPROACH TO ART IN *OTHERWISE THAN BEING*

Every discourse, even when said inwardly, is in proximity and does not include the totality.

Emmanuel Levinas (*OBBE*, p. 171)

Perhaps a certain aesthetics does constitute a part of ethics.

Adriaan Peperzak[41]

For Levinas, language is made up of the saying and the said: it is the task of philosophy to interrupt the said to reveal the saying. Levinas takes philosophy as the 'royal road' to uncover the saying, by interruption. So central is the action of philosophical discourse for Levinas that it appears *only* philosophical language can cause this interruption. His explicit declared position on the aesthetic, that it comprises essences resounding, shows that art certainly cannot achieve this disruption. It is at this point that a self-contradiction in Levinas's thought on art becomes clear. Put simply, in *Otherwise than Being*, Levinas's view of art, especially literature, correlates neither with his concept of language nor with his concept of the task of philosophy and its relation to language.

At the end of his attack on Heidegger, as one who writes as a poet, letting essence resound, Levinas writes that the language of essence, the said, is interrupted by a voice that 'comes from the other shore' which 'interrupts the saying of the already said' (*OBBE*, p. 183). Here, after denouncing a philosopher for being a poet, for speaking only of essence and in the language of essence, Levinas chooses a phrase that, in a work so permeated with *Hamlet* as *Otherwise than Being*, recalls Hamlet's discussion of the bourn from which no traveller returns in the first scene of Act III. The other is a voice which calls across the transcendence of death, from the other shore, which would break open Hamlet's inwardness. The question remains of why Levinas chooses this significant phrase. This section will argue that he chooses it because, vitally, the saying does take place in art. Moreover, and despite Levinas's stated position on the aesthetic, the text of *Otherwise than Being* itself shows this to be the case. This moment, this 'voice' (*OBBE*, p. 183) is just one instance of this.

Levinas's own writing in *Otherwise than Being*, despite his position on aesthetics, suggests that literary art must also be composed of the interaction of the saying and the said, and is not merely the resounding of the said. Three factors suggest this: first, Levinas's understanding of language in general; second, the use of, and appeal to, literature in *Otherwise than Being*; third, the text's own potential 'literary' status. As a consequence, it seems clear that literature does incorporate the saying. In turn, this implies that there might be an 'event' or 'process' analogous to the philosophical reduction Levinas outlines, which can actively reveal the saying in literature, an ethical criticism.

Saying in Literature 1: the Nature of Language

Levinas's argument about language, summarised in the metaphor of the thread with knots along its length, applies to all language. Literature, like philosophy, occurs in language. This implies that literature, too, must comprised the saying and the said, the condition of language, and it, too, should exhibit the amphibology of language. Therefore, literary art cannot be purely the said resounding. Just as a work of philosophy is an example of discourse as the knotted thread, literature, as language, should have these knots. The saying must also exist in 'non-philosophical' texts, 'non-philosophical' discourse. Indeed, Levinas writes that '[E]very discourse . . . is in proximity and does not include the totality' (*OBBE*, p. 171): that is, *every* discourse reveals the saying, proximity, and threatens the totalising imposition of the said. Levinas discusses the exposure of the other in terms of 'communication' in general, not any specific form of communication (*OBBE*, p. 120). It is 'discourse *qua discourse*' (*OBBE*, p. 170, italics added), not just philosophical discourse, which disrupts the said. Language, not just philosophy, or philosophical language, 'is already scepticism' (*OBBE*, p. 170) because it is in language that the saying questions the said of language. This disruptive power of language is not only not limited to philosophical language, as Levinas seems to suggest, but also must occur in other uses of language, not least in aesthetic uses of language.

However, this seemingly straightforward argument could be contested by suggesting that, while literary language certainly disrupts the said, its 'referent' may not be the other and thus it may not partake of the ethical saying. Instead, literary language might open up to what Blanchot and Levinas name the *Il y a*, the 'There is', the neuter or the other night. These terms refer to the anonymous insistent 'sensation' of existence, which for Blanchot, and for Levinas in his early work, underlies identity or self. It is the experience of existence without focus, 'vigilance without objects' (*EE*, p. 65) uncovered by insomnia for example (*EE*, pp. 65–7). It is what Blanchot tries to evoke at the start of his novel *Thomas the Obscure*.

If this is the case, if literary language opens to this anonymous insistent neutrality which is the bare experience of existence and not to the other, to the horizon of ethics, then literature has no access to the saying. The words of a work of literature, resounding as the essence of words, could only serve either to recall us to our essence in the world of essence formed by the said, or to a strange 'suspension' of the ethical.

This, however, is not the case *Otherwise than Being* makes. Although this in itself is not enough to demonstrate the opening of literary language to the ethical saying, by working through Levinas's self-contradictions between language, aesthetics and the task of philosophy, and by taking his position on language in the context of his other positions, it becomes clear that the 'referent' of literary language is the other, and that literature – after Levinas, at least – does partake of the saying. The interruptions of language in literature open to the saying, and so to the ethical responsibility for the other, for Levinas first because he shows precisely this in his appeals to literature, and second and more importantly because of the performative 'literary' nature of *Otherwise than Being* itself.

Saying in Literature 2: Levinas's Appeal to Literature

In direct contradiction to his declarations on the aesthetic in *Otherwise than Being*, and creating a tension through the text, there are a number of other occasions where Levinas suggests that artworks as well as philosophic works embody the saying by making an appeal to, or through, works of literature. For example, Levinas asks the core question of his philosophy three times, articulated in three different discourses: '[W]hy does the other concern me? What is Hecuba to me? Am I my brother's keeper?' (*OBBE*, p. 117). Each of these questions is in a different discourse, a different sort of said. The first, with its use of philosophic 'key words', 'why' (for what reason), 'other', 'concern' (*sorge* – care or concern in Heidegger), is a question in the discourse of philosophy which interrupts and calls for, or to, philosophy. Levinas writes close to this language in *Otherwise than Being*, in which philosophy tries to interrupt the *logos* to access the saying. The third question is taken from the Hebrew Scriptures, the book of Genesis (4:9). This question demands an answer drawn from or compatible with scriptural discourse, in the work of Karl Barth, for example, or in Levinas's 'confessional writings'[42].

However, the question 'what is Hecuba to me?' is a question asked in and of literature, asking how and why literature might have ethical meaning. It requires an answer compatible with the same discourse. If one were to follow the argument of *Otherwise than Being* on art, where art is said and supports western ontology, the answer would be that Hecuba meant nothing to me. This is clearly very different to the answer to the other two questions. If the saying, the revelation of 'my ethical exposure to the other' could not take place in art, the question of what Hecuba is to me is meaningless and out of place. If, on the other hand, the question can have an answer that shares a trajectory with the other two questions, not only is it not out of place, but also it suggests that art can be a locus for the saying and that there might be a literary or critical equivalent of the 'reduction' to expose this saying.

Another example of Levinas's suggestion that, despite his explicit stated position, art is not simply said, comes in his defence of the saying from the accusation that it is platitudinous. Levinas writes, movingly, that the signification of the saying

> is not a poverty of the saying received in exchange for the infinite richness of the said, fixed and admirably mobile, in our books and our traditions, our sciences and our poetry, our religions and our conversations; it is not a barter of the duped. The caress of love,

always the same, in the last accounting (for him that thinks in counting) is always different and overflows with exorbitance the songs, poems and admissions in which it is said in so many different ways and through so many themes, in which it is apparently forgotten. (*OBBE*, p. 184)

Here, again, the exorbitance of the saying, surpassing the logocentric constrictions of the said, is clearly understood to occur in art. The saying, the caress of love, overflows through the songs and poems in which it is said. This contradicts Levinas's writing on the aesthetic in *Otherwise than Being*, in which the caress of love – the saying – cannot be achieved by art. These moments in *Otherwise than Being* then suggest that a literary art work is, in fact, an interweaving of the saying and the said, and not simply the said resounding.

Levinas also makes a number of appeals to literary works. These appeals are in two forms. First he simply uses literary texts as examples. Valéry on architecture reveals how the said resounds in poetry (*OBBE*, p. 40, p. 129); Pushkin illustrates the 'unconditionality of the subject' (*OBBE*, p. 195, fn. 15); Rimbaud's alienation is differentiated from the self alienated as 'hostage' (*OBBE*, p. 118); Tolstoy shows how the 'imperialism of the ego' (*OBBE*, p. 128) – Heidegger's Dasein, amongst others – is 'comical' (*OBBE*, p. 129). These sort of appeals, although they show that Levinas holds literary works in some regard, do not challenge his understanding of art as said.

The other sort of use, however, is an appeal to literary texts as authorities, as 'expert witnesses'. In *Otherwise than Being*, of all texts, this appeal to authority must be an appeal to the saying. Dostoyevsky reveals our responsibility to the other, in a phrase that Levinas cites on more than one occasion (*OBBE*, p. 146). If this literary use of language simply restates essence, if it is delusory, it can carry no weight as a 'witness' in an argument, yet Levinas does use it as an appeal, in a way that he did not use literary texts in *Totality and Infinity*. Claudel chooses an epigraph which illustrates the voice of exteriority, in a discourse that is not the discourse of philosophy, but which Levinas takes as valid. Levinas writes that Claudel's epigraph 'can be understood in the sense we have just put forth' (*OBBE*, p. 147). Claudel's aesthetic use of language parallels a philosophic use of language in which the saying can be traced. Levinas (*OBBE*, p.99) uses a phrase from Paul Celan's poem, 'In Praise of Remoteness', as an epigraph: 'Ich bin du, wenn/ich ich bin' (I am you only if/I am I). This suggests that this piece of poetry runs in parallel with the philosophic trajectory of *Otherwise than Being*. The work aims to disrupt the *logos* in order to expose the saying:

Levinas must consider that the poem does too. The poem must interrupt in the name of the saying. Levinas calls these works of literature as 'witnesses' to his argument. As literary texts, they work as 'prophecy', fracturing the said, and echo the aim of his work in the discourse of philosophy. For this to be the case, for Levinas to use them, they must, in some way, be more than just the said resounding, foregrounding its own essence. They must open to the other: they are saying as well as said.

The Saying in Literature 3: Otherwise than Being *as a 'gift of literature'*

> How can philosophy be talked about, opened up, and presented, without, by that very token, using a particular language, contradicting itself, mortgaging its own possibility? Must not the philosopher be a writer and thus forgo philosophy, even while pointing out the philosophy implicit in writing?
>
> Maurice Blanchot[43]

Blanchot offers a more radical suggestion. Perhaps Levinas's work, pre-eminently *Otherwise than Being*, is literature, which performatively appeals to the saying. Derrida suggested that *Totality and Infinity* was 'a work of art and not a treatise' (*VM*, p. 312 fn. 7); the reasons for this ascription of Levinas's work as literature are even more evident in *Otherwise than Being*. For Derrida, literature is 'the place or experience of this 'trouble' we . . . have with the essence of language, with truth and with essence, the language of essence in general'.[44] In *Otherwise than Being: or, Beyond Essence* the central concerns – philosophically and stylistically – are the language of essence and the essence of language. Blanchot, too, suggests that Levinas's philosophy is 'a gift of literature'.[45] That Levinas writes obliquely, in a way 'one might call literary' is plain (*ED*, p. 153).

The work has its own metaphorical consistency in its use of linguistic terms – saying, said, noun, verb, amphibology, for example. The emphasis Levinas puts on breathing, exhalation and speech also fall within this trope of language. His writing lays metaphor on dizzying metaphor. These metaphors are, as has been shown, not strict terms which demand rigid definitions as counters in a philosophical argument. In fact, the ideas in themselves (the saying) and the metaphors in which they appear (the said) explicitly refuse this very schematic. They can be equally well be understood as poetic concepts, as those things to which poetry points.

Levinas's technique of writing in questions, which has already been highlighted, opens up his discourse to interruption. It performs what the discourse discusses. The questions, too, refuse the more traditional attempts to close off philosophical discussion. For Levinas, philosophy is not a attempt to offer a final answer, a system of systems which will explain everything and leave no questions; instead, it represents a continuing and infinite series of questions and re-expressions. His interrogative style echoes this.

Levinas continuously and ceaselessly redefines and repeats, fugue-like, key ideas in different phrases in order to deny simple definition or stultification in the said. This is done to resist rigid, exclusary philosophic discourse, the said. His repetitive, complex, Proustian syntax make interpreting *Otherwise than Being* an activity closer to reading poetry rather than philosophy. Phrases have indeterminate referents, and unambiguous meaning comes not from one clear definition, but from a series of phrases which continuously echo each other. *Otherwise than Being* is not a linear work, but a tapestry, weaving ideas and concerns together in shifting patterns. To concentrate on one fragment is, like looking only at part of a tapestry, to see only individual threads and small, seemingly incoherent patterns and images. Only together, as a whole, does its significance become apparent. By trying to escape the said of philosophy, by trying to be an 'unheard of graphics', the work gestures towards literature, carrying more than the implication that literary texts can also escape and rupture the said. The literary style of *Otherwise than Being*, trying to interrupt its own discourse to break open the saying, is a pivotal part of its 'argument'. The style of this text opens it towards the saying.

The text, like a work of literature, explicitly performs itself, and as a result, echoes literary writing, especially perhaps self-reflexive contemporary postmodern poetry and prose. As an example of this self-reflexivity, Levinas writes that the 'very discussion which we are at this moment elaborating . . . [is] bringing back into the bosom of being all signification allegedly conceived beyond being' (*OBBE*, p. 155). Levinas's text is aware of its own discursiveness and its own performativity. Indeed, no small part of the text's 'argument' aims to draw attention to its own, and others', use of language. In his style of writing and choice of metaphors Levinas performatively foregrounds language in order to disrupt the said. Instead of simply making essence resound, Levinas tries to uncover the traces of the saying.

As a 'gift of literature', *Otherwise than Being* is part of literature, a literary saying and said given out, without expecting a return, to (rupture) philosophy. As a 'gift of literature' it is also a gift given to literature by philosophy, opening up literature to the possibility of the ethical saying. It exists as both these possibilities, as a performative, inconclusive amphibology.

If Levinas's writing can do this, other writings, even if they do not claim to be in philosophical discourse, can also disrupt the said. Levinas's belief in the power of philosophy to interrupt the said does not exclude other attempts to interrupt the said, the *logos*, using other discourses and traditions. The saying can be understood as occurring in literary discourse as much as in philosophical discourse. The text of *Otherwise than Being*, despite its opposition to the aesthetic, endorses this view, because of its understanding of language, its appeal to literature as a discourse in which the saying appears and its own 'literariness'.

However, it is not necessarily clear that the said, in a 'literary' tradition, can be disrupted in the same way that the said in a 'philosophic' tradition can be disrupted. *Otherwise than Being* aspires to interrupt and open the *logos*, both explaining how the interruption works and, by its shifting terms and refusal of simple definition, performatively enacting the interruption – the reduction – of the said by the saying, by using philosophy. Whatever strange sort of text *Otherwise than Being* is, the discourse of philosophy is its 'indispensable guiderail' (*OG*, p. 158). It arises from a philosophical tradition and it seeks to fracture the logos by using this tradition. That it comes from this tradition does not mean that the 'literary' way in which it uses language should be ignored, but reflects the fact that philosophy is special for Levinas because of its ethically motivated power to interrupt, its relationship with scepticism. However, although Levinas' text does not explicitly offer an equivalent of this power for literature, his text calls for an equivalent. By focusing attention on the ethical significance of language itself, Levinas provides an understanding of language and ethics which will underlie ethical criticism.

INTERRUPTION AND INTERPRETATION:
TRANSLATING THE REDUCTION FROM
PHILOSOPHICAL DISCOURSE TO LITERARY DISCOURSE

Criticism as Interpretation

Criticism is interpretation. Criticism, from its development in modernity, stands as a relatively new discipline offering interpretation of specifically defined literary texts. This focus on interpretation, which existed in other disciplines (such as biblical hermeneutics, for example) before it existed in relation to vernacular literature, is central to criticism. Anglophone critical practice, following certain implicit or explicit assumptions and agendas, *is*, in the profoundest sense, interpretation. Before, in the modernist paradigm of criticism, critical interpretation was governed at the deepest level by a modernist humanism, which has been eroded over time. After a reading of Levinas, a new understanding of the ethics which underlies criticism is clear.

Interruptive Interpretation

As Levinas has argued, the ethical saying in communication is always under threat: the relation between communication, including writing, and saying is one of 'uncertainty' (*OBBE*, p. 120). To explore it is 'a dangerous life, a fine risk to run' (*OBBE*, p. 120) yet 'the ethical interruption of essence' (*OBBE*, p. 44) is the duty of philosophy. The risk is that the saying will be utterly engulfed in the said. In philosophy, this risk is run in Levinas's idea of the reduction, aiming to extract the saying, the 'otherwise than being from the said' (*OBBE* p. 7). This risk is also taken in forms of discourse other than philosophy. As the saying exists in literature, there is a corresponding literary version of the philosophical reduction which reveals the saying.

The reduction of 'the said to the saying beyond the *logos*, beyond being and non-being, beyond essence, beyond true and non-true' (*OBBE*, p. 45) occurs for Levinas, in philosophy, through the constant interruption of the said, called for by the saying. Yet the reduction is not a philosophical process, it has no prescribed method: it resembles a form of 'prophecy' or 'witness'. It also resembles scepticism, constantly interrupting and challenging. As 'prophecy', or 'witness', or scepticism, it can occur in any discourse – it is not just philosophy which opens up to the saying. It is 'discourse qua discourse . . . [it] belies the very claim to totalise' (*OBBE*, p. 170), belies the said. Language itself 'is already scepticism' (*OBBE*, p. 170), any use of language already invokes the distinctions between the saying and the said.

This ethical call for interruption occurs in relation to literature as well. Literature, criticism and philosophy have an analogous relationship to the call for interruption. *Otherwise than Being*, despite its disavowal of art, suggests this. Levinas argues that language is beyond the limits of thought, and through the saying has a 'meaning' beyond systems and definition, beyond totalisable meaning. He writes that this 'possibility is laid bare in the poetic said and the interpretation it calls for ad infinitum' (*OBBE*, p. 170). The saying in poetry, interwoven in poetic language with the said, calls for infinite interruption. Just as interruption is 'the only possible end' (*OBBE*, p. 20) of philosophy, interruption is the only possible end of literature.

Levinas writes that a book is

interrupted discourse catching up with its own breaks. But books have their fate; they belong to a world they do not include, but recognize by being written and printed, and by being prefaced and getting themselves preceded with forewords. They are interrupted, and call for other books and in the end are interpreted in a saying distinct from the said. (*OBBE*, p. 171)

Any book, literary, philosophical or otherwise, is 'pure said' (*OBBE*, p. 171), but at the same time the result of 'interrupted discourse'. A book is the moment of encryptment of the saying in the said, and bears the signs of this encryptment. Books reveal the ferment of the saying and the said, constantly interrupting themselves and each other. Yet, they 'have their fate': what was an interruption becomes part of the said and loses its power as an ethical interruption of essence.[46] It is the process of texts becoming said that asks for interruption and calls for other books. In the (impossible) beginning, as it were, the saying in the said is clear in a book. Through writing, through prefaces and the sedimentation of time, a book becomes only said, which calls out for interpretation as interruption. This interpretation as interruption is a saying, 'distinct from the said'.

It is this process of interruption and interpretation which makes up the ethics of criticism and which underlies critical practice. The question the saying asks, calling to our responsibility, is unsayable. It can be spoken of, encrypted in language, 'only by an abuse of language' (*OBBE*, p. 196). Levinas hears this call in the 'abuse of language' that is philosophy: for him, the question posed by the saying is uncovered by considering the question 'why does the other concern me?'. This abuse, this 'translation' from what cannot be spoken into a concrete language, from the saying to the said, is an 'indiscretion . . . which is probably the very task of philosophy' (*OBBE*, p. 7). However, to consider the question posed by the saying in art, to ask 'what is Hecuba to me?', is only to translate or abuse the unsayable question of the saying into another discourse. Levinas's attempt to interrupt the *logos* in philosophical language in the name of the other can be transferred into an attempt to do the same in the discourse of literature and criticism. The saying in literature calls for this. Despite his opposition to the aesthetic, this is suggested by *Otherwise than Being*, and is only an extension of Levinas's thought. Literary discourse, too, is an abuse of language which can speak of the unsayable. This is the ethics which underlies any criticism.

This process – ethical criticism – cannot be reduced to a methodology. There cannot be a Levinasian ethical criticism *per se*, because as soon as a way of reading becomes a methodology, an orthodoxy or a totalising system, it loses its ability to interrupt, to fracture the said. The saying calls for constant reflection in order to interrupt the said in the name of the other. It might be suggested that because the reduction takes place only in relation to texts, criticism should have a special awareness of the textual nature of the texts it explores. However, to suggest that criticism exclusively pays attention to the text, to the 'the words on the page' (*ER*, p. 6), is to threaten to limit its ability to interrupt. To return critical practice to this results in criticism becoming no more than a game, a play of essences, arguing which word sounds most fitting. In a sense, this was Miller's conclusion, when he discovered that he was unable to tell whether he was subject to a linguistic demand or an ethical demand. For Miller, concentrating on the 'real situation of a man or a woman reading a book' (*ER*, p. 4), only the material of language, the said, existed. However, this is not to deny the rupturing power of this sort of reading. It is to suggest, against Miller, that other sorts of criticism are able to rupture the said in order to bring out the saying. Any reading which interrupts the said and proposes that the art work is a site of fracture makes us aware of the constant force of our responsibilities. In contrast, any critical method, like Miller's or Nussbaum's, which claims to offer the last word, the last interpretation, is open to question. To finish interpreting is to finish interrupting, to stop trying to expose the saying in an art work.

For Levinas, perhaps, the difficulty of exposing the saying from the said of art is great – perhaps, the 'fine risk' (*OBBE*, p. 120) is just too fine for him to suggest outright that the saying is present in an artwork. He can find no way of 'unforgetting' the said in art, and is suspicious of the ethical or transcendent claims so often made for the aesthetic. However, if the saying is present in all discourse, in literature as well as in 'the peaks' of philosophical thought, there is a need to uncover this saying.

Apart from the 'risk', it is possible to suggest why this 'critical' reduction was not suggested explicitly by Levinas. Perhaps his long-standing suspicion of art prevented such a development; perhaps his belief in the vital importance and centrality of philosophy prevented him from developing a 'literary or aesthetic' reduction, even after his renewed understanding of how ethics signifies in language. Perhaps, more simply, it is a question of historical contingency: the literary critical tradition which he was familiar did not, perhaps, have the heterogeneous tools or developing strategies to uncover the saying in the said which now exist. Criticism in the anglophone world, *pace* Arnold and Leavis, has been deeply concerned with ethics. In France, Germany and Lithuania, however, literary studies developed in different ways – there is very little of what might be called 'literary criticism' in France (as opposed to, for example, literary biography, literary history or theories of literature). As a result, the question of the ethics of criticism, which has been at the centre of many debates and lies the at the heart of the discourse of anglophone literary studies, is not as central as in other traditions.

It might also be a question of canons. Deleuze suggests that English and American literature flies out, traces 'a line, lines, a whole cartography. One only discovers worlds through a long, broken flight'.[47] This idea runs parallel to Levinas's demand that philosophy move from the same to the other, like Abraham, and does not return to the same. This movement, this flight to the other, might be offered much more clearly in Anglo-American literature: the shifting viewpoints of *Bleak House*, the undermining of subjectivity in *Tristram Shandy* and *Ulysses*. In contrast, for Deleuze, other literatures are inward-looking, interior. Proust, who with Dostoyevsky was one of the quintessential novelists for Levinas, wrote that

> in reality, every reader is, while he is reading, the reader of his own self. The writer's work is merely a kind of optical instrument which he offers to the reader to enable him to discern what, without this book, he would perhaps never have perceived in himself. And the recognition of the reader in his own self of what the book says is proof of its veracity.[48]

Here, the inward-looking trajectory of Proust's work is clear. It shows a self-absorption and a single-minded search for the individual's place in the sun, which, as Levinas's citation from Pascal makes clear, 'is how the usurpation of the world began' (*OBBE*, frontispiece). This, Deleuze argues is characteristic of non-English continental literatures, which might suggest to Levinas that this form of literature does not and could not uncover the saying.

Criticism, like philosophy, must continually seek to be interpretation as interruption. The reduction in philosophy of the said to the saying, never complete and never pure, is rearticulated in criticism and literature. Again, just as in philosophy, the reduction has no set method. Levinas is at his most perceptive when his work finds the saying exceeding the said in the 'highest, exceptional hours' of philosophy, where it states the 'beyond being and the one distinct from being' (*OBBE*, p. 178).[49] By the same token, the 'critical' reduction finds the saying in a number of places and in a number of ways, wherever it finds the said of literature exceeded by its saying. The 'critical' reduction is not and could not be a literary critical method. It underlies method: it is the reason for a critical reading and is presupposed by any criticism with a concern for ethics. The reduction in relation to literature is the constant interruption enacted in certain forms of interpretation. There can be no last word, no final interpretation beyond interruption.

The reduction in criticism, just like the action of philosophy, risks the overwhelming of the saying into the said: as soon as the saying 'is conveyed before us it is betrayed in the said that dominates the saying which states it' (*OBBE*, p. 7). Critical writing, like philosophy, must be a continual process of interruption. As soon as one critical strategy occurs, in which the unveiling of the saying takes place, it has always already become *doxa*, said. Without interruption, interpretation becomes an example of the oppressive and imperialistic language of ontology.

CONCLUSION: ETHICS BEYOND CRITICISM

Levinas' thinking appears in a new light as soon as one recognises that his goal is not to generate an ethics . . . his task is to find the sense of ethics and not to construct an ethics. The world is not suffering from a lack of ethical systems. To exist in society is to find an ethics already in place.

Robert Bernasconi[50]

The aim of understanding the ethics of criticism by the 'schema' (which is not a schema) of the saying and the said is not to offer a new system of ethical criticism. It is not to provide protocols like Miller's rules of reading, insisting that good reading is 'guided by the presupposition of a possible heterogeneity in the text' (*VP*, p. 33). Nor is it to suggest simply that 'novels share certain ethical commitments' and that criticism hones our own ethical perceptions, as Nussbaum argues (*LK*, p. 190). Nor is it to draw criticism into an area of philosophy which evaluates 'ethical criteria' (an idea that itself denies an understanding of ethics as first philosophy).[51]

In *Totality and Infinity*, a speaker 'must . . . present a face' (*TI*, p. 182). In *Otherwise than Being*, Levinas writes that the 'reference to an interlocutor permanently breaks through the text that the discourse claims to weave in thematising and enveloping all things' (*OBBE*, p. 170). Levinas's new understanding of language means that the ethical is understood to signify through language, in the *reference to*, the *representation* of, *but no longer* the actual presence of, an interlocutor. The saying, which 'opens me to the other [and] . . . is already the testimony of this responsibility', occurs in the said, in the very braid of language.[52] It occurs in representation – indeed, it underlies the very act of representation. The ethical is in language, if at the cost of a betrayal in the said of language.

This offers a way to understand the ethical moment which underlies any act of criticism. Criticism seeks to break open the said and show the saying's exorbitant overflow – to reveal the exposure of the one to the other in the 'prehistory' of the ego posited for itself (*OBBE*, p. 117). Like philosophy, it can only do this through the said, through language permeated by ontological thought which demands a methodology, protocols of reading, an engagement with the said. Thus, like philosophy, it will always fail. Like philosophy, criticism must be 'an endless critique, or scepticism . . . destroying the conjunction into which its saying and said continually enter' (*OBBE*, p. 44). Criticism chooses a different tradition and discourse from philosophy in which to do this.

This understanding of the ethics which underlie criticism allows a renegotiation of the opposition between Miller and Nussbaum, as representatives of fundamental distinctions in reading strategies.

Interruption and Nussbaum's Criticism

Nussbaum's ethically minded criticism found the ethical significance of literature 'behind the screen' of language, in the fictional events. However, language does not refer back to actual events or individuals, fictional or real. Language is, however, where the saying is made manifest. Language, in fiction as much as in philosophy, calls us to our responsibilities because it is the locus of the saying beyond essence. Fiction appeals to ethics not because it is narrative but because it is in language. What Nussbaum does not account for is the puncturing of the said, of the logocentric language of ontology, by the saying. In fact, Nussbaum's work does the opposite. Because she reduces ethics to a subsection of philosophy, and because she considers characters and events as self-contained 'theatre', she is unable to exceed the language of ontology and reach a moment of transcendence.

For Nussbaum, literature is a play of essence, which occurs in front of an observer who can choose to watch or not. In narration, the 'unnarratable other loses his face as a neighbour' (*OBBE*, p. 166). Nussbaum argues that the reader or observer absorbs characters, as in, for example, her account of how the audience and Hecuba become identified with each other. This rides over the call of the other in the saying of language, precisely because language itself is not of interest to Nussbaum. What would interrupt her omnivorous philosophy, the saying, is passed over in order to explore the 'essential renewal' (*OBBE*, p. 40) of the said. She cannot explain *why* it is that literature can have a bearing on ethics, only that it does: she understands that bearing as a result of the said, of narrative. For Nussbaum, the ethical does not interrupt.

Interruption and Miller's Reading

Perhaps unsurprisingly, taking into account the influence of Levinas on Derrida and vice versa, Miller's position is slightly closer to Levinas's. Miller argues that it is in the actual language from which a text is constructed that the interruption of the *logos* occurs. Miller's criticism agrees with the ethical impulse developed from Levinas in focusing on language as the way in which obligations have always already taken us up. However, perhaps influenced by his New Critical modernist heritage, for Miller language is a selection of meanings, circulating in the said, to be encoded and decoded in surprising new ways. For Miller language as said makes language resound and he is unable to escape this play of essence. There is no other, no saying, in his critical approach. Moreover, he also understands ethics as a traditional area of philosophy, separate from language, even if the ethical is entrapped in language. This is why he is unable to tell whether the ethical demand he is subject to in relation to reading is 'a linguistic necessity or an ontological one' (*ER*, p. 127). Levinas's understanding of language resolves this dilemma. The ethical demand which Miller calls 'ontological', which Levinas would name as the saying actually antecedent to ontology, is simultaneous with a linguistic demand. There is no difference between the two terms: language is both delimiting said and ethical saying.

Levinas writes that the 'revelation of the beyond being is perhaps indeed but a word, but this 'perhaps' belongs to an ambiguity in which the anarchy of the infinite resists the univocity of an originary or a principle' (*OBBE*, p. 156). Levinas's thought in *Otherwise than Being* shows how the ethical, beyond being, appears in literature. This revelation in language, in a 'word', is able to counter, to 'resist' the continual pressure of the said. The saying, the resistance to and interruption of ontological thought, is shown in the reduction of the said to the saying. This reduction which underlies criticism, analogous with the reduction which underlies philosophy, provides a way to understand the ethical impulse in criticism. Criticism, or literary interpretation, as interruption and in many different forms, is a 'witness' to the saying in the language of literature: this witnessing is its responsibility and its duty.

NOTES

1. There is some debate about these lines. The First Quarto has '[F]or Hecuba, why what is Hecuba to him or he to Hecuba?' (London: Scholars Press, 1969). The Second Quarto has '[W]hat's Hecuba to him, or he to her?' (London: Scholars Press, 1969). See also Harold Jenkins, 'Playhouse Interpolations in the Folio Text of *Hamlet*', *Studies in Bibliography*, vol. 13 (1960), pp. 31–47.

2. Drucilla Cornell, *The Philosophy of the Limit* (London: Routledge, 1992), pp. 70–1.
3. Tamara Wright, Peter Hughes, Alison Ainley, 'The Paradox of Morality: an Interview with Emmanuel Levinas', in *The Provocation of Levinas*, eds Robert Bernasconi and David Wood (London: Routledge, 1988), pp. 169–80 (pp. 170–1).
4. For two good accounts of this, see: Robert Bernasconi, 'Levinas: Philosophy and Beyond', in *Philosophy and Non-Philosophy since Merleau-Ponty*, ed. Hugh J. Silverman (London: Routledge, 1988), pp. 232–58; Simon Critchley, 'The Chiasmus: Levinas, Derrida and the Ethical Demand for Deconstruction', *Textual Practice*, vol. 3 (1989), pp. 91–106.
5. Emmanuel Levinas, 'The Trace of the Other', and Jacques Derrida, 'Différence', both in *Deconstruction in Context: Literature and Philosophy*, ed. Mark C. Taylor (London: University of Chicago Press, 1986), pp. 345–59, pp. 396–420. See also: Derrida, *Of Grammatology*, p. 70; Michael J. Macdonald, 'Jewgreek and Greekjew: the Concept of Trace in Derrida and Levinas', *Philosophy Today*, vol. 35 (1991), pp. 215–27.
6. This dialogue is continued specifically in Emmanuel Levinas, 'Wholly Otherwise', trans. Simon Critchley, in *Rereading Levinas*, eds Robert Bernasconi and Simon Critchley (London: Athlone Press, 1991), pp. 3–10; Jacques Derrida, 'At This Moment in This Work Here I Am', trans. Ruben Berezdivin, in *Rereading Levinas*, pp. 11–48.
7. Joseph Libertson, *Proximity: Levinas, Blanchot, Bataille and Communication* (The Hague: Martinus Nijhoff, 1982), p. 286. For another mostly negative account of Derrida's essay, see Richard A. Cohen. *Elevations: the Height of Good in Rosenzweig and Levinas* (Chicago: Chicago University Press, 1994), pp. 305–21.
8. Robert Bernasconi, 'Deconstruction and the Possibility of Ethics', in *Deconstruction and Philosophy*, ed. John Sallis (London: University of Chicago Press, 1987), pp. 122–39 (p. 124).
9. This quotation, from *Culture and Anarchy*, is perhaps more apposite than accurate. Arnold's complex orientalism is clear not just here but also, for example, in his essay on Heine:

    > [Heine] had in him both the spirit of Greece and the spirit of Judaea; both these spirits reach the infinite, which is the true goal of all poetry and all art – the Greek spirit of beauty, the Hebrew spirit of sublimity. By his perfection of literary form, by his love of cleanness, by his love of beauty, Heine is Greek; by his intensity, by his untamableness, by his 'longing that cannot be uttered' he is Hebrew. (Matthew Arnold, *Lectures and Essays in Criticism: Complete Prose Works*, vol. 3, ed. R. H. Super (Ann Arbor: University of Michigan press, 1962) pp. 127–8)

    This seems to inscribe Arnold's own ideologies on to Greeks and Hebrews. However, it finds echoes in Levinas' own thought. In an interview, Levinas said: 'I often say, though it is a dangerous thing to say publicly, that humanity consists of the Bible and the Greeks. All the rest can be translated: all the rest – all the exotic – is dance' (in Raoul Mortley, *French Philosophers in Conversation* (London: Routledge, 1991) p. 18). Levinas has acute and unsettling insight into the process of colonialism and its relation to philosophy: he writes that '(W)estern philosophy has most often been an ontology . . . A philosophy of power, ontology is . . . a philosophy of injustice . . . ontology . . . leads inevitably to another power, to imperialist domination, to tyranny (*TI*, pp. 43, 46–7). He is also acutely aware of the capability of human suffering, as his thought and his biography make clear. However, he is still able to make these claims which exclude cultures who do not claim an inheritance from either the Greeks or the Judeo-Christian tradition, and Derrida's citation from Arnold seems to emphasise this.

    Works like Said's *Orientalism* and Bernal's *Black Athena* have begun to show how a number of discourses are deeply imbued with, if not in fact dependent on, colonialist and racist assumptions. In philosophy this process is only beginning to occur. Despite Derrida's intention in *Of Grammatology* 'to focus attention on the *ethnocentrism* which . . . had controlled the concept of writing' (p. 3), the ethnocentric assumptions which underlie philosophy as a whole have not yet been fully explored. That the ethnocentrism of philosophical discourse, including Levinas's own discourse, is now being interrupted in and by the name of the other is, in some small part, a response to the influence of Levinas's thought, despite his comments. Levinas's ethics is one which helps us to see 'this Europe where they are never done talking of Man, yet murder men everywhere they find them' and knows 'with what sufferings humanity has paid for every one of [Europe's] triumphs of the mind' (Franz Fanon, *The Wretched of the Earth*, trans. Constance Farrington (Harmondsworth: Penguin, 1990) p. 251). See also: Robert Bernasconi, 'Heidegger and the Invention of the Western Philosophical Tradition', *Journal of the British Society for Phenomenology*, vol. 26 (1995), pp. 240–54; Simon Critchley, 'Black Socrates: Questioning the Philosophical Tradition', *Radical Philosophy*, vol. 69 (1995), pp. 17–26; Robert Eaglestone, 'The Imperialist

Logic of Philosophy: Athens, Jerusalem and the Metaphor of the City', *Diatribe* vol. 6 (1996), pp. 9–16.

10. Simon Critchley, 'The Problem of Closure in Derrida (part two)', *Journal of the British Society for Phenomenology*, vol. 23 (1992), pp. 127–45 (p. 140).

11. Christopher Johnson, *System and Writing in the Philosophy of Jacques Derrida* (Cambridge: Cambridge University Press, 1993), p. 64.

12. Emmanuel Levinas, 'Meaning and Sense', in *Collected Philosophical Papers*, trans. Alphonso Lingis (Dordrecht: Kluwer Academic Publishers, 1987), pp. 75–108 (p. 77).

13. It is at this point, after his analysis of Derrida's essay, that Christopher Norris stops his critique of Levinas and criticism which draws on Levinas's work (*Truth and The Ethics of Criticism* (Manchester: Manchester University Press, 1994). As Chapter 4 has shown, Norris is correct for reasons beyond those he gives when he finds Levinas's work problematic for criticism. However, Norris does not take into account Levinas's response to Derrida, and because of this Norris fails to do justice to Levinas's work.

14. Edith Wyschogrod, 'God and 'Being's Move', in the Philosophy of Emmanuel Levinas', *The Journal of Religion*, vol. 62 (1982), pp. 145–55 (p. 150).

15. Richard Kearney, *Dialogues with Contemporary Continental Thinkers* (Manchester: Manchester University Press, 1984), p. 108.

16. 'In Other Words' is the title of the final, concluding section of the book, which consists of only Chapter IV, entitled 'Outside'. This chapter takes its epigram – epigrams are rare in Levinas's work – from Goethe's *Faust II*, Act I. Faust, against Mephistopheles' advice, is about to travel to a nether world:

> Mephistopheles: [So narrow-minded? Scared by a new world?]
> Or will you only hear what you have already heard?
> You're too long used to miracles to fear
> However strange the thing's sound you may hear
> Faust: Nothing good is gained by standing still
> Knowledge of fear is what gives man's spirit wings
> [The world does not allow this feeling cheaply
> but once felt, the unknown vastness moves us deeply]

(J. W. von Goethe, *Faust I and II*, trans. Robert David Macdonald (Birmingham: Oberon Books, 1988), p. 146)

The new world of which Mephistopheles speaks, for Levinas, may be the outside of the world which is envisioned by philosophy, but for another reading, see John Llewelyn, *Emmanuel Levinas: The Genealogy of Ethics* (London: Routledge, 1995), p. 159.

17. Jacques Derrida, 'Letter to a Japanese Friend', in *Derrida and Différance*, eds David Wood and Robert Bernasconi (Coventry: Parousia Press, 1985), pp. 1–8 (pp. 4–5).

18. Kearney, *Dialogues with Contemporary Continental Thinkers*, p. 108.

19. Maurice Blanchot, 'Our Clandestine Companion', in *Face to Face with Levinas*, ed. Richard A. Cohen (New York: State University of New York Press, 1986) pp. 41–50 (p. 50).

20. Blanchot, 'Our Clandestine Companion', p. 49.

21. Emmanuel Levinas, 'God and Philosophy', in *Collected Philosophical Papers*, pp. 153–73 (p. 172).

22. See also: Kearney, *Dialogues with Contemporary Continental Thinkers*, p. 67; Levinas, *Ethics and Infinity*, p. 101; Levinas, 'God and Philosophy', p. 168.

23. John Caputo, *Against Ethics* (Bloomington: Indiana University Press, 1993), p. 4. See also Wendy Farley, 'Ethics and Reality: Dialogue between Caputo and Levinas', *Philosophy Today*, vol. 36 (1992), pp. 211–20.

24. Robert Bernasconi, 'The Trace of Levinas in Derrida', in *Derrida and Différence*, pp. 17–44 (p. 26).

25. 'Witness' is a key term in Paul Ricoeur's analysis of Levinas. See Paul Ricoeur, 'Emmanuel Levinas, Penseur du Témoinage', in *Répondre D'Autrui Emmanuel Levinas*, ed. Jean-Cristophe Aeschlimann (Boudry-Neuchâtel: Éditions de la Baconnière, 1989), pp. 17–40. On Ethical Language, see also Paul Davies, 'On Resorting to an Ethical Language', in *Ethics as First Philosophy*, ed. Adriaan Peperzak (London: Routledge, 1995), pp. 95–104.

26. William Large, 'Ethics and the Ambiguity of Writing in the Philosophy of Emmanuel Levinas' (unpublished doctoral thesis, University of Essex, 1990), p. 19.

27. Adriaan Peperzak, 'Beyond Being', *Research In Phenomenology*, vol. 8 (1978), pp. 239–61 (p. 249).

28. See: Genesis 22:1, 7, 11; 27:1, 18; 31:11; 37:13; 46:2; Exodus 3:4; 1 Samuel 3:4, 5, 6, 8, 16; 12:3;

22:12; 2 Samuel 1:7; 15:26; Isaiah 6:8; 58:9. Although Levinas is thinking of the Hebrew scriptures, the phrase also occurs in Acts 9:10.

29. Peperzak, 'Beyond Being', p. 260.

30. For a similar discussion of closure, see: Simon Critchley, 'The Problem of Closure in Derrida (part one)', *Journal of the British Society for Phenomenology*, vol. 23 (1992), pp. 3–19; 'The Problem of Closure in Derrida (part two)', *Journal of the British Society for Phenomenology*, vol. 23 (1992), pp. 127–45.

31. Robert Bernasconi, '"Failure of Communication" as a Surplus: Dialogue and Lack of Dialogue between Buber and Levinas', in *The Provocation of Levinas*, pp. 100–35 (p. 128).

32. Emmanuel Levinas, 'The Trace of the Other', trans. Alphonso Lingis, in *Deconstruction in Context*, ed. Mark C. Taylor, pp. 345–59 (p. 348).

33. [This] putting into question of the same by the Other . . . is, beyond knowledge, the condition of philosophy . . . not only attested by the articulations of Husserlian thought . . . but also appears at the summits of philosophies: it is the beyond-being of Plato, it is the entry through the door of the agent intellect in Aristotle; it is the idea of God in us, surpassing our capacity as finite beings; it is the exaltation of theoretical reasoning in Kant's practical reason; it is the study of the recognition by the Other in Hegel himself; it is the renewal of duration in Bergson; it is the sobering of lucid reason in Heidegger. (Emmanuel Levinas, 'Philosophy and Awakening', trans. Mary Quaintance, in *Who Comes after the Subject?*, eds Eduardo Cadava, Peter Connor and Jean-Luc Nancy (London: Routledge, 1991), pp. 206–16 (p. 215).)

34. See Robert Bernasconi, 'Scepticism in the face of Philosophy', in *Rereading Levinas*, pp. 149–61 (p. 152).

35. Jacques Derrida, 'At this Very Moment in this Work Here I am', trans. Ruben Berezdivin, in *Rereading Levinas*, pp. 11–48.

36. Simon Critchley, 'Bois – Derrida's Final Word on Levinas', in *Rereading Levinas*, eds Robert Bernasconi and Simon Critchley, pp. 162–89 (p. 178).

37. Critchley, 'Bois – Derrida's Final Word on Levinas', p. 178.

38. The caress is a key gesture for Levinas, and is discussed in all his major works. Marc-Alain Ouaknin understands the caress as the pre-eminent Levinasian gesture, the key to a postmodern ethics. The caress, which adores, follows, but does not impose violence, is 'un relativisme, un scepticisme sans nihilism . . . la "caresse" incarne la sagesse de l'incertitude' (Marc-Alain Ouaknin, *Méditations Érotiques* (Paris: Éditions Balland, 1992), pp. 133, 137).

39. *Otherwise than Being* does however make a number of references to art works: to the painter Dufy (*OBBE*, p. 30) and to Xenakis's *Nomos Alpha for Unaccompanied Cello* (*OBBE*, p. 41). Writers referred to include Valéry (*OBBE*, p. 40), Dostoyevsky (*OBBE*, p. 146), Claudel (*OBBE*, p. 147), Paul Celan (an epigraph, *OBBE*, p. 99), Pushkin (*OBBE*, p. 195, fn. 15), Rimbaud (*OBBE*, p. 118), Tolstoy (*OBBE*, p. 129), Goethe (*OBBE*, p. 175) and Shakespeare (*OBBE*, pp. 3, 87, 117). Levinas also refers to science-fiction (*OBBE*, p. 116). From myth he refers to Ulysses (*OBBE*, pp. 79, 81, 132), Gyges (*OBBE*, p. 145, 149), Deucalion (*OBBE*, p. 159) and the tunic of Nessus (*OBBE*, p. 109, p. 195 fn. 10). He refers to the Hebrew scriptures a number of times, for example to the book of Job (*OBBE*, pp. 122–3), Ecclesiastes (*OBBE*, p. 182) and the Song of Songs (*OBBE*, p. 192).

40. See also Llewelyn, *Emmanuel Levinas: the Genealogy of Ethics*, p. 181.

41. Adriaan Peperzak, 'Levinas on Technology and Nature', *Man and World*, vol. 25 (1992), pp. 469–82 (p. 480).

42. Karl Barth attempted to use the discourse of theology and biblical exegesis. He wrote that the 'Gospel is not a truth amongst other truths. Rather it sets a question-mark against all truths' (Karl Barth, *The Epistle to the Romans*, 6th edn, trans. Edwyn Hoskins, (Oxford: Oxford University Press, 1968), p. 35). See also: Steven G. Smith, *The Argument to the Other: Reason beyond Reason in the thought of Karl Barth and Emmanuel Levinas* (Chico, California: Scholar Press, 1983). Levinas, in a sentiment similar to Barth's, writes that 'theological language destroys the religious situation of transcendence. The infinite 'presents' itself anarchically, but thematisation loses the anarchy which alone can accredit it. Language about God rings false or becomes a myth, that is, can never be taken literally' (*OBBE*, p. 197, fn. 25).

43. Blanchot, 'Our Clandestine Companion', p. 45.

44. Derrida, 'This Strange Institution Called Literature', p. 48.

45. Blanchot, 'Our Clandestine Companion', p. 49.

46. Levinas's phrase 'world they do not include' is deeply ambiguous. On the one hand, this harks back to 'Reality and its Shadow' and its discussion of the dark 'hither' world of art: the book, if an art work, belongs to this 'wicked' world of art. By being printed and prefaced, an art work, in this

sense, comes into the 'real' world. However, this explanation leaves the 'written' as ambiguous. It is impossible for a book to exist without being written. By being 'written' – in fact, by its own existence – a book comes into the 'real' world: this would imply that a book is always in the real world, even if the 'cowardly' urge to 'bewitching' art is not. This interpretation of the passage would imply that, in the abstract, art is not of the world, but any actual art works are of the world: this position would seem to be nonsensical. On the other hand, and as a result of this position's unfeasiblity, another interpretation is offered by the suggestion that the 'world they do not include' is the 'world' beyond being, the 'other shore' (*obbe*, p. 183) from which the interrupting voice comes, the 'world' of the saying which books uncover. This in turn is lost in writing, in being prefaced, in the process of a text becoming said, which in turn calls for interruption.

47. Giles Deleuze and Claire Parnet, 'On the Superiority of Anglo-American Literature', in *Dialogues*, trans. Hugh Tomlinson and Barbara Habberjam (London: Athlone Press, 1987), pp. 36–76 (p. 36).

48. Marcel Proust, *Remembrance of Things Past*, 3 vols, trans. C. K. Scott-Moncrieff, Terence Kilmartin, Andreas Mayor (Harmondsworth: Penguin, 1983), vol. 3, *Time Regained*, p. 949. This ideas in this passage are echoed by Harold Bloom talking on criticism: he says that people 'cannot stand the saddest truth I know about the very nature of reading and writing imaginative literature, which is that poetry does not teach us to talk to other people; it teaches us to talk to ourselves . . . Criticism is as solitary as lyric poetry' (Imre Salusinszky, *Criticism in Society* (London: Methuen, 1987), pp. 70, 71). Bloom finds criticism to be a solitary affair, the aim only to improve the individual self; it is in part against this that ethical criticism stands.

49. See Levinas, 'Philosophy and Awakening', p. 215, and Robert Bernasconi, ' Scepticism in the Face of Philosophy', in *Rereading Levinas*, pp. 149–61.

50. Robert Bernasconi, 'The Ethics of Suspicion', *Research in Phenomenology*, vol. 20 (1990), pp. 3–18 (p. 9).

51. Wayne Booth, *The Company We Keep: An Ethics of Fiction* (London: University of California Press, 1988), p. 10.

52. Levinas, 'God and Philosophy', p. 170.

Conclusion

—————— • ——————

INTERPRETATION CONTINUAL INTERRUPTION

Maurice Blanchot describes three different ways of reading:

> [T]here is an active, productive way of reading which produces text and reader and thus transports us. There is a passive kind of reading which betrays the text while appearing to submit to it, by giving the illusion that the text exists objectively, fully, sovereignly: as one whole. Finally, there is the reading that is no longer passive, but is passivity's reading. It is without pleasure, without joy; it escapes both comprehension and desire. It is like the nocturnal vigil, that 'inspiring' insomnia when, all having been said, 'Saying' is heard, and the testimony of the last witness is pronounced.[1]

The first, active way of reading, and the ethical understanding of literature it evokes, has been exemplified by the epi-reading of Martha Nussbaum. Her work argues that literature transports us into the world of the literary work, where, as we experience the events, our ethical perceptions are sharpened. However, as Chapter 2 argued, her position is not without its problems. For literature to work as part of moral inquiry, Nussbaum has to assume that a text is not a linguistic artifact but a surface behind which there are real situations and real events. In contrast, the work of J. Hillis Miller, an exemplary graphi-reader, argued that we can respond to the text alone. This offers a 'thin' conception of ethics which, in addition, does not seem to come to terms with Blanchot's third, uneasy sense of reading.

Blanchot's third description of reading uses 'saying' in a Levinasian sense. The 'saying' in literature is precisely that uncanny moment when we are made to feel not at home with the text or in ourselves. We are neither transported to a nether world of virtual life, nor do we simply mouth our misinterpretation of the text. It is in these moments when our sense of our selves and our relation to the *logos* is interrupted and put into question that the ethics of literature are at their clearest. These moments of fragmentation are a testimony to the irreducible otherness of the other and to our responsibility. The difficulty lies in pointing out these flaws in the said through critical practice. Each text requires reading in such a way as that its saying can be heard, that the flaws in the said appear.

This book was begun out of a dissatisfaction with the ethical commitment of criticism. This dissatisfaction arose from three areas. It came from a reaction to claims made by critics and philosophers like Olsen, who argued that '[s]tyle, content and structure are the subjects of literary criticism, and it is difficult to see what else it can be about'.[2] This seems to lose precisely the moments of saying in literature and, as a consequence, what made it important. It arose from a dissatisfaction with the modernist paradigm of criticism, which, as it decays, also loses these moments. It also arose from a dissatisfaction with the new ways of criticism called 'theory' because these various different approaches did not seem to have made clear their ethical commitments.

As a result of this, this book sought to explore the possibilities of an 'ethical criticism' by turning to the ethical philosophy of Emmanuel Levinas. His thought, despite its self-contradictory antipathy to art, offered a way of understanding ethical criticism. Just as the role of philosophy is to draw attention to the saying in the said through philosophy, the task of criticism is to interrupt the said in the name of the saying in literary works. Criticism, like philosophy, could say the saying, although at a 'fine risk' (*OBBE*, p. 120).

The question of the form this critical saying remains. Levinas's thought cannot be turned into a methodology: it is not a philosophy that can be 'applied'. Rather, he refuses a philosophic programme and insists that his task 'does not consist in constructing ethics; I only try to find its meaning'.[3] In contrast to Nussbaum's or Miller's approach to this same question, Levinas's thought could not become a critical method. It underlies methodology – as soon as criticism becomes an orthodoxy, it loses its ability to interrupt, to fracture the said. To ask for a Levinasian critical method is to ask for something that cannot and should not exist. This is the 'fine risk' that criticism takes: it risks becoming said, and covering up the saying, in the very moment of exposing the saying.

How the saying might be recognised in criticism is, then, a problem. To approach it the subject for another work and can only be gestured towards here. Criticism, through an awareness of the way the ethical signifies in language, must explode the said and draw attention, momentarily, to the saying. Criticism, dealing first and foremost with language, even more perhaps than the discourse of philosophy, is born of the tension between the saying and the said, and must always remain awake, energetic, able to fracture the said in the name of the saying. There is obviously no one critical process which embodies Levinas's ideas, no one answer. Rather, the saying can be recognised in all critical approaches which interrupt established understandings, the said. In this, currently, the various different strands of 'theory' are perhaps the clearest examples of the saying in criticism. As Denis Donoghue writes, theory 'whatever in addition it may be, is another technique of trouble, a device to make trouble for ourselves'.[4] 'Theory' can be seen as the introduction of new and challenging questions into critical discourse – questions of history, concerning colonialism for example, or questions about understandings of gender relations. Their very disruptive power is ethical. The saying, the ethical, and 'the interpretation it calls for ad infinitum' (*OBBE*, p. 170) means that the only path for criticism to take is to make its interpretation continual interruption. 'Theory', understood as interruption, opens the saying in criticism: it should make discussions that appear to be closed open, turn the expected into the unexpected and show the last word only to be the most recent word.

Terence Hawkes, by re-examining moments of tension in Arnold and Eliot, challenges literary criticism to be 'anxious'.[5] Using Freud's distinction of the *heimlich* and the *unheimlich*, he argues that criticism needs to

> not merely raise the spectre of the *unheimlich*, but also [be] intent, not on nullifying it, but on somehow including and promoting the *unheimlich* within the material it examines – indeed of openly scrutinising those elements that its initial impulse is to try to occlude or swallow.[6]

He goes on to cite Adorno, ' "it is part of morality not to be at home in one's home" ', and then suggests that 'the sort of homeless, 'hooligan' criticism that I am advocating must eventually subscribe to a morality of that sort'.[7] Hawkes's account can be paralleled with an understanding of the task of criticism derived from Levinas. The said, at home, is the quiescence resulting from a familiar, often-used critical method, interpretations of texts that no longer threaten or interrupt. The saying is the state of not being at home, the strangeness of the ineluctable call to responsibility: criticism, renewed by 'theory', is the question, the interruption, put to the said by the saying.

This understanding of criticism allows a reinterpretation of Paul de Man's statement 'the main theoretical interest of literary theory consists in the impossibility of its definition'.[8] To define (de-fine) means to set limits to, to delimit. 'Theory', as the interruption of the saying in criticism, understood in the light of Levinas's thought, cannot be de-fined. To do so would be to make it a said, to take from it its opening to the (impossible) moment of saying. This is precisely what the 'anti-theorists', examined in the first chapter, seek to do, by delimiting the area, range and depth of questions that can be put by criticism. To limit criticism to a 'humanism' is, at the same moment, to lose the ethical impulse, the saying, which first stimulated that humanism. 'Humanism' Levinas writes 'has to be denounced because it is not sufficiently human' (*OBBE,* pp. 127–8). In the name of what they call ethics, which now is but a husk, said, the anti-theorists seek to stop the continual movement of 'ethics', the saying, fracturing.

Alternatively, a number of contemporary critical strategies embody the saying. Edward Said's *Orientalism,* for example, 'reminds us most forcefully of our scholarly responsibilities and speaks to our calling'.[9] Said's work – and much post-colonial theory it inspired – draws attention to the injustices which underlie western discourse. This 'drawing attention to' is a process of interruption or disturbance of that western discourse. Derrida's work, especially in the extraordinarily productive way it has been taken up by literary studies, is another example of the momentary explosion of the said to reveal the saying. Deconstructive criticism represents a way of fracturing the said. That these will always represent such an interruption is not certain because of the way that interruptions are reincorporated back into the logocentric said.

Perhaps this understanding of perpetual questioning and interruption is also applicable to disciplines other than philosophy and criticism. Right across the humanities and social sciences, new understandings are emerging. These differ from more traditional changes that a discipline undergoes over time because, echoing the ethical 'structure' of the saying and the said and the continual need for interruption, these changes – often reductively understood as 'postmodern' – eschew claims that they are universally true, or represent understandings that are uninterruptable. The structure of the saying puncturing the said might occur outside language in the visual arts: Roland Barthes discusses the 'punctum', the moment when some small detail fractured the 'separateness' of a photograph.[10] John Berger shares a similar sort of intuition in relation to both photographs and paintings. It is permissible to hope that these changes within academic disciplines might be the starting point of wider changes in our world.

Frank Kermode wrote that it is 'not expected of critics as it is of poets that they should help us to make sense of our lives; they are bound only to the attempt the lesser feat of making sense of the ways in which we try to make sense of our lives'.[12] The aim of this book has not been to offer a new version of a literary work, nor to explore literary history – it has been to understand the ethical moment which underlies criticism. It has tried to analyse the ethical understandings of criticism which makes sense of those who make sense of our lives. It hopes to stress the ethical importance of the task of criticism by offering a clearer understanding, in Levinas's terms, of the ethics and responsibility which underlie criticism. It hopes to show that criticism in the future must embrace new questions, and only by doing so can it maintain its necessary commitment to the ethical – only then can it be ethical criticism. Perhaps most importantly, it hopes to show that, like philosophy, which must always fail for Levinas, criticism too must fail, must always be open to interruption. There can be no final reading, no last word.

NOTES

1. Maurice Blanchot, *The Writing of the Disaster*, trans. Ann Smock (London: University of Nebraska Press, 1986), p. 101.
2. Stein Haugom Olsen, *The End of Literary Theory* (Cambridge: Cambridge University Press, 1987), p. 3.
3. Emmanuel Levinas, *Ethics and Infinity*, trans. R. A. Cohen (Pittsburg: Duquesne University Press, 1985), p. 90.
4. Dennis Donoghue, *The Pure Good of Theory* (Oxford: Blackwell, 1992), p. 32.
5. Terence Hawkes, 'The *Heimlich* Manoeuvre', *Textual Practice*, vol. 8 (1994), pp. 302–18.
6. Hawkes, 'The *Heimlich* Manoeuvre', p. 312.
7. Hawkes, 'The *Heimlich* Manoeuvre', p. 313.
8. Paul de Man, *The Resistance to Theory* (Minneapolis: University of Minnesota Press, 1986), p. 3.
9. Gordon Johnson, review of Edward Said, *Orientalism*, (2nd edn), *Times Higher Education Supplement*, 24 February 1995, pp. 20, 22 (p. 22). Professor Johnson kindly provided the reference from David Ford, with which the introduction began.
10. Roland Barthes, *Camera Lucida*, trans. Richard Howard (London: Flamingo, 1984).
11. John Berger, *And Our Faces, My Heart, Brief as Photos* (London: Granta Books, 1992).
12. Frank Kermode, *The Sense of an Ending* (Oxford: Oxford University Press, 1967), p. 3.

BIBLIOGRAPHY

Aeschlimann, Jean-Christophe (ed.), *Répondre D'Autrui Emmanuel Levinas* (Boudry-Neuchâtel: Éditions de la Baconnière, 1989)

Anderson, Perry, 'Components of the National Culture', *New Left Review*, vol. 50 (1968), pp. 3–57

Arac, Jonathan, Godzich, Wlad and Martin, Wallace (eds), *The Yale Critics: Deconstruction in America* (Minneapolis: University of Minnesota Press, 1983)

Armstrong, Isobel, 'Textual Harassment: The Ideology of Close Reading, or How Close is Close?', *Textual Practice* vol. 9(3), pp. 401–20

Arnold, Matthew, *Culture and Anarchy*, ed. J. Dover Wilson (Cambridge: Cambridge University Press, 1960)

Arnold, Matthew, *Lectures and Essays in Criticism: Complete Works Volume III*, ed. R. H. Supir (Ann Arbor: University of Michigan Press, 1962)

Atkins, G. Douglas, 'Dehellenizing Literary Criticism', *College English*, vol. 41 (1980), pp. 769–79

Bakhtin, Mikhail, *The Dialogic Imagination*, trans. Michael Holoquist and Caryl Emerson, ed. Michael Holoquist (Austin: University of Texas Press, 1981)

Baldick, Chris, *The Social Mission of English Criticism, 1848–1932* (Oxford: Clarendon Press, 1983)

Barth, Karl, *The Epistle to the Romans*, trans. Edwyn Hoskyns (Oxford: Oxford University Press, 1968)

Barthes, Roland, *Camera Lucida*, trans. Richard Howard (London: Flamingo, 1984)

Bauman, Zygmunt, *Modernity and the Holocaust*, 2nd edn (Oxford: Polity Press/Blackwell, 1993)

Bauman, Zygmunt, *Postmodern Ethics* (Oxford: Blackwell, 1993)

Bell, Michael, *F. R. Leavis* (London: Routledge, 1988)

Benhabib, Selya, *Critique, Norm, Utopia* (New York: Columbia University Press, 1986)

Bennington, Geoffrey, 'Deconstruction and the Philosophers (the Very Idea)', *Oxford Literary Review*, vol. 10 (1988), pp. 73–130

Berger, John, *And Our Faces, My Heart, Brief as Photos* (London: Granta Books, 1992)

Bergonzi, Bernard, *Exploding English: Criticism, Theory, Culture* (Oxford: Clarendon Press, 1990)

Bernasconi, Robert, 'Fundamental Ontology, Meontology and the Ethics of Ethics', *Irish Philosophical Journal*, vol. 4 (1987), pp. 76–93

Bernasconi, Robert, 'The Ethics of Suspicion', *Research in Phenomenology*, vol. 20 (1990), pp. 3–18

Robert Bernasconi, 'Heidegger and the Invention of the Western Philosophical Tradition', *Journal of the British Society for Phenomenology* vol. 26 (1995), pp. 240–54

Bernasconi, Robert and Critchley, Simon (eds), *Rereading Levinas* (London: Athlone Press, 1991)

Bernasconi, Robert and Wood, David (eds), *Derrida and Différence* (Coventry: Parousia Press, 1985)

Bernasconi, Robert and Wood, David, (eds), *The Provocation of Levinas: Re-thinking the Other* (London: Routledge, 1988)

Berthoff, Warner, *Literature and the Continuances of Virtue* (Princeton: Princeton University Press, 1986)

Bhabha, Homi K., *The Location of Culture* (London: Routledge, 1994)

Blamires, Harry, *A History of Literary Criticism* (London: Macmillan, 1991)

Blanchot, Maurice, *The Writing of the Disaster*, trans. Ann Smock (London: University of Nebraska Press, 1986)

Bloom, Allan, *The Closing of the American Mind* (New York: Simon and Schuster, 1987)

Bloom, Harold (ed), *Deconstruction and Criticism* (London: Routledge and Kegan Paul, 1979)

Booth, Wayne, *The Rhetoric of Fiction* (London: University of Chicago Press, 1961)

Booth, Wayne, *The Company We Keep: An Ethics of Fiction* (London: University of California Press, 1988)

Bouckraet, Luk, 'Ontology and Ethics: Reflections on Levinas' Critique of Heidegger', *International Philosophical Quarterly*, vol. 3 (1970), pp. 402–19

Bové, Paul, *Mastering Discourse: The Politics of Intellectual Culture* (London: Duke University Press, 1992)

Bradford, Richard (ed), *The State of Theory* (London: Routledge, 1993)

Brooker, Peter and Humm, Peter, *Dialogue and Difference; English into the 90s* (London: Routledge, 1989)

Burggraeve, Roger, *Emmanuel Levinas: une bibliographie primaire et secondaire (1929–1985) avec complément (1985–1989)* (Leuven: Peeters, 1990)

Burke, Seán, *The Death and Return of the Author: Criticism and Subjectivity in Barthes, Foucault and Derrida* (Edinburgh: Edinburgh University Press, 1992)

Burt, E. S., 'Developments in Character: Reading and Interpretation in "The Children's Punishment" and "The Broken Comb"', *Yale French Studies*, vol. 69 (1984), pp. 192–210

Cadava, Eduardo, Connor, Peter, and Nancy, Jean-Luc (eds), *Who Comes After the Subject?* (London: Routledge, 1991)

Caputo, John, *Against Ethics* (Bloomington: Indiana University Press, 1993)

Carey, John, *The Intellectuals and The Masses* (London: Faber & Faber, 1992)

Casey, John, *The Language of Criticism* (London: Methuen, 1966)

Cavell, Stanley, *Must We Mean What We Say?* (Cambridge: Cambridge University Press, 1976)

Chalier, Catherine and Abensour, Migel (eds), *L'Herne Emmanuel Levinas* (Paris: Éditions de l'Herne, 1991)

Chanter, Tina, *Ethics of Eros: Irigaray's Rewriting of the Philosophers* (London: Routledge, 1995)

Ciaramelli, Fabio, 'L'appel infini à l'interprétation: Remarques sur Levinas et l'art', *Revue Philosophique de Louvain*, vol. 92 (1994), pp. 32–52

Cohen, Richard A. (ed), *Face to Face with Levinas* (Albany: State University of New York Press, 1986)

Cohen, Richard A., *Elevations: the Height of Good in Rosenzweig and Levinas* (Chicago: Chicago University Press, 1994)

Cook, Albert, *Canons and Wisdoms* (Philadelphia: University of Pennslyvania Press, 1993)

Cornell, Drucilla, *The Philosophy of the Limit* (London: Routledge, 1992)

Cornell, Drucilla, Rosenfeld, Michael and Carlson, David Gray (eds), *Deconstruction and the Possibility of Justice* (London: Routledge, 1992)

Cornford, F. M. (originally anonymous), *Microcosmographia Academica: Being a Guide for the Young Academic Politician* (Cambridge: Bowes and Bowes, 1908)

Critchley, Simon, 'The Chiasmus: Levinas, Derrida and the Ethical Demand for Deconstruction', *Textual Practice*, vol. 3 (1989), pp. 91–106

Critchley, Simon, 'The Problem of Closure in Derrida (part one)', *Journal of the British Society for Phenomenology*, vol. 23 (1992), pp. 3–19

Critchley, Simon, 'The Problem of Closure in Derrida (part two)', *Journal of the British Society for Phenomenology*, vol. 23 (1992), pp. 127–45

Critchley, Simon, *The Ethics of Deconstruction* (Oxford: Blackwell, 1992)

Critchley, Simon, 'Black Socrates?', *Radical Philosophy*, vol. 69 (1995), pp. 17–26

Cunningham, Valentine, *In the Reading Gaol: Postmodernity, Texts, History* (Oxford: Blackwell, 1994)

Dallery, Arleen B., and Scott, C. E. (eds), *The Question of the Other* (Albany: State University of New York Press, 1989)

Davis, Lennard J., and Mirabella, M. Bella (eds), *Left Politics and the Literary Profession* (New York: Columbia University Press, 1990)

Day, Gary (ed), *The British Critical Tradition: A Re-evaluation* (Basingstoke: Macmillan, 1993)

Deleuze, Giles, and Guattari, Felix, *A Thousand Plateaus*, trans. Brian Massumi (London: Athlone Press, 1988)

Deleuze, Giles, and Parnet, Claire, *Dialogues*, trans. Hugh Tomlinson and Barbera Habberjam (London: Athlone Press, 1987)

De Man, Paul, *Allegories of Reading* (London: Yale University Press, 1979)

De Man, Paul, *The Resistance to Theory* (Minneapolis: University of Minnesota Press, 1986)

De Man, Paul, *Wartime Journalism, 1939–1943*, eds Werner Hamacher, Neil Hertz and Thomas Keenan (London: University of Nebraska Press, 1988)

Derrida, Jacques, 'White Mythology: Metaphor in the Text of Philosophy', *New Literary History*, vol. 6 (1974), pp. 8–74

Derrida, Jacques, *Of Grammatology*, trans. Gayatri Chakravorty Spivak (London: Johns Hopkins University Press, 1976)

Derrida, Jacques, *Writing and Difference*, trans. Alan Bass (London: Routledge and Kegan Paul, 1978)

Derrida, Jacques, *Dissemination*, trans. Barbara Johnson (London: Athlone Press, 1981)

Derrida, Jacques, 'Racisms' Last Word', trans. Peggy Kamuf, *Critical Inquiry*, vol. 12 (1985), pp. 291–9

Derrida, Jacques, 'Like the Sound of the Sea Deep within a Shell: Paul de Man's War', *Critical Inquiry*, vol. 14 (1988), pp. 590–652

Derrida, Jacques, *Acts of Literature*, ed. Derek Attridge (London: Routledge, 1992)

Derrida, Jacques, *Spectres of Marx*, trans. Peggy Kamuf (London: Routledge, 1994)

Dews, Peter, *Logics of Disintegration* (London: Verso, 1987)

Docherty, Thomas, *Postmodernism: A Reader* (London: Harvester, 1993)

Docherty, Thomas, *Alterities: Criticism, History, Representation* (Oxford: Clarendon Press, 1996).

Donoghue, Denis, *Ferocious Alphabets* (London: Faber & Faber, 1981)

Donoghue, Denis, *The Pure Good of Theory* (Oxford: Blackwell, 1992)

Eaglestone, Robert, 'The Face of Emmanuel Levinas and Philip II of Macedon', in *Diatribe* vol. 4 (1994–5), pp. 9–20.

Eaglestone, Robert, 'The Imperialist Logic of Philosophy: Athens, Jerusalem and the Metaphor of the City', *Diatribe* vol. 6 (1996), pp. 9–16.

Eagleton, Terry, *Criticism and Ideology* (London: New Left Books, 1976)

Eagleton, Terry, *Literary Theory* (Oxford: Blackwell, 1983)

Eagleton, Terry, *The Function of Criticism* (London: Verso, 1984)

Eagleton, Terry, *Against the Grain: Selected Essays* (London: Verso, 1986)

Eagleton, Terry, *The Significance of Theory* (Oxford: Blackwell, 1990)

Eagleton, Terry, 'Discourse and Discos: Theory in the Space between Culture and Capitalism', *Times Literary Supplement*, 15 July, 1994, pp. 3–4

Easthope, Anthony, *British Post-Structuralism since 1968* (London: Routledge, 1988)

Eldridge, Richard, *On Moral Personhood* (London: University of Chicago Press, 1989)

Eliot, T. S., *After Strange Gods* (London: Faber & Faber, 1934)

Eliot, T. S., *Selected Prose*, ed. Frank Kermode (London: Faber & Faber, 1975)

Ellis, John, *Against Deconstruction* (Princeton: Princeton University Press, 1989)

Elton, G. R., *Return to Essentials* (Cambridge: Cambridge University Press, 1991)

Fackenheim, Emil L., *To Mend the World* (New York: Schocken Books, 1982)

Falck, Colin, *Myth, Truth and Literature: Towards a True Postmodernism* (Cambridge: Cambridge University Press, 1989)

Fanon, Franz, *The Wretched of the Earth*, trans. Constance Farrington (Harmondsworth: Penguin, 1990)

Farley, Wendy, 'Ethics and Reality; Dialogue between Caputo and Levinas', *Philosophy Today*, vol. 36 (1992), pp. 211–20

Faur, José, *Golden Doves with Silver Dots: Semiotics and Textuality in Rabbinic Tradition* (Bloomington: Indiana University Press, 1986)

Felman, Shoshona and Laub, Dori, *Testimony* (London: Routledge, 1992)

Felperin, Howard, 'The Anxiety of Deconstruction', *Yale French Studies*, vol. 69 (1984), pp. 254–66

Felperin, Howard, *Beyond Deconstruction: the Uses and Abuses of Literary Theory* (Oxford: Clarendon Press, 1985)

Fisch, Harold, *Poetry with a Purpose: Biblical Poetics and Interpretation* (Bloomington: Indiana University Press, 1988)

Fischer, Michael, *Does Deconstruction Make Any Difference?* (Bloomington: Indiana University Press, 1985)

Fish, Stanley, 'Anti-Professionalism', *New Literary History*, vol. 17 (1985–6), pp. 89–108

David Ford, 'Obedience and the Academic Vocation Today: Lessons for Universities', *Cambridge: The Magazine of the Cambridge Society*, vol. 35 (1994–5), pp. 90–5

Frank, Joseph, 'The Voices of Mikhail Bakhtin', *New York Review of Books*, 23 October 1986, pp. 56–9

Freadman, Richard, and Miller, Seumas, *Rethinking Theory* (Cambridge: Cambridge University Press, 1992)

Gasché, Rodolphe, 'Deconstruction as Criticism', *Glyph 6* (London: Johns Hopkins University Press, 1979), pp. 177–216

Gasché, Rodolphe, *The Tain of the Mirror* (London: Harvard University Press, 1986)

Gerber, Rodolph J., 'Totality and Infinity: Herbraism and Hellenism – The Experiential Ontology of Emmanuel Levinas', *Review of Existential Psychology and Psychiatry*, vol. 7 (1967), pp. 177–88

Gibbs, Robert, 'The Other comes to Teach Me: a Review of Recent Levinas Publications', *Man and World*, vol. 24 (1991), pp. 219–33

Gibbs, Robert, *Correlations in Rosenzweig and Levinas* (Princeton: Princeton University Press, 1992)

Gibson, Andrew, *Towards a Postmodern Theory of Narrative* (Edinburgh: Edinburgh University Press, 1996)

Giles, Judy and Middleton, Tim (eds), *Writing Englishness 1900–1950* (London: Routledge, 1995)

Gillon, G., 'Interview with Emmanuel Levinas', *Substance*, vol. 14 (1976), pp. 54–7

Goethe, J. W. von, *Faust I and II*, trans. Robert David MacDonald (Birmingham: Oberon Books, 1988)

Goodheart, Eugene, *The Skeptic Disposition in Contemporary Criticism* (Princeton: Princeton University Press, 1984)

Grant, Patrick, *Literature and Personal Values* (Basingstoke: Macmillan, 1992)

Graff, Gerald, and Warner Michael (eds), *The Origins of Literary Studies in America*, (London: Routledge, 1989)

Griffiths, A. Phillips (ed), *Ethics: Royal Institute of Philosophy Supplement 35*, (Cambridge: Cambridge University Press, 1993)

Hamacher, Werner, Hertz, Neil and Keenan, Thomas, (eds), *Responses to Paul de Man's Wartime Journalism* (London: University of Nebraska Press, 1989)

Handelman, Susan A., *The Slayers of Moses: The Emergence of Rabbinic Interpretation in Modern Literary Theory* (Albany: State University of New York Press, 1982)

Handelman, Susan A., *Fragments of Redemption: Jewish thought and Literary Theory in Benjamin, Scholem and Levinas* (Bloomington: Indiana University Press, 1991)

Harpham, Geoffrey Galt, 'Language, History and Ethics', *Raritan*, vol. 7 (1987), pp. 128–46

Hartman, Geoffrey, *Criticism in the Wilderness* (London: Yale University Press, 1980)

Hawkes, Terence, 'The *Heimlich* Manoeuvre', *Textual Practice*, vol. 8 (1994), pp. 302–18

Hegel, G. W. F., *Introductory Lectures on Aesthetics*, trans. Reginald Bosanquet, ed. Michael Inwood (Harmondsworth: Penguin, 1993)

Heidegger, Martin, *Being and Time*, trans. John Macquarrie and Edward Robinson (Oxford: Blackwell, 1962)

Heidegger, Martin, *Poetry, Language, Thought*, trans. Albert Hofstadter (London: Harper and Row, 1971)

Heidegger, Martin, *Basic Writings*, ed. David Farrell Krell (London: Harper Row, 1977)

Inglis, Fred, *Radical Earnestness: English Social Theory, 1880–1980* (Oxford: Martin Robinson, 1982)

Jabès, Edmond, *The Book of Questions*, trans. Rosmarie Waldrop (Connecticut: Wesleyan University Press, 1976)

James, Henry, *The Art of the Novel* (New York: Scribner, 1934)

James, Henry, *The Golden Bowl* (Harmondsworth: Penguin, 1985)

Jameson, Fredric, *The Political Unconscious* (London: Methuen, 1981)

Jardine, Alice and Smith, Paul (eds), *Men in Feminism* (London: Methuen, 1987)

Jenkins, Harold, 'Playhouse Interpolations in the Folio Text of *Hamlet*', *Studies in Bibliography*, vol. 13 (1960), pp. 31–47

Johnson, Barbara, 'Rigorous Unreliability', *Yale French Studies*, vol. 69 (1985), pp. 73–80

Johnson, Barbara, *The Wake of Deconstruction* (Oxford: Blackwell, 1994)

Johnson, Christopher, *System and Writing in the Philosophy of Jacques Derrida* (Cambridge: Cambridge University Press, 1993)

Johnson, Gordon, review of Edward Said, *Orientalism* (2nd edn), *Times Higher Education Supplement*, 24 February 1995, pp. 20, 22

Julius, Anthony, *T. S. Eliot: Anti-semitism and Literary Form* (Cambridge: Cambridge University Press, 1996)

Kant, Emmanuel, *The Moral Law*, trans. H. J. Paton (London: Hutchinson, 1948)

Kaufmann, David, 'The Profession of Theory', *PMLA*, vol. 105 (1990), pp. 519–30

Kavanagh, T. M., *The Limits of Theory* (Stanford: Stanford University Press, 1989)

Kearney, Richard, *Dialogues with Contemporary Continental Thinkers: The Phenomenological Heritage* (Manchester: Manchester University Press, 1984)

Kermode, Frank, *The Sense of an Ending* (Oxford: Oxford University Press, 1967)

Keyes, C. D., 'An Evaluation of Levinas' Critique of Heidegger', *Research in Phenomenology*, vol. 11 (1972), pp. 121–42

Krieger, Murray, 'In the Wake of Morality: the Thematic Underside of Recent Theory', *New Literary History*, vol. 15 (1983), pp. 119–36

LaCapra, Dominick, *History and Criticism* (London: Cornell University Press, 1985)

Large, William, 'Ethics and the Ambiguity of Writing in the Philosophy of Emmanuel Levinas' (unpublished thesis, University of Essex, 1990)

Lawton, P. N. 'A Difficult Freedom: Levinas' Judaism', *Tijdschrift voor Filosofie*, vol. 4 (1975), pp. 681–91

Leavis, F. R., *The Common Pursuit* (London: Chatto and Windus, 1952)

Leavis, F. R., *The Critic as Anti-philosopher: Essays and Papers*, ed. G. Singh (London: Chatto and Windus, 1982)

Lehman, David, *Signs of the Times: Deconstruction and the Fall of Paul de Man* (London: Poseidon Press, 1991)

Lentricchia, Frank, *After the New Criticism* (London: Methuen, 1983)

Lescourret, Marie-Anne, *Emmanuel Levinas* (Paris: Flammarion, 1994)

Levinas, Emmanuel, 'Le Réalité et Son Ombre', *Les Temps Modernes*, vol. 38 (1948), pp. 771–89

Levinas, Emmanuel, 'La Transcendance des Mots', *Les Temps Modernes*, vol. 44 (1949), pp. 1090–5

Levinas, Emmanuel, *Sur Maurice Blanchot* (Monpellier: Fata Morgana, 1975)

Levinas, Emmanuel, 'About Blanchot: an Interview', *Substance*, vol. 14 (1976), pp. 54–7

Levinas, Emmanuel, *Otherwise than Being: or, Beyond Essence*, trans. Alphonso Lingis (The Hague: Martinus Nijhoff, 1981)

Levinas, Emmanuel, *Ethics and Infinity: Conversations with Phillipe Nemo*, trans. R. A. Cohen (Pittsburg: Duquesne University Press, 1985)

Levinas, Emmanuel, *Time and the Other*, trans. Richard A. Cohen (Pittsburg: Duquesne University Press, 1987)

Levinas, Emmanuel, *Collected Philosophical Papers*, trans. Alphonso Lingis (Dordrecht: Kluwer Academic Publishers, 1987)

Levinas, Emmanuel, *Existence and Existents*, trans. Alphonso Lingis (London: Kluwer Academic Publishers, 1988)

Levinas, Emmanuel, 'As If Consenting to Horror', trans. Paula Wissing, *Critical Inquiry*, vol. 15 (1989), pp. 485–88

Levinas, Emmanuel, *The Levinas Reader*, ed. Seàn Hand (Oxford: Blackwell, 1989)

Levinas, Emmanuel, *De l' Obliteration: Entretien avec Françoise Armengaud à propos de l' oeuvre de Sosno* (Paris: Éditions de la Différence, 1990)

Levinas, Emmanuel, *Totality and Infinity: An Essay on Exteriority*, 3rd printing, trans. Alphonso Lingis (London: Kluwer Academic Publishers, 1991)

Levinas, Emmanuel, 'Transcending Words: Concerning Word-erasing', trans. Didier Maleuvre, *Yale French Studies*, vol. 81 (1992), pp. 145–50

Libertson, Joseph, *Proximity: Levinas, Blanchot, Bataille and Communication* (The Hague: Martinus Nijhoff, 1982)

Lindberg, Kathryne and Kronick, Joseph, (eds), *America's Modernisms: Revaluing the Canon* (London: Louisiana State University Press, 1996)

Llewelyn, John, *Emmanuel Levinas: The Genealogy of Ethics* (London: Routledge, 1995)

Lyotard, Jean François and Thébaud, Jean-Loup, *Just Gaming*, trans. Wlad Godzich, (Minneapolis: University of Minnesota Press, 1985)

MacDonald, Michael J., 'Jewgreek and Greekjew: the Concept of the Trace in Levinas and Derrida', *Philosophy Today*, vol. 35 (1991), pp. 215–27

MacIntyre, Alasdair, *Three Rival Versions of Moral Inquiry* (London: Duckworth, 1990)

Manning, Robert John Sheffer, 'Thinking the Other without Violence? An Analysis of the Relation between the Philosophy of Emmanuel Levinas and Feminism', *Journal of Speculative Philosophy*, vol. 5 (1991), pp. 132–43

Manning, Robert John Sheffer, *Interpreting Otherwise than Heidegger* (Pittsburgh: Duquesne University Press, 1993)

Marion, Jean-Luc, *God Without Being*, trans. Thomas A. Carlson (London: University of Chicago Press, 1991)

Miller, J. Hillis, 'Theory and Practice: Response to Vincent Leitch', *Critical Inquiry*, vol. 6 (1980), pp. 609–14

Miller, J. Hillis, *The Ethics of Reading* (New York: Columbia University Press, 1987)

Miller, J. Hillis, 'Presidential Address 1986: The Triumph of Theory, the Resistance to Reading and the Question of the Material Base', *PMLA*, vol. 102 (1987), pp. 281–91

Miller, J. Hillis, *Versions of Pygmalion* (London: Harvard University Press, 1990)

Miller, J. Hillis, *Hawthorne and History: Defacing it* (Oxford: Blackwell, 1990)

Mitchell, W. J. T. (ed.), *Against Theory* (London: University of Chicago Press, 1985)

Mortley, Raol, *French Philosophers in Conversation* (London: Routledge, 1991)

Mouffe, Chantal (ed.), *Deconstruction and Pragmatism* (London: Routledge, 1996)

Mueller-Vollmer, Kurt (ed.), *The Hermeneutics Reader* (Oxford: Blackwell, 1985)

Mulhern, Francis, *The Moment of Scrutiny* (London: New Left Books, 1979)

Nettleship, H., *The Study of Modern European Languages and Literatures in the University of Oxford* (Oxford: Parker, 1887)

Nettleship, H., *The Moral Influence of Literature; Classical Education in the Past and Present: Two Popular Addresses* (London: Percival, 1890)

Newton, Adam, *Narrative Ethics* (London: Harvard University Press, 1995)

Nicholson, Linda (ed.), *Feminism/Postmodernism* (London: Routledge, 1990)

Norris, Christopher, *Derrida* (London: Fontana, 1987)

Norris, Christopher, *Paul de Man: Deconstruction and the Critique of Aesthetic Ideology* (London: Routledge, 1988)

Norris, Christopher, *Deconstruction and the Interests* of Theory (London: Pinter, 1988)

Norris, Christopher, *What's Wrong with Postmodernism* (London: Harvester Wheatsheaf, 1990)

Norris, Christopher, *Uncritical Theory: Postmodernism, Intellectuals and the Gulf War* (London: Lawrence and Wishart, 1992)

Norris, Christopher, *Truth and The Ethics of Criticism* (Manchester: Manchester University Press, 1994)

Nussbaum, Martha, 'Reply to Richard Wollheim, Patrick Gardiner and Hilary Putnam', *New Literary History*, vol. 15 (1983–4), pp. 201–7

Nussbaum, Martha, 'Sophistry about Conventions', *New Literary History*, vol. 17 (1985–6), pp. 129–40

Nussbaum, Martha, *The Fragility of Goodness* (Cambridge: Cambridge University Press, 1986)

Nussbaum, Martha, *Love's Knowledge: Essays on Philosophy and Literature* (Oxford: Oxford University Press, 1990)

Olsen, Stein Haugom, *The End of Literary Theory* (Cambridge: Cambridge University Press, 1987)

Ouaknin, Marc-Alain, *Méditations érotiques* (Paris: Éditions Balland, 1992)

Palmer, D. J., *The Rise of English Studies* (London: Oxford University Press/Hull University Press, 1965)

Palmer, Frank, *Literature and Moral Understanding* (Oxford: Clarendon Press, 1992)

Parriner, Patrick, *The Failure of Theory* (Brighton: Harvester Press, 1987)

Peperzak, Adriaan, 'Beyond Being', *Research in Phenomenology*, vol. 8 (1978), pp. 239–61

Peperzak, Adriaan, 'Emmanuel Levinas: Jewish Experience and Philosophy', *Philosophy Today*, vol. 27 (1983), pp. 297–306

Peperzak, Adriaan, 'Phenomenology–Ontology–Metaphysics: Levinas' Perspective on Husserl and Heidegger', *Man and World*, vol. 16 (1983), pp. 113–27

Peperzak, Adriaan, 'The One for the Other: the Philosophy of Emmanuel Levinas', *Man and World*, vol. 24 (1991), pp. 427–59

Peperzak, Adriaan, 'Levinas on Technology and Nature', *Man and World*, vol. 25 (1992), pp. 469–82

Peperzak, Adriaan, *To the Other: An Introduction to the Philosophy of Emmanuel Levinas* (West Lafayette: Purdue University Press, 1993)

Peperzak, Adriaan (ed.), *Ethics as First Philosophy* (London: Routledge, 1995)

Peters, Gary, 'The Rhythm of Alterity: Levinas and Aesthetics', *Radical Philosophy*, vol. 82 (1997), pp. 9–16.

Proust, Marcel, *Remembrance of Things Past*, 3 vols, trans. C. K. Scott Moncrieff, Terence Kilmartin and Andreas Mayor (Harmondsworth: Penguin, 1983)

Putnam, Hilary, 'Taking Rules Seriously – A Response to Martha Nussbaum', *New Literary History*, vol. 15 (1983), pp. 193–200

Rapaport, Herman, *Heidegger and Derrida: Reflections on Time and Language* (London: University of Nebraska Press, 1989)

Rawls, John, *A Theory of Justice* (Oxford: Clarendon Press, 1972)

Rée, Jonathan, *Philosophical Tales: An Essay on Philosophy and Literature* (London: Methuen, 1987)

Richards, I. A., *Practical Criticism* (London: Routledge and Keegan Paul, 1973)

Ricoeur, Paul, *Time and Narrative*, vol. 3, trans. Kathleen McLaughlin and David Pellauer (London: University of Chicago Press, 1988)

Robbins, Jill, *Prodigal Son/Elder Brother; Interpretation and Alterity in Augustine, Petrarch, Kafka, Levinas* (London: University of Chicago Press, 1991)

Robbins, Jill, '*Visage, Figure*: Reading Levinas' *Totality and Infinity*', *Yale French Studies*, vol. 79 (1991), pp. 135–49

Rorty, Richard, *Contingency, Irony and Solidarity* (Cambridge: Cambridge University Press, 1989)

Rorty, Richard, *Philosophical Papers*, 2 vols (Cambridge: Cambridge University Press, 1991)

Rose, Gillian, *The Broken Middle* (Oxford: Blackwell, 1992)

Rose, Gillian, *Judaism and Modernity* (Oxford: Blackwell, 1993)

Rose, Gillian, *Mourning Becomes the Law: Philosophy and Representation* (Cambridge: Cambridge University Press, 1996)

Said, Edward, *Culture and Imperialism* (London: Vintage, 1994)

Sallis, John (ed), *Deconstruction and Philosophy: The Texts of Jacques Derrida* (London: University of Chicago Press, 1987)

Salusinszky, Imre, *Criticism in Society* (London: Methuen, 1987)

Saussure, Ferdinand de, *Course in General Linguistics*, 2nd edn, trans. Roy Harris (London: Duckworth, 1983)

Schiralli, M., 'Reconstructing Literary Value', *Journal of Aesthetic Education*, vol. 25 (1991), pp. 115–19

Schroeder, Brian, *Altared Ground: Levinas, History and Violence* (London: Routledge, 1996)

Siebers, Tobin, *The Ethics of Criticism* (London: Cornell University Press, 1988)

Shakespeare, William, *Hamlet: First Quarto Facsimile* (London: Scholars Press, 1969)

Shakespeare, William, *Hamlet: Second Quarto Facsimile* (London: Scholars Press, 1969)

Shakespeare, William, *Hamlet*, ed. Harold Jenkins (London: Routledge, 1982)

Silberstein, L. and Cohn, R. L., *The Other in Jewish Thought and History* (London: New York University Press, 1994)

Silverman, Hugh (ed.), *Philosophy and Non-philosophy since Merleau Ponty* (London: Routledge, 1988)

Silverman, Hugh (ed.), *Postmodernism: Philosophy and the Arts* (London: Routledge, 1990)

Smith, Steven G., *The Argument to the Other: Reason Beyond Reason in the Thought of Karl Barth and Emmanuel Levinas* (Chico: Scholars Press, 1983)

Steiner, George, *Real Presences* (London: Faber & Faber, 1989)

Tallis, Raymond, *Not Saussure: A Critique of Post-Saussurian Theory* (London: Macmillan, 1988)

Taylor, Mark C., *Deconstruction in Context: Literature and Philosophy* (London: University of Chicago Press, 1986)

Thurley, Geoffrey, *Counter-modernism in Current Literary Theory* (London: Macmillan, 1983)

Tillyard, E. M. W., *The Muse Unchained: An Intimate Account of the Revolution in English Studies at Cambridge* (London: Bowes and Bowes, 1958)

Ting-Toomey, Stella (ed.), *The Challenge of Facework: Cross-cultural and Interpersonal Issues* (Albany: State University of New York Press, 1994)

Viswanathan, Gauri, *Masks of Conquest: Literary Study and British Rule in India* (New York: Columbia University Press, 1989)

Washington, Peter, *Fraud: Literary Theory and the End of English* (London: Fontana, 1989)

Wellek, René and Warren, Austin, *Theory of Literature*, 3rd edn (Harmondsworth: Peregrine, 1963)

White, Hayden, *Metahistory* (London: Johns Hopkins University Press, 1973)

White, Hayden, *Tropics of Discourse: Essays in Cultural Criticism*, paperback edn (London: Johns Hopkins University Press, 1985)

Widdowson, Peter (ed.), *Rereading English* (London: Methuen, 1982)

Williams, Bernard, *Ethics and the Limits of Philosophy* (London: Fontana/Collins, 1985)

Wimsatt, William and Brooks, Cleanth, *Literary Criticism: A Short Introduction* (London: Routledge and Kegan Paul, 1957)

Wollheim, Richard, 'Flawed Crystals: James's *The Golden Bowl* and the Plausibility of Literature as Moral Philosophy', *New Literary History*, vol. 15 (1983), pp. 185–91

Wyschogrod, Edith, *Emmanuel Levinas, The Problem of Ethical Metaphysics* (The Hague: Martinus Nijhoff, 1974)

Wyschogrod, Edith, 'God and 'Being's Move' in the Philosophy of Emmanuel Levinas', *The Journal of Religion*, vol. 62 (1982), pp. 145–55

INDEX